The WORLD of SPORT examined

2nd Edition

WITHDRAWN FROM STOCK

Paul Beashel   Andy Sibson   John Taylor

First published in 1997 by:
Thomas Nelson and Sons Ltd

Second edition published in 2001 by:
Nelson Thornes Ltd
Delta Place
27 Bath Road
CHELTENHAM
GL53 7TH
United Kingdom

02 03 04 05 / 10 9 8 7 6 5 4 3 2

A catalogue record for this book is available from the British Library

ISBN 0 17 438752 0

Illustrations by Roger Goode, Steve Noon, Darrell Warner
Beehive Illustration
Page make-up by The Junction

Printed and bound in Italy by STIGE

Acknowledgements
The authors and publishers are grateful to the sports organisations
who have given their permission to reproduce logos in chapters 9
and 11. Every attempt has been made to contact copyright holders,
and we apologise if any have been overlooked.

Photo credits
All photos © Allsport or Nelson Thornes Ltd with the exception of
pp. 172, 176, 177 (Hulton Getty Images) and p. 100 (Action Images).
Cover photos © Allsport

The World of Sport Examined

(Second Edition)

Sport is important to us all. It plays an ever-increasing part in the life of the nation. If our national teams and our Olympic sportspeople are doing well, it lifts us all. Understanding sport in our society is essential. We believe our new book will help you to analyse, appreciate and understand the worldwide phenomenon of sport.

As sportspeople we always strive for perfection. Our book will help you achieve your sporting targets. Through greater knowledge and understanding of the ingredients of sporting excellence, your own performance will certainly improve.

We live in an information-rich world, but finding the information we need is often a problem. Recognising this challenge, we have linked our book with a brand new website. Finding what you want will be easy and will keep you at the cutting edge of sporting knowledge. Visiting our website will open up a world of sporting opportunity that should not be missed.

We hope you find this new edition a good read and helpful for your exam course.

Paul Beashel   Andy Sibson   John Taylor

Contents

Introduction

Our body systems

We need all our body systems to be in good working order for healthy living and our best sports performances.

Energy in action

We need efficient energy systems for everyday living, but sport makes extra demands on our energy.

Fitness for health and performance

Everyone needs basic fitness for health. Sportspeople must build up special fitness for their chosen sport.

Foundation

The sports development continuum

Participation

Training for success

Improving our performance depends on the effort we put into our training. Our body responds to strenuous exercise.

Skill in sport

Skilled performances need basic ability, sound techniques and good skills. Teaching skills is an art based on understanding the learning process.

Care of our bodies

Our bodies need looking after. We should exercise regularly, eat sensibly, watch our weight and resist drugs of all kinds.

Safety in sport

Preventing accidents and injuries is better than dealing with them. We should prepare our bodies for sport and respect our opponents. Knowledge of first aid can return us to sport quickly and may even save a life.

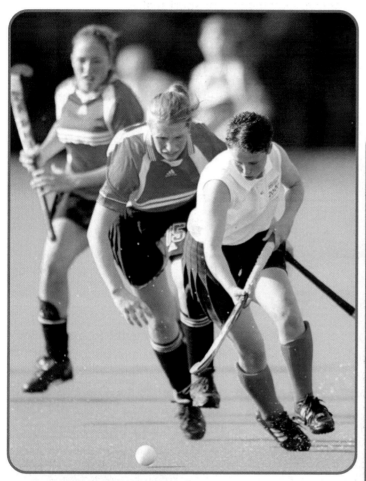

Performance

Providing for sport

We need facilities of all types at a fair price. Clubs provide the organisation and opportunities for us to take part. Private enterprise is replacing government support in sport.

Taking part in sport

Playing sport is a popular activity. Our reasons for taking part are many and varied. The influence of our family and teachers is critical. Some people are disadvantaged through gender, race, disability or age.

The changing face of sport

Sport has developed through the ages from the village feast days to the Olympic spectacle. Gentleman amateurs have been replaced by wealthy television sports stars. Modern technology has made dramatic changes but sport is still built on the amateurs playing in the parks and halls of Britain.

Excellence

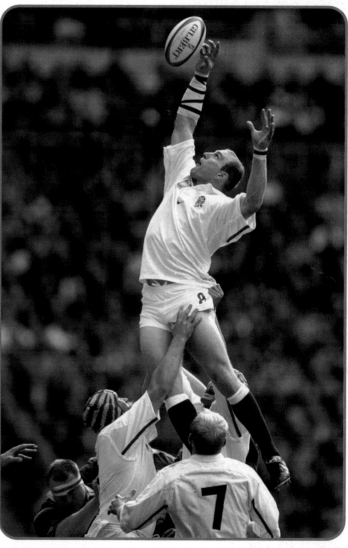

Sport as a spectacle

The entertainment industry, sponsoring companies, and the media have taken control of much sport. The excitement offered by sport makes it compulsive viewing.

1 Our body systems

What do we need to stay alive? We need air, food, sleep, shelter and clothes. We need to breathe, move about and know what is going on around us. We need to be able to get supplies of energy into our bodies and convert them so that we can use them. We then need to get rid of any waste products.

Our bodies have developed special systems so that these and other life-preserving activities can be carried out. Although we will look at a number of these body systems separately, it is important to remember that they all work together to keep our bodies working.

Our nervous system
page 10

Our nervous system keeps all the parts of the body in touch with each other. It allows us to control our muscles for sport while other functions such as our heartbeat carry on automatically.

Our muscular system
page 22

All our movements need muscular action. Skilful movement results from many skeletal muscles working smoothly together. Our muscles work non-stop in order to keep our body working, even when it is at rest.

Our skeletal system
page 12

Bones give shape to our bodies and protect vital organs. They also provide attachments for muscles and allow movement to take place through our joints.

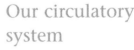

Our circulatory system
page 36

Our heart and blood vessels ensure that oxygen and nutrients are carried to all the cells of the body. At the same time, waste products are removed.

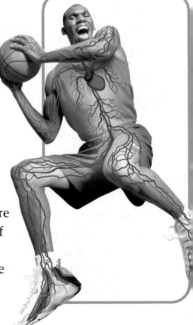

Our bodies are designed for action. Nowhere is this more apparent than in sport. Different sports make different demands on our bodies. Our bodies are machines that learn and are able to change to meet a wide variety of different stresses. They do this by improving and combining our separate body systems effectively.

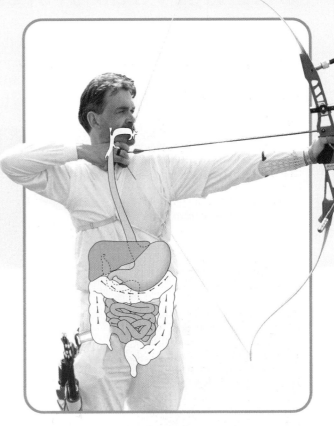

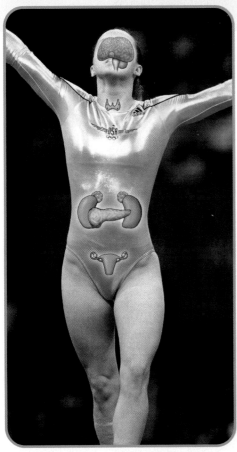

Our hormonal system
page 54

Hormones are chemical messengers. They are released into the bloodstream so that they can send messages around our body. These messengers control the workings of our body.

Our digestive system
page 55

All our energy for muscular work is provided by the food we eat. We need a balanced diet for good sporting performance and a healthy body. When in action, our bodies produce more waste products. These have to be removed by our excretory system.

Our respiratory system
page 46

Our bodies need oxygen to be able to make use of the energy available in food. Our lungs allow oxygen from the air to be exchanged with waste products from our body.

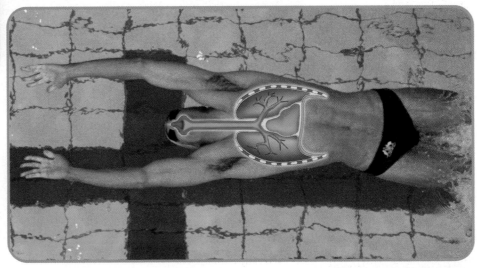

Our nervous system

All **sports** need our body systems to work smoothly together. The task of running all our body systems is carried out by our nervous system, which controls everything that goes on in our body.

Our nervous system keeps all parts of our body in touch with each other. It allows us to control our muscles for sport while other functions such as our heartbeat carry on automatically.

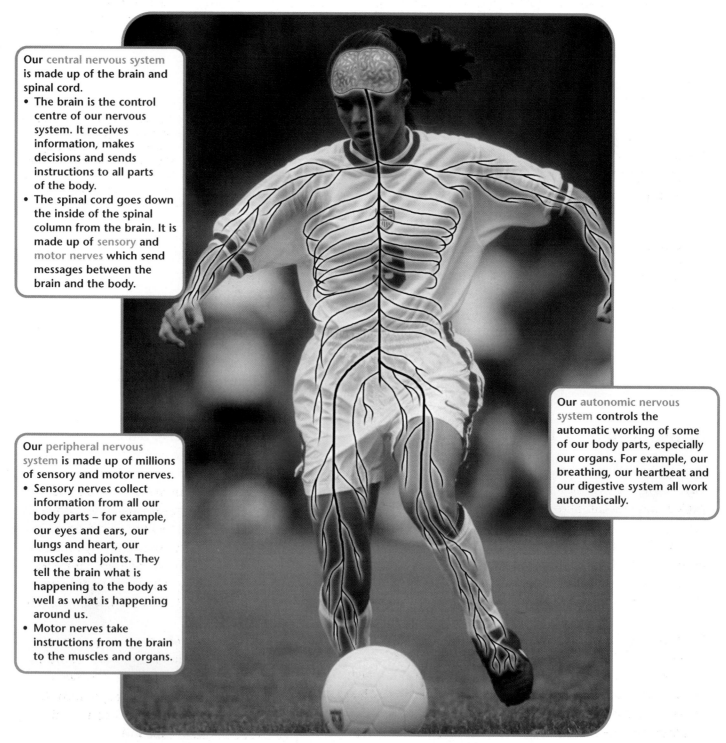

Our central nervous system is made up of the brain and spinal cord.
- The brain is the control centre of our nervous system. It receives information, makes decisions and sends instructions to all parts of the body.
- The spinal cord goes down the inside of the spinal column from the brain. It is made up of **sensory** and **motor nerves** which send messages between the brain and the body.

Our peripheral nervous system is made up of millions of sensory and motor nerves.
- Sensory nerves collect information from all our body parts – for example, our eyes and ears, our lungs and heart, our muscles and joints. They tell the brain what is happening to the body as well as what is happening around us.
- Motor nerves take instructions from the brain to the muscles and organs.

Our autonomic nervous system controls the automatic working of some of our body parts, especially our organs. For example, our breathing, our heartbeat and our digestive system all work automatically.

The nervous system

Our nervous system in action

The eyes take in information about the bowler, the speed of his run up, the flight of the ball and the position of the fielders. The ears hear the talking of the players and the noise of the crowd.

The hormone adrenaline is pumped around the body. This prepares all our body organs for sporting action. Heart rate and breathing both increase. Blood is diverted away from parts such as the digestive system towards the muscles that are working.

The sense organs in the muscles and joints tell the batsman about the position of his limbs and how he is holding the bat.

The brain receives a lot of information from the sensory nerves. Using previous experience it makes decisions about what to do. It then sends messages to the muscles about how to move to play the ball or let it go by.

The sense organs continue to send messages back to the brain as the cricketer plays the ball. The brain may alter its instructions to the muscles even as the ball is played.

Conditioned reflexes

If you are a skilled batsman you will have learned how to play many different strokes. Your brain can choose any of these strokes and you can play it automatically. These strokes have become conditioned reflexes. You will also have learned that the stroke you choose depends on the type of ball bowled. This means you can concentrate on the speed and direction of the ball and can decide where to play it. You do not have to worry about how to play the shot.

We learn many complex skills in our lifetime. For example, the movements in riding a bike, in swimming and throwing a ball become automatic. These patterns of movement, which we have learned, are called conditioned reflexes. We use them a lot in sport. However, we must take care to learn the correct technique. Changing an incorrect conditioned reflex can be very difficult, as golfers with a poor swing find out.

Our nervous system and sport

Our nervous system plans, controls and co-ordinates all our movements. Therefore sporting activity is totally dependent on it working efficiently. But a superbly muscled and conditioned person will not necessarily be skilful. Sporting skills need to be learned and are closely linked to the working of our nervous system.

Any damage to our nervous system is likely to reduce our ability to play sport. In contact sports there is always a danger of serious injury to the brain or spinal cord. Any such injury must be treated with the greatest care (see Chapter 6).

Our skeletal system

Without our skeletal systems we would look very different indeed. Our bodies would have no framework, our delicate organs would be unprotected, and we would be unable to move. Our skeletal systems all vary in size. This will limit our ability in some sports.

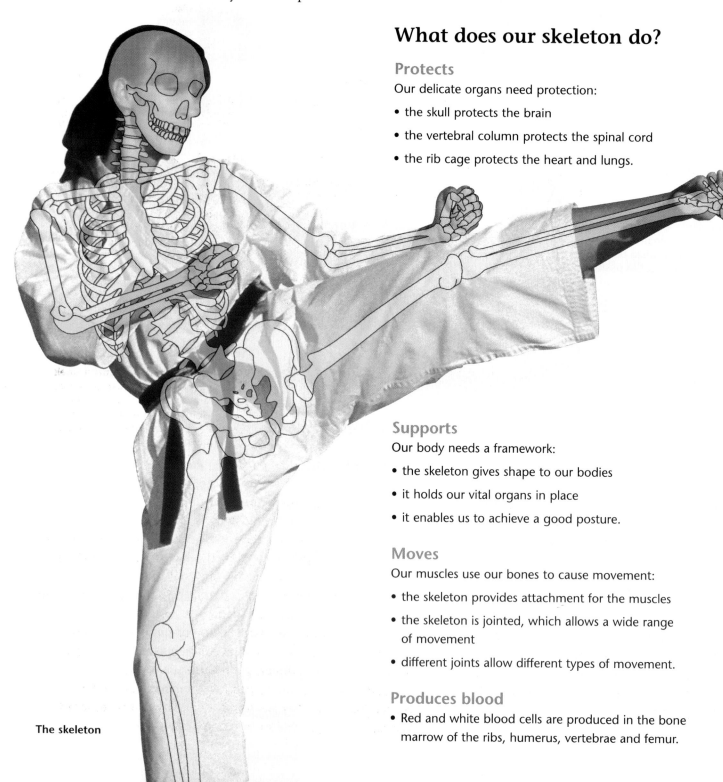

The skeleton

What does our skeleton do?

Protects
Our delicate organs need protection:

- the skull protects the brain
- the vertebral column protects the spinal cord
- the rib cage protects the heart and lungs.

Supports
Our body needs a framework:

- the skeleton gives shape to our bodies
- it holds our vital organs in place
- it enables us to achieve a good posture.

Moves
Our muscles use our bones to cause movement:

- the skeleton provides attachment for the muscles
- the skeleton is jointed, which allows a wide range of movement
- different joints allow different types of movement.

Produces blood
- Red and white blood cells are produced in the bone marrow of the ribs, humerus, vertebrae and femur.

How do our bones grow?

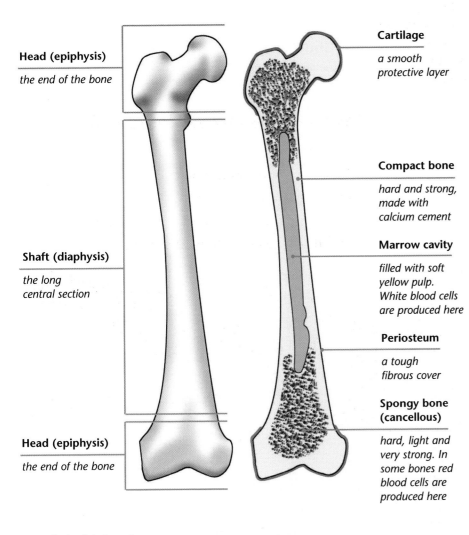

Head (epiphysis)

the end of the bone

Shaft (diaphysis)

*the long
central section*

Head (epiphysis)

the end of the bone

A typical adult long bone

Cartilage

*a smooth
protective layer*

Compact bone

*hard and strong,
made with
calcium cement*

Marrow cavity

*filled with soft
yellow pulp.
White blood cells
are produced here*

Periosteum

*a tough
fibrous cover*

**Spongy bone
(cancellous)**

*hard, light and
very strong. In
some bones red
blood cells are
produced here*

In the embryo

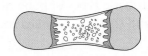

In the embryo (our state before birth)
most of the skeleton is made up of
cartilage. Cartilage is a firm, but
elastic material.

Young person

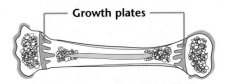

Growth plates

As the embryo grows so cartilage is
changed to bone. The development of
bone from cartilage is called ossification.
Ossification also continues through
childhood until adulthood. Bones
increase in length as the cartilage at the
growth plates is changed into bone.

Adult

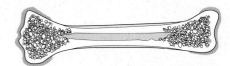

When we are fully grown only a small
amount of cartilage remains at the bone
ends. The bones have become hard and
rigid. Calcium compounds give them
hardness. Collagen fibres make them
strong and light.

Our bones change even when we are fully
grown. They adapt to any pressure that is
put upon them by making new bone and so
become stronger. Regular load-bearing
exercise throughout life will keep our bones
strong and healthy. When we get older this
process stops and our bones become lighter.
This condition is called osteoporosis and it
affects many older people. If we do not
strengthen our bones enough when we are
young they may weaken and break easily
when we are older.

Our skeletal system and sport

Exercise helps the development of the skeleton in young people.
Exercise can increase bone width, bone density and therefore
bone strength. It has no effect on bone length.

However, lifting heavy weights during the growing period can
damage the growth plates and lead to abnormal growth. If
muscle strength develops faster than skeletal strength, bones
can break up at the attachment point of the tendon, as happens
in Osgood–Schlatters disease at the knee. Strength training
during adolescence must be planned and supervised by a
qualified instructor. Injuries to bone need careful treatment to
avoid damage to growth areas.

What are the different bone types?

We have four basic types of bone in our body.
Their sizes and shapes are linked to how we use them.

● Long bones

These are the large bones in our legs, arms, fingers and toes. We use them in the main movements of our body.

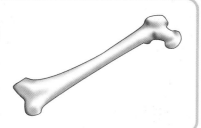

● Short bones

These are the small bones at the joints of our hands and feet. We use them in the fine movements of our body.

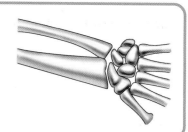

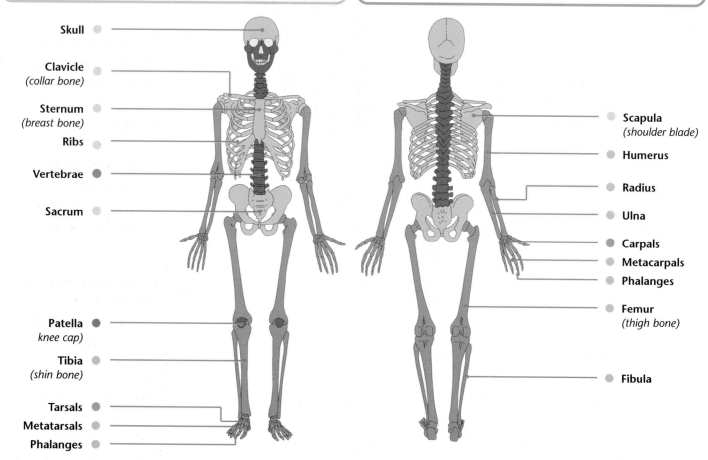

Skull

Clavicle
(collar bone)

Sternum
(breast bone)

Ribs

Vertebrae

Sacrum

Patella
(knee cap)

Tibia
(shin bone)

Tarsals

Metatarsals

Phalanges

Scapula
(shoulder blade)

Humerus

Radius

Ulna

Carpals

Metacarpals

Phalanges

Femur
(thigh bone)

Fibula

● Flat bones

These are the bones of our skull, shoulder girdle, ribs and pelvic girdle. We use them to protect the organs of our body. We can attach large muscles to our flat bones.

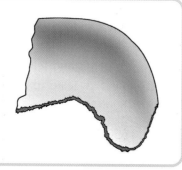

● Irregular bones

These are the bones in our face and vertebral column. We use them to give our body protection and shape.

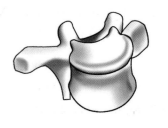

Note: ● The sesamoid bones are a special type of short bone within a tendon, for example, the patella (knee cap).

What are the main parts of our skeleton?

Our skeleton is divided into the **axial skeleton** and the **appendicular skeleton**.

Appendicular skeleton

- Shoulder girdle
- Arms
- Hip girdle
- Legs

Shoulder girdle

- Made up of two clavicles and two scapulas
- Is only linked by muscles to our vertebral column. This gives us great flexibility in our arms and shoulder. However, it limits the force we can use

Arms

- Humerus, radius and ulna
- There are eight carpal bones in the wrist
- Five metacarpal bones in the hand
- 14 phalanges in each hand

Hip girdle

- Made up of two halves, each formed by three bones, which are fused together on each side
- Forms a very stable joint with the vertebral column and passes the weight of the body to the legs
- Supports the lower abdomen and provides a strong joint for the femur
- The female pelvis is wider and shallower than the male pelvis. This is to make childbearing easier, but it does make running less efficient

Legs

- Femur, tibia and fibula
- There are seven tarsals in each foot
- Five metatarsals in the foot
- 14 phalanges in each foot

Axial skeleton

- Skull
- Vertebral column
- Sternum
- Ribs

Skull

- Made up of 28 bones
- There are also 14 bones in the face and six in the ear
- Fused together in early childhood
- Protects the brain, eyes and ears
- Balance mechanisms found in the ears

Sternum

- A large flat bone at the front of the ribcage
- Helps to make the rib cage stronger.

Ribs

- Made up of 12 pairs joined to the vertebral column
- Seven pairs are joined to the sternum
- Three pairs are joined to the seventh rib (false ribs)
- Two ribs are unattached (floating ribs)
- The ribcage protects our lungs and heart

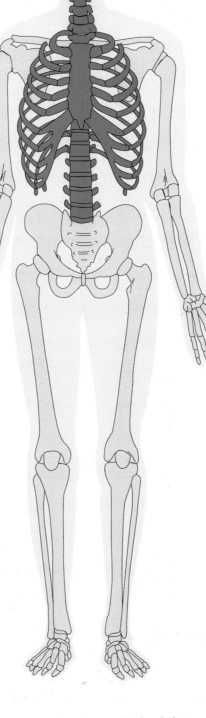

The axial and appendicular skeleton

Our vertebral column

The vertebral column is also called the spine or spinal column. It is made up of 33 small specialised bones called vertebrae. The vertebral column is divided into five regions. Each region has its own type of vertebrae which work in their own way.

Vertebral discs

There is a disc of cartilage between each vertebra. Each disc is a thick circle of tough tissue. It acts as a shock absorber for the vertebral column and allows movement between the vertebrae.

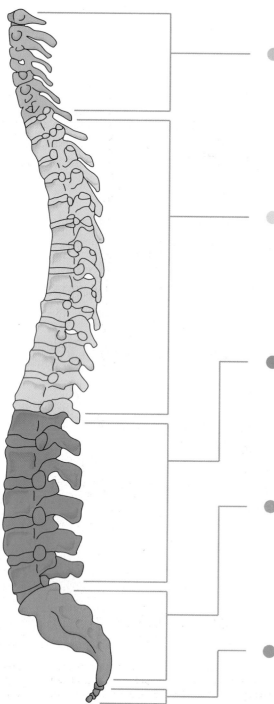

Seven cervical vertebrae
- Our smallest vertebrae
- The neck muscles are attached to them
- They support our head and neck
- The top vertebra, the Atlas, fits into the skull and lets the head nod
- The second vertebra, the Axis, lets the head rotate

Twelve thoracic vertebrae
- Our larger vertebrae
- Our ribs are attached to them
- They support the ribcage
- They allow us some slight movement, bending forward, backward and from side to side

Five lumbar vertebrae
- The largest vertebrae
- Our back muscles are attached to them
- They allow much bending forward, backward and from side to side
- The large range of movement means that this region can be easily injured

Five sacral vertebrae
- These vertebrae are fused together. They are also fused to the pelvic girdle
- They make a very strong base, which supports the weight of the body
- They also pass force from the legs and hips to the upper body

Four coccyx
- Our other fused vertebrae
- They have no special use

Functions of the vertebral column

Our vertebral column:
- protects the spinal cord
- supports the upper body
- gives us a wide range of movement
- is important for posture
- passes force to the other body parts.

Our vertebral column and sport

The vertebral column is important to all sporting movements. It has many joints and is both flexible and strong. This allows us to bend and stretch our bodies into very many different positions. You must always learn the correct technique in your sport to help avoid injury.

This is especially important in weight lifting, rugby, bowling in cricket and the throws in athletics. All spinal injuries should be treated very seriously. The injury can become permanent or even be life threatening.

This gymnast has bent her back into a hyperextension position. This should only be tried after much specialised training. Sportspeople can develop back injuries as a result of hyperextension.

The vertebral column of this badminton player is able to extend to allow him to play a high shot with strength.

This diver is able to change her body position with great precision whilst moving at speed through the air. Our vertebrae and discs are arranged to form a flexible but strong unit.

It is very important for this rugby player that the weight pushing against his shoulders is passed to his legs through a straight vertebral column. A bent back with his vertebrae out of line could lead to injury.

How do we move?

The skeleton has many joints. These allow our muscles to move our bones and let the whole body move. We have over 100 different joints in our bodies.

A joint is a place where two bones meet. Joints can be put into three different groups, based on the amount of movement they allow.

What is cartilage?

Cartilage is a tough but flexible tissue. Hyaline cartilage is found on the ends of our bones in all our synovial joints. It is different from other forms of cartilage found in the body. For example, we have pads of tough cartilage in the knee and vertebral column which act as shock absorbers.

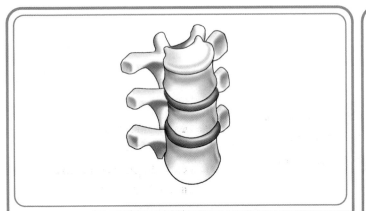

Slightly movable joints (cartilaginous joints)

- The bones are linked by cartilage.
- Slight movement is possible between the bones.
- Examples are found in the joints of the vertebral column and the joints between the ribs and sternum.

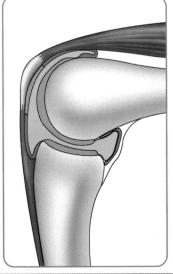

Freely movable joints (synovial joints)

- **Synovial joints** are complex joints.
- The bones are linked by ligaments.
- A wide variety of movement is possible.
- Examples are found throughout the body including knee, hip and shoulder.

● Hyaline cartilage
- Covers the heads of the bones at a joint
- A hard, tough, slippery layer
- Protects our bones
- Reduces friction in the joints

○ Joint capsule
- Made of fibrous tissue
- Holds the bones together at a joint
- Protects the joint

Ligaments (not shown)
- Bands of tough fibrous tissue
- Come in different shapes and sizes
- Hold bones together at joints
- Limit our range of movement
- Prevent dislocation
- Will stretch to a limited amount

● Synovial fluid
- Found in the joints
- Lubricates the joints
- Allows friction-free movement

● Synovial membrane
- A layer on the inside of our joint capsule
- Produces synovial fluid

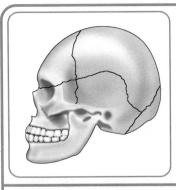
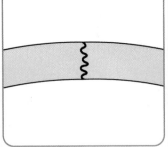

Immovable joints (fibrous joints)

- These are fixed joints.
- No movement is possible between the bones.
- Examples are found between the flat bones of the skull (sutures) and between the bones of the pelvic girdle.

Types of synovial joint

Synovial joints have different structures, depending on how they work. This means the shape of the bones varies, as does the arrangement of any ligaments. We can put joints into groups based on their structures.

There are six basic types of synovial joint:

- ball and socket
- hinge
- pivot
- saddle
- condyloid
- gliding (plane).

We can look at some joints in more than one way. For example, the knee joint has a condyloid joint structure, but actually works as a hinge joint. The knee joint can fit into more than one category of synovial joint.

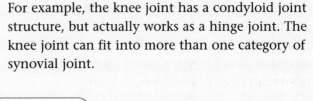

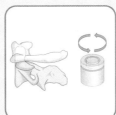

Pivot joint

- Only rotation is possible because it has a 'ring on a peg' structure
- Example: between the atlas and axis vertebrae in the neck

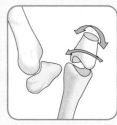

Saddle joint

- Allows movement in two planes at right angles to each other
- Bones are shaped like saddles and fit neatly together
- Movement is back and forward and side to side
- Movement is limited because of the shape of the bones
- Example: thumb

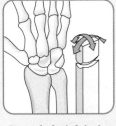

Condyloid joint

- Movement is possible in two planes
- The rounded end of one bone fits into the hollow of another
- Movement is back and forward and side-to-side
- Ligaments prevent rotation
- Example: wrist

Hinge joint

- Movement in one plane only
- Will open until it is straight
- Movement is limited because of the shape of the bones and the position of ligaments
- Example: elbow

Ball and socket joint

- Moves freely in all directions
- Ligaments are often used to keep the joint stable
- Examples: hip, shoulder

Gliding (plane) joint

- One bone slides on top of another
- A little movement is possible in all directions
- Ligaments limit the movement
- Example: vertebrae, carpal bones in the hand

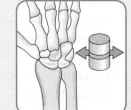

Our joints and sport

Our different joints work smoothly together when we make skilled sporting movements. They must be capable of a full range of movement in order to work well. The muscles and ligaments surrounding each joint must be strong enough to give stability to the joint.

The demands of sport put severe stress on our joints. We must warm up thoroughly before activity and should warm down afterwards.

Joints can be injured as a result of impact, internal forces or a mixture of both. Common examples include sprained ankle, torn knee ligaments and dislocated shoulder (see Chapter 7).

Type of joint	Movement allowed
Ball and socket	Flexion and extension Abduction and adduction Rotation and circumduction
Hinge	Flexion and extension
Pivot	Rotation only
Saddle	Flexion and extension Abduction and adduction
Condyloid	Flexion and extension Abduction and adduction
Gliding	Some gliding in all directions (no bending or circular movements)

Most joints extended

Most joints flexed

Examination-type questions: Our skeletal system

There are 12 marks for each question.

1 (a) Name two of the three bones of the arm. *(2 marks)*

(b) Name one organ of the body and the bones that protect it. *(2 marks)*

(c) Where do we find the following types of synovial joint in the body?
Give one example for each.
(i) Ball and socket
(ii) Hinge. *(2 marks)*

(d) Give three functions of the skeleton and explain what is meant
by each function. *(6 marks)*

2 (a) Give an example of:
(i) a flat bone
(ii) an irregular bone. *(2 marks)*

(b) In what part of the body are the following bones found:
(i) tibia
(ii) metacarpals? *(2 marks)*

(c) In a synovial joint, what is the function of:
(i) the synovial membrane
(ii) the synovial fluid? *(2 marks)*

(d) Two movements at a joint are flexion and extension. Explain each
movement by referring to a particular joint and the action taking place. *(6 marks)*

3 (a) Name the type of synovial joint found
(i) at the hip
(ii) between the thumb and the hand. *(2 marks)*

(b) The vertebral column consists of five regions. Name any two regions. *(2 marks)*

(c) Explain the difference between cartilage and bone. *(2 marks)*

(d) Describe the difference between the appendicular and axial
skeletons by naming three major bones for each. *(6 marks)*

4 (a) Give two functions of the vertebral column. *(2 marks)*

(b) Synovial joints are very common in the body.
Name two other types of joint. *(2 marks)*

(c) Explain the difference between the movements adduction and
abduction at a joint. *(2 marks)*

(d) Describe the development of bone from the embryo until maturity. *(6 marks)*

Answers are given in the World of Sport Examined Teacher Resource and Student Workbook.

Our muscular system

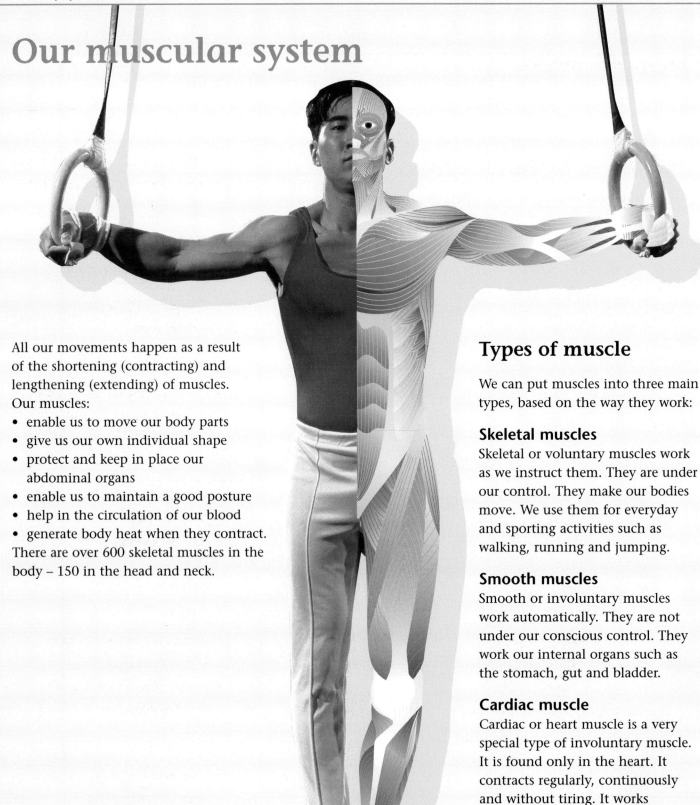

All our movements happen as a result of the shortening (contracting) and lengthening (extending) of muscles. Our muscles:

- enable us to move our body parts
- give us our own individual shape
- protect and keep in place our abdominal organs
- enable us to maintain a good posture
- help in the circulation of our blood
- generate body heat when they contract.

There are over 600 skeletal muscles in the body – 150 in the head and neck.

Types of muscle

We can put muscles into three main types, based on the way they work:

Skeletal muscles

Skeletal or voluntary muscles work as we instruct them. They are under our control. They make our bodies move. We use them for everyday and sporting activities such as walking, running and jumping.

Smooth muscles

Smooth or involuntary muscles work automatically. They are not under our conscious control. They work our internal organs such as the stomach, gut and bladder.

Cardiac muscle

Cardiac or heart muscle is a very special type of involuntary muscle. It is found only in the heart. It contracts regularly, continuously and without tiring. It works automatically but is under constant nervous and chemical control.

Our main muscles

Our major muscles

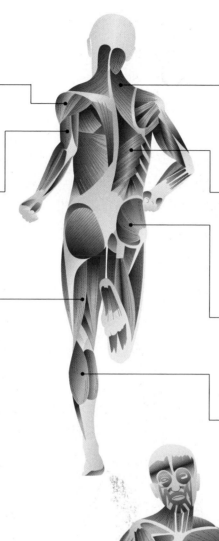

Deltoids:

- move the arm in all directions at the shoulder.
- Example: bowling in cricket.

Triceps:

- extends the forearm at the elbow
- extends the arm at the shoulder.
- Example: a smash in badminton.

Hamstrings:

- extend the hip joint
- flex the knee joint.
- Example: drawing the leg back before kicking a ball.

Trapezius:

- helps to control the shoulder girdle.
- Example: a player holding his head up in a rugby scrum.

Latissimus dorsi:

- adducts and extends the arm at the shoulder
- Example: swimming the butterfly stroke.

Gluteals:

- abduct and extend the hip joint.
- Example: stepping up during rock climbing.

Gastrocnemius:

- flexes the knee joint
- points the toes.
- Example: running.

Biceps:

- flexes the forearm at the elbow.
- Example: drawing a bow in archery.

Abdominals:

- rotate and raise the trunk
- strengthen the abdominal wall
- help with breathing.
- Example: performing upward circles on the bar in gymnastics.

Pectorals:

- adduct the arm and shoulder
- used for deep breathing.
- Example: playing a forehand drive in tennis .

Quadriceps:

- flexes the hip joint
- extends the knee joint.
- Example: taking off in high jump.

Note: These movement terms are explained on pages 32–33.

Our muscles in action

Different sports develop different muscle groups

Our muscles and sport

Successful sporting action depends on our muscles
working together to produce skilful movement. The
muscles we use depend on the sporting activity. For
example, in archery we use a limited number of
muscles in the upper body to work very closely
together for a short period of time. In contrast, for
wrestling we use most of the muscles of the body
vigorously for a longer period of time.

Sometimes we use different muscles at different
phases of an activity. For example, when throwing the
javelin we use our leg muscles in the run-up and our
upper body for the delivery.

How do our muscles work?

Our muscles can work in different ways.
There are three main types of muscular contraction:

- isotonic and concentric
- isotonic and eccentric
- isometric.

Isotonic contraction with muscles working concentrically

- Our muscles shorten as they contract
- The ends of the muscle move closer together
- Our biceps work in this way when we do a pull-up
- Most sporting movements are of this type

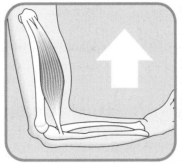

Muscle shortening

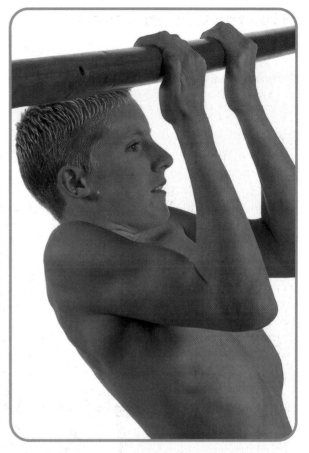

Isotonic contraction with muscles working eccentrically

- Our muscles lengthen as they contract under tension.
- The ends of the muscle move further apart
- Our biceps work in this way when we lower our body from a pull-up position
- Plyometric exercise uses eccentric contractions

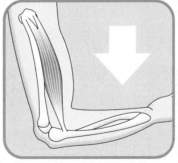

Muscle lengthening

Isometric contraction

- Our muscles stay the same length as they contract
- There is no movement, so the ends of the muscles stay the same distance apart
- Our shoulder muscles work in this way when we pull in a tug of war.
- In many sporting movements the stabilising muscles hold parts of the body steady as other parts move

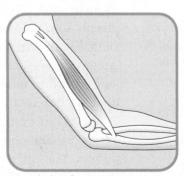

No movement

How do our muscles work together?

Our muscles can pull by contracting but they cannot push. If one muscle contracts across a joint to bring two bones together, another muscle is needed to pull the bones apart again. Therefore muscles always work in pairs. We need a large number of pairs of muscles to work together in different ways for even simple body movements. Our muscles take on different roles depending on the movement we are performing.

They can work as:

- **flexors**, contracting to bend our joints
- **extensors**, contracting to straighten our joints
- **prime movers** (or agonists), contracting to start a movement
- **antagonists**, relaxing to allow a movement to take place
- **fixators**, contracting to steady parts of the body to give the working muscles a firm base
- **synergists**, reducing unnecessary movement when a prime mover contracts. They can also fine tune our movement.

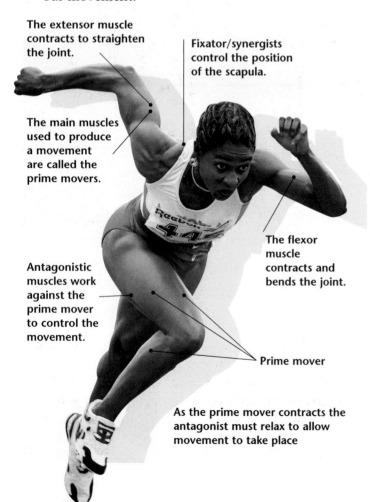

The extensor muscle contracts to straighten the joint.

Fixator/synergists control the position of the scapula.

The main muscles used to produce a movement are called the prime movers.

Antagonistic muscles work against the prime mover to control the movement.

The flexor muscle contracts and bends the joint.

Prime mover

As the prime mover contracts the antagonist must relax to allow movement to take place

ICT and muscle analysis

We can use a digital camcorder to record a sporting movement – for example, a sprint start. By playing it back in slow motion and using the freeze-frame facility we can see exactly how the muscles work. We can determine which muscles are the prime movers and the antagonists in the leg action, which muscles are acting as extensors and which as flexors. We can also identify the fixators and synergists.

By moving the video on a number of frames we can see how the roles of the muscles change. If a printer is available we can print out each of the still frames and label the muscles and their actions.

How are our muscles attached to our bones?

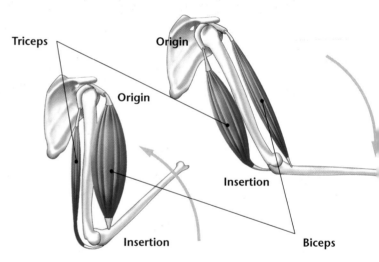

Triceps

Origin

Origin

Insertion

Insertion

Biceps

Our muscles are usually attached to two or more different bones. The muscle fibres end in a strong, flexible cord, called a **tendon**. The tendon is fixed deeply into the bone and very strongly attached. Tendons vary in shape and size. Some of our muscles are divided up into more than one part. They may end in two or more different tendons, which may be fixed to different bones.

When our muscles make the bones around a joint move, usually one bone stays fixed and the other moves. The end of the muscle that is attached to the fixed bone is called the **origin**. The other end of the muscle is called the **insertion**. It is attached to the bone which moves. As the muscle contracts the insertion moves towards the origin.

How do our muscles work in pairs?

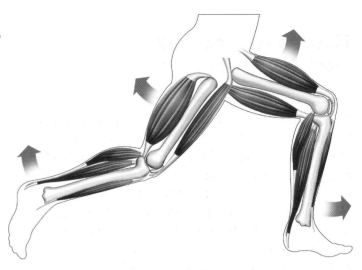

When a prime mover contracts the antagonist must relax to allow a movement to take place. However, the antagonist muscle will keep some fibres contracting. This is to stop our prime mover moving the joint so hard that the antagonists are damaged. Sometimes this system fails, for example when sprinters are running flat out. They may tear their hamstrings and quickly come to a painful stop.

In sport our muscles work in pairs

Muscle tone

The way our prime movers and antagonists work against each other also gives us **muscle tone.** All the time some muscle fibres are contracted whilst others are relaxed. This is true even when we are not moving. These contractions tighten the muscles a little, but are not strong enough to cause movement.

Different fibres contract at different times in order to prevent tiredness setting in.

This continuous slight contraction of our muscles is called muscle tone. It is very important for good **posture** and keeps the body ready for instant action.

Our posture

Our bodies are unstable when we are upright. This is because we have a high centre of gravity and a small base of support.

If we have good posture we can keep our bodies upright easily by keeping our centre of gravity over our base of support. Most of the weight of the body will be supported by the bones. We need only a little help from the muscles, which hold us upright. Good muscle tone, particularly in the lower back, leg and abdominal muscles, will help posture.

Good posture reduces the strain on our muscles, tendons and ligaments. It allows our body systems to work more easily and makes us less tired.

When we slouch, however, the upper back muscles must contract to move the body to the correct posture. If we continue to slouch the muscles will gradually adapt to that position. Poor posture may then become permanent.

Bad Posture

Good Posture

How can we have good posture when standing and walking?

- Stand with head up
- Stretch the back upward
- Keep shoulders straight and chest high and open
- Balance weight evenly on both feet
- Relax the knees
- Wear sensible shoes

How can we have good posture when sitting?

- Choose chairs that support the small of the back
- Sit back in the chair to support the lower back
- Have feet flat on the floor in front of you
- Try to have the knees higher than the hips
- Check that working surfaces are at the correct height
- Have a break every 20 minutes to gently exercise arms and shoulders

How can we have good posture when lifting?

- Never bend forward without bending the knees
- Keep back flat and straight
- Try to avoid lifting anything above the level of the elbows
- Keep objects as close to the body as possible
- Extend legs in order to lift objects
- Keep head up and eyes looking forward

Sporting posture

When we play sport we use a wide variety of body positions. We must take up the right body position for the situation we find ourselves in our sport.

Posture is important in two ways:
- starting position – examples include golf, discus and fencing
- position during the activity. We must maintain our **core stability**. This means that we are in a comfortable, balanced position. We are ready to perform the next sporting movement with power and control. Our centre of gravity is over our base of support. Muscle tone is essential for core stability.

Posture and sport

We often take up a special position when preparing to start our sport. For example, for golf we need to stand in a particular way to swing through and hit the ball well. If we fence we use a body position which allows us to move backwards and forwards very quickly in a sideways-on position. When preparing to putt a shot we position ourselves facing away from the direction of the putt.

Core stability is essential for all sports. Some sports require a special posture throughout the activity – as, for example, when we ski or ride a horse. However, we will adjust our posture to deal with different situations such as a slalom ski course or jumping fences on a horse.

In sports requiring a great deal of movement and uncertainty, core stability is essential in order to react quickly. For example, in football and netball we need to respond to the position of the ball and other players.

How are our muscles and leverage linked together?

We move because our skeletal muscles pull hard enough on our bones to make them move. Our muscles use our bones as levers. Levers have a hinge (or pivot), a load and a force working on them. In our bodies, our joints are the hinges. The load is the weight of our body, together with anything else in our hands such as a ball, racket or dumb-bell. The force is the muscular power we use to move our body and the object in our hands.

There are three different types of lever system in our body. The third-order system is the one we most commonly use. We can see it at work when we do biceps curls.

The length of the limb has an important effect on the movement around a joint. For example, a gymnast with short arms and legs can produce speed more quickly than one with long limbs. However, long limbs allow us to use force over a greater distance when we throw a discus. Our own particular physical build will give us an advantage in some physical activities and a disadvantage in others.

For biceps curls, the load is the dumb-bell, the force is the biceps contracting and the pivot is the elbow joint

A long arm allows force to be applied over a range of movement

What happens to our muscular system as we exercise?

- There is an increased flow of blood to the working muscles
- Muscles take up more of the oxygen from the blood
- The muscles contract more often and more quickly
- More of the muscle fibres contract
- There is a rise in temperature in the muscles

- Our stores of adenosine triphosphate (ATP) and creatine phosphate (CP) in the muscles are used up
- Waste products such as carbon dioxide and lactic acid build up in the muscles
- These waste products may lead to tiredness and cramp (muscle fatigue)
- Our stores of muscle glucose are used up
- Our ability to carry on will be affected
- Overuse of muscles can lead to soreness and strains

Muscle changes and sport

Our muscles increase in size and strength when we follow a regular strength training programme. This is called muscle hypertrophy. When we do not use our muscles regularly they get smaller and weaker. We call this muscle atrophy. This loss of size and strength often happens when we are recovering from an injury. If we are waiting for a particular injury to heal we should try to exercise the rest of the body as much as possible.

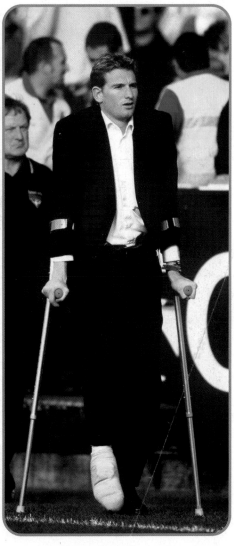

How does our body move?

When we play sport we move our limbs in many different directions. We use special words to describe these movements – extension, flexion, abduction, adduction, rotation and circumduction.

Extension
• Our limbs straighten at a joint

Flexion
• Our limbs bend at a joint.

Abduction
- Our limbs are moved away from a line down the middle of the body.

Adduction
- Our limbs are moved towards a line down the middle of the body.

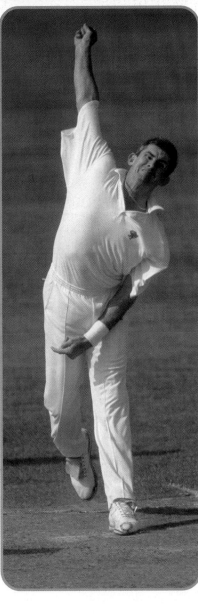

Rotation
- This is a circular movement – part of the body turns whilst the rest remains still.

Circumduction
- The end of a bone moves in a circle, for example swinging your arm in a circle at the shoulder.

What are muscle fibres?

Our muscles are made up of many tiny threadlike fibres packed together in bundles. We have two different types of fibres in our skeletal muscle: fast twitch and slow twitch.

Slow-twitch muscle fibres:
• have a very good oxygen supply
• work for a long time without tiring
• are not as strong as our fast-twitch fibres
• take longer to contract
• are used in all types of exercise
• are used especially in aerobic activities.

Our fast-twitch muscle fibres:
• do not have a good oxygen supply
• tire very quickly
• are stronger than our slow-twitch fibres
• contract very quickly
• are used when we need fast, powerful movements
• are used only in high-intensity exercise
• are used in anaerobic activities

Sprinters develop fast-twitch fibres

Distance runners develop slow-twitch fibres

Our muscle fibres and sport

If we jog slowly, only a few of our slow-twitch muscle fibres contract to move our legs. When we increase our speed we use more slow-twitch fibres. As we run faster our fast-twitch fibres also start to contract to help out. More and more will start to work as we run even faster. At top speed, all of our fast and slow twitch muscle fibres will be working.

In many sports we need to use the different fibres at different times. In hockey, for example, we need to use our fast-twitch fibres for quick sprints and our slow-twitch fibres for jogging when not involved in the action.

Our muscles are usually an equal mixture of both fast and slow-twitch muscle fibres. A person with more slow-twitch fibres is likely to be better at sports needing endurance such as cycling, running and swimming. Someone with more fast-twitch fibres is likely to be better at sprinting, throwing and jumping. We can train our muscle fibres to either contract more often (slow twitch) or more powerfully (fast twitch) – see Chapter 4.

Examination-type questions: Our muscular system

There are 12 marks for each question.

1 (a)   In what parts of the body are these muscles found:
   (i)   triceps
   (ii) trapezius?   *(2 marks)*

   (b)   Give two functions of muscles.   *(2 marks)*

   (c)   Describe the main action of the following muscles:
   (i)   biceps
   (ii) quadriceps.   *(2 marks)*

   (d)   Explain what is meant by good posture. Give two points to remember
        for each of standing, sitting and lifting.   *(6 marks)*

2 (a)   Name two major muscles of the leg.   *(2 marks)*

   (b)   A tendon joins two parts of the body together. Name the two body parts. *(2 marks)*

   (c)   Muscular contraction can be isotonic or isometric.
        Describe one example of each.   *(2 marks)*

   (d)   Name the three different types of muscle and give one example of each.   *(6 marks)*

3 (a)   Many muscles work in pairs. One muscle will flex a limb, the other
        will straighten it. Name one such pair of muscles.   *(2 marks)*

   (b)   Explain what is meant by:
   (i)   prime movers,
   (ii) fixators.   *(2 marks)*

   (c)   Voluntary and involuntary muscles work in different ways.
        Explain this difference.   *(2 marks)*

   (d)   Explain what happens to our muscles as we exercise. Give six changes.   *(6 marks)*

4 (a)   Cardiac muscle is found in the heart.
        Give two important points about cardiac muscle.   *(2 marks)*

   (b)   What is meant by muscle tone?   *(2 marks)*

   (c)   Describe the different effects on muscle of hypertrophy and atrophy.   *(2 marks)*

   (d)   Explain the main differences between fast and slow-twitch muscle fibres.
        Give two examples to show the importance of each fibre type for
        different sports.   *(6 marks)*

Answers are given in the World of Sport Examined Teacher Resource and Student Workbook.

Our circulatory system

Our circulatory system is made up of blood, blood vessels, pulmonary circulation, systemic circulation and the heart.

Our circulatory system:
- takes oxygen and nutrients to every cell
- removes carbon dioxide and other waste products from every cell
- carries hormones from the hormonal (endocrine) glands to different parts of the body
- maintains temperature and fluid levels
- prevents infection from invading germs.

Our systemic circulation carries oxygenated blood from the heart to the rest of our body. The deoxygenated blood returns to the heart with waste products, which have to be removed from our body.

Our pulmonary circulation carries deoxygenated blood from our heart to our lungs. Here carbon dioxide is exchanged for oxygen. Oxygenated blood is then carried back to the heart.

● Oxygenated blood flowing away from the heart

● Deoxygenated blood flowing towards the heart

Circulatory system

How does our heart work?

The heart is a muscular pump. It is made up of special cardiac muscle which contracts regularly, without tiring. It pumps blood first to the lungs, to exchange carbon dioxide for oxygen. Then blood with the new oxygen is returned to the heart to be pumped out around the body.

The three stages of heart action are shown below.

- Our cardiac cycle is one complete cycle of these three stages
- Our heartbeat is one complete contraction of the heart
- Our heart rate (pulse) is the number of heartbeats per minute

At rest our heart pumps between 50 and 80 times a minute. It pumps about 4.7 litres of blood around the body. At rest this journey takes about 20 seconds.

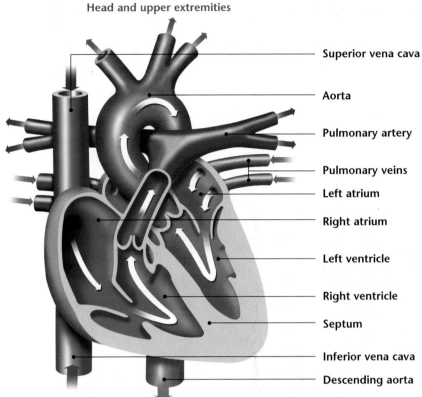

Head and upper extremities

Superior vena cava

Aorta

Pulmonary artery

Pulmonary veins

Left atrium

Right atrium

Left ventricle

Right ventricle

Septum

Inferior vena cava

Descending aorta

Trunk and lower extremities

Stage 1

- Blood flows into the heart when it is between beats and relaxed
- Deoxygenated blood from our body enters the right atrium through the two vena cava veins
- At the same time newly oxygenated blood from our lungs enters the left atrium through the pulmonary veins

Stage 2

- Our right atrium muscles contract to pump blood through the tricuspid valve into the right ventricle
- At the same time our left atrium muscles contract to pump blood through the mitral valve into the left ventricle

Stage 3

- Our right ventricle muscles contract to pump blood through the semilunar valves into the pulmonary artery to travel to the lungs
- Our left ventricle muscles contract to pump blood through the semilunar valves into the aorta, to travel around our body again

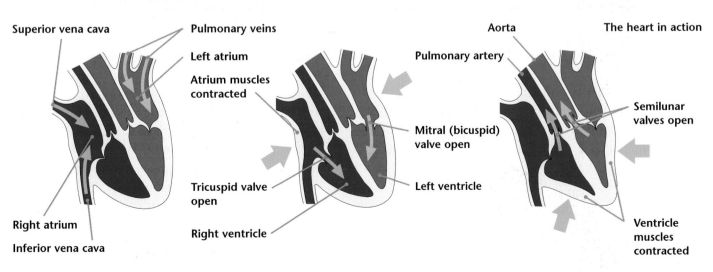

Superior vena cava

Pulmonary veins

Left atrium

Atrium muscles contracted

Tricuspid valve open

Right ventricle

Right atrium

Inferior vena cava

Aorta

Pulmonary artery

Mitral (bicuspid) valve open

Left ventricle

Aorta

The heart in action

Semilunar valves open

Ventricle muscles contracted

How does blood move around the body?

The heart is actually a double pump. It is divided into two parts by a muscular wall called the septum.

The right-hand side of the heart deals with blood returning from our body through the vena cava veins. During its journey, our blood has given up much of its oxygen. It has picked up waste products, including carbon dioxide. It is now a dull red colour. The heart pumps this blood to our lungs in our pulmonary artery. This is the only artery which carries deoxygenated blood.

Our blood vessels include arteries, arterioles, veins, venules and capillaries. These carry blood to all parts of the body and back again to the heart.

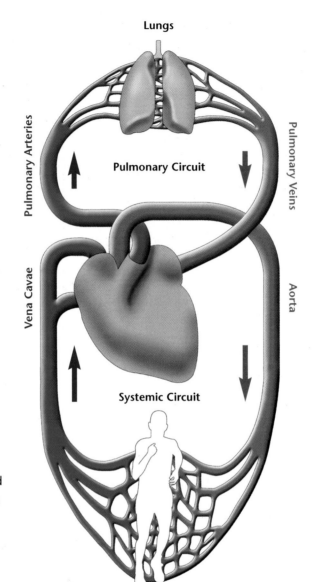

Lungs

Pulmonary Arteries

Pulmonary Veins

Pulmonary Circuit

Vena Cavae

Aorta

Systemic Circuit

● Deoxygenated blood   ● Oxygenated blood

The left-hand side of the heart deals with the blood returning from our lungs in our pulmonary veins. These are the only veins that carry oxygenated blood. In our lungs the blood releases carbon dioxide and other waste products, and is supplied with fresh oxygen. When blood returns to the heart it is bright red. The heart pumps this blood into our largest artery, the aorta, to travel around the body.

Our arteries carry freshly oxygenated blood from the heart. They become smaller and smaller. The smallest arteries are called arterioles. They take blood into the tissue where they join up with our smallest vessels – the capillaries. In turn the capillaries join up with venules, which increase in size to become veins. Our veins return deoxygenated blood to our heart.

Our heart and sport

As we work harder our muscles need more oxygen. The oxygen is delivered by our blood. The right type of training can increase the size and pumping ability of the heart (see Chapter 4). In this way we can increase the amount of oxygen going to our working muscles. This will help us to work harder and for longer in our sport. During hard physical activity, our heart rate can increase to over 200 beats per minute. The heart of a trained athlete can pump up to 45 litres of blood a minute.

Our blood circulation and sport

The body can alter the flow of blood to different areas. At rest our skeletal muscles need little oxygen, so only 15–20% of our heart's output goes to them. During exercise more blood is directed to these working muscles and away from such areas as the digestive system. As much as 80% of the heart's output may go to our working muscles during exhausting exercise.

How does oxygen get to our muscles?

1. Arteries:

- thick walled
- elastic, expand to carry blood
- blood under high pressure
- no valves needed, artery walls contract to move blood
- carry blood away from the heart
- carry oxygenated blood (except pulmonary artery)

2. Capillaries:

- microscopic blood vessels linking arterioles and venules
- extremely thin walls, one cell thick
- allow food and oxygen to pass out to our body tissues
- allow carbon dioxide and other waste to pass into blood from our body tissues

3. Veins:

- thin walled
- non-elastic
- blood under low pressure
- have valves to stop blood flowing backwards
- carry blood to the heart
- carry deoxygenated blood (except pulmonary veins)

Smooth inner lining
Elastic fibre and muscle
Non-elastic fibres

Artery   Vein

What happens in our capillaries?

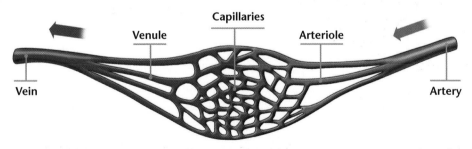

Venule — Capillaries — Arteriole

Vein   Artery

Our capillary network is extremely large. It is also very dense in active tissue such as muscles. Arterioles bring oxygen and nutrients to the capillaries. In muscle tissue the oxygen and nutrients squeeze out through the thin capillary walls. This enables the muscle to work. As a muscle contracts it produces waste products, including carbon dioxide, which squeeze back into the capillaries. The capillaries then join up with venules, which lead to veins and back to the heart. Carbon dioxide is then removed by our lungs. Other waste is removed by our kidneys.

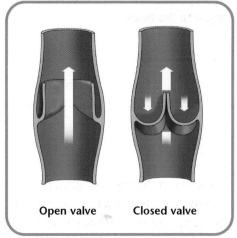

Open valve   Closed valve

Valves

- Blood returning to our heart is under low pressure.
- Valves are needed to stop the blood flowing backwards

What makes up our blood?

The total volume of blood in the body is different for different people. It depends mainly on body size. Men on average have 5–6 litres and women 4–5 litres.

Blood is made up of 55% plasma and 45% formed elements. The formed elements are red blood cells (called erythrocytes), white blood cells (called leukocytes), and platelets (called thrombocytes).

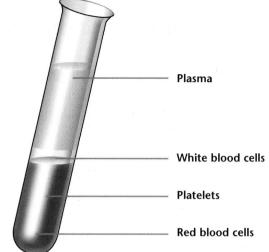

Plasma

White blood cells

Platelets

Red blood cells

Plasma:

- is a watery liquid
- is pale yellow in colour
- contains dissolved substances: salts and calcium, nutrients including glucose, hormones, carbon dioxide and other waste from our body cells.

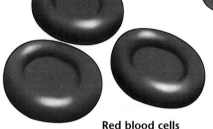

Red blood cells

Red blood cells:

- are made in the red marrow of our long bones, sternum, ribs and vertebrae
- are extremely numerous
- give blood its colour
- contain haemoglobin, which carries oxygen from the lungs to all our body cells
- have no nucleus and last for about 120 days
- are replaced in very large numbers.

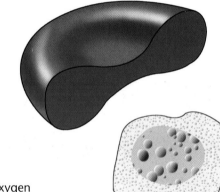

White blood cells

Platelets:

- are made in our bone marrow
- stick to each other easily
- produce clots when a blood vessel is damaged
- work with fibrinogen to make blood clot.

White blood cells:

- are made in our bone marrow, lymph nodes and spleen
- are far fewer than red blood cells
- are three times the size of red blood cells
- are a mobile guard system to deal with infection and disease: some eat up germs, some produce antibodies to destroy germs.

Our blood and sport – altitude training

At high altitude it is more difficult for people to carry sufficient oxygen in their blood to supply their working muscles. As a result people who live at high altitude have more red blood cells and haemoglobin than those who live at sea level. This helps them to take in sufficient oxygen for their activities.

Endurance athletes from high-altitude areas usually have an advantage when they compete at sea level. They can carry extra oxygen in their blood, which helps their performance. For this reason, sportspeople will train at high altitude to improve their stamina (aerobic capacity).

How do our red cells carry oxygen?

Our red blood cells contain an iron-based substance called haemoglobin. When the blood travels to our lungs the oxygen in the air joins up with the haemoglobin in the blood to form oxyhaemoglobin.

Our blood is now oxygenated and bright red. In this way the oxygen is carried by our blood around our body.

When blood arrives at our capillaries, the oxyhaemoglobin breaks down, setting the oxygen free to pass out to our body cells.

Our blood is now deoxygenated and dull red in colour. It is pumped back first to our heart then to our lungs to pick up more oxygen.

What does our blood do?

Our blood links all the tissues and organs of our body together. It has four main functions.

Transportation

- Carries nutrients from our digestive system to all our body cells
- Takes oxygen from our lungs to our working muscles
- Removes carbon dioxide from our body in our lungs
- Removes waste products and excess water in our kidneys
- Takes hormones to where they are needed

Protection

- Carries white cells to sites of infection
- Carries antibodies to destroy germs
- Carries platelets to damaged areas to form clots

Functions of blood

Temperature regulation

- Carries heat away from working muscles to skin
- Carries heat away from centre of body to skin
- Maintains temperature within the body

Maintaining body's equilibrium

- Reduces the effect of lactic acid produced in the working muscles
- Regulates fluid balance
- Enables hormones and enzymes to work

How well does our heart pump?

The heart is made up of cardiac muscle and we cannot control its action. Fortunately cardiac muscle never tires. The speed and force of each heartbeat is controlled by the brain. Our brain is affected by what we are doing. If we start running, our brain tells our heart to pump more blood to supply our working leg muscles with more oxygen.

Heart muscle can get stronger when exercised, like any other muscle.

The amount of blood pumped by the heart depends on heart rate and stroke volume.

Heart rate

Heart rate is the number of times the heart beats per minute. At each heartbeat, blood is pumped out of the heart into the arteries. Our arteries are forced to expand and then contract, which is called our pulse. The number of pulses in one minute is the heart rate. For a normal adult when resting this will be about 70 beats per minute.

A pulse can be felt at points in the body where arteries are near to the skin.

Carotid – in the neck, in the groove beside the windpipe

Radial – at the wrist, below the thumb

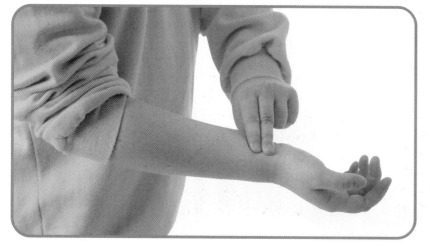

Our heart rate and sport

Resting heart rates can vary between people, due to factors such as sex, age and health. For a healthy, resting adult it is about 70 beats per minute. Endurance sportspeople will have a much lower rate, perhaps as low as 30 beats per minute. This is because their hearts are stronger and are able to pump more blood in fewer beats than an unfit person. Their stroke volume is therefore greater.

Resting heart rate can be one way to show fitness level. The speed at which heart rate returns to normal after exercise is called the recovery rate. This rate can also be used to measure fitness.

Stroke volume

Stroke volume is the amount of blood pumped by the heart in each beat.

Whenever we exercise stroke volume increases for a number of reasons. Working muscles squeeze blood in our veins, forcing more blood back to the heart. The heart stretches as it fills up with the extra blood and in turn it contracts more strongly. This results in more blood being pumped out of the heart for each beat.

Cardiac output

Cardiac output is the amount of blood pumped out of the heart per minute.

It is controlled by both heart rate and stroke volume:

heart rate × stroke volume = cardiac output

In sport we usually want to increase the amount of blood going to the working muscles – that is, our cardiac output. We can do this by increasing stroke volume, heart rate or both.

What is blood pressure?

Blood pressure is the force of the blood against the walls of the blood vessels. It is different in different blood vessels. It depends on how much blood is flowing into the blood vessels and how easily it can flow out.

In our arteries the blood pressure is high because the arteries are narrow and a lot of blood is being forced into them from the heart. Blood flows only slowly in the wider veins, which are a long way from the heart. Here blood pressure is low and so valves are needed to prevent blood from flowing backwards.

How do we measure blood pressure?

We use a special instrument to measure the pressure needed to stop the blood flowing through an artery. It is always measured in our upper arm and two readings are taken. Blood pressure should be taken when we are relaxed and resting. It will therefore be at its lowest.

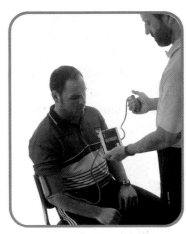

What will affect blood pressure?

- Age: blood pressure increases as we grow older because our arteries are less elastic.
- Exercise: blood pressure increases when we exercise but returns to normal after exercise. Regular exercise helps to lower resting blood pressure and prevent cardiovascular disease.
- Stress: stress causes hormones to be released into the blood, which increases blood pressure.

Exercise affects blood pressure

- Smoking: smoking increases blood pressure because nicotine reduces the efficiency of our capillaries.
- Diet: a diet high in fat or salt may lead to increased blood pressure. This is because fatty deposits may block up or harden arteries. Excess salt intake may lead to an imbalance in the body's chemistry.
- Weight: being overweight puts an extra strain on the circulatory system and so raises blood pressure.

What does high blood pressure mean?

A person has high blood pressure (called hypertension) if readings stay high over a long period of time. Hypertension may be caused by blockages in the smaller blood vessels, which means that the heart has to work harder to force blood around the body. Arteries taking blood to the heart muscle can also become blocked. Sudden activity can cause a sharp pain (called angina) or even a heart attack.

Our blood pressure and sport

During sport the heart beats faster and pumps out more blood. Blood pressure rises. This is quite normal. Regular sensible exercise linked with a healthy diet and lifestyle will actually lower resting blood pressure. In sport, illegal blood doping raises blood pressure. Recently some drugs such as erythropoietin (EPO), which has been taken by some cyclists, have reduced blood pressure to dangerously low levels.

What happens to our circulatory system when we exercise?

- The hormone adrenaline is released even before we start to exercise. It prepares the body for action.
- Adrenaline in the bloodstream causes the heart to beat more quickly – heart rate increases.

- The heart contracts more powerfully. It sends out a greater amount of blood with each contraction. Stroke volume increases.

- Blood circulation speeds up and greater amounts of oxygen-carrying blood reach the working muscles. Cardiac output increases.

- The pumping action of muscles forces more deoxygenated blood back to the heart more quickly.
- Blood flow to the areas of the body not in urgent need of oxygen, for example our digestive system, is reduced.
- Blood flow to the areas in greatest need of oxygen, for example our skeletal muscles, is increased.

- Blood vessels to skin areas become enlarged. This allows excess heat from muscles and organs to be lost more easily from the skin.
- During very hard exercise even these blood vessels will be reduced in size. Body temperature will then rise very quickly. It can cause overheating and fatigue.

- The oxygen going to the muscles can be up to three times the resting amount.
- Blood flow can be increased up to 30 times. Therefore, the working muscles can receive up to 90 times the amount of oxygen they receive at rest.

Examination-type questions: Our circulatory system

There are 12 marks for each question.

1 (a)   Name two of the major components of blood.   *(2 marks)*

   (b)   Where is blood carried to in
         (i)   the aorta
         (ii) the vena cava?   *(2 marks)*

   (c)   Describe two differences between arteries and veins.   *(2 marks)*

   (d)   Explain how the heart, lungs and circulatory system work together to
         get blood to working muscles.   *(6 marks)*

2 (a)   Name two functions of the circulatory system.   *(2 marks)*

   (b)   Give two factors that might affect blood pressure.   *(2 marks)*

   (c)   Blood arrives at the working muscles in the capillaries.
         Explain what happens to it then.   *(2 marks)*

   (d)   Our circulatory system responds to exercise. Describe six changes
         that occur when we exercise.   *(6 marks)*

3 (a)   Name the components of blood which:
         (i)   help clotting
         (ii) carry oxygen.   *(2 marks)*

   (b)   What is meant by:
         (i)   heart rate
         (ii) stroke volume?   *(2 marks)*

   (c)   Explain why our pulse increases when we exercise.   *(2 marks)*

   (d)   Name three functions of blood and give one example to illustrate
         each function.   *(6 marks)*

4 (a)   The heart has four chambers, called the upper and lower ventricles
         and atria. Where does blood go when it leaves
         (i)   the right ventricle
         (ii) the left ventricle?   *(2 marks)*

   (b)   Suggest two ways in which the pulse can be used to show our level
         of fitness.   *(2 marks)*

   (c)   Describe the difference between the systemic and pulmonary
         circulation systems.   *(2 marks)*

   (d)   Explain why an efficient circulatory system is important for sportspeople. *(6 marks)*

Answers are given in the World of Sport Examined Teacher Resource and Student Workbook.

Our respiratory system

Our bodies are made up of millions of cells, all of which use oxygen to break down the nutrients from food. This sets free the energy the cells need to work. Our respiratory system takes in oxygen from the air and transfers it to the blood in our lungs. The oxygen travels to the cells in our blood, where it is exchanged for carbon dioxide. Our respiratory system then removes the carbon dioxide.

What happens as we breathe?

- Air enters through the nose and mouth.
- The **nasal cavity** contains mucus and hair. It moistens, filters and warms the air.

- The **palate** separates the nasal cavity from the mouth. It allows us to chew and breathe at the same time.

- The **epiglottis** is a flap at the back of the throat. It closes when we swallow to stop food from going down the trachea.

- The **trachea** (windpipe) has rings of cartilage to hold it open. It divides into two bronchi. Each bronchus branches out into smaller tubes which in turn become bronchioles.
- The **bronchioles** split up and end in **alveoli**.
- The **alveoli** are thin-walled, spongy, air sacs. Most of our lung tissue is made up of large numbers of alveoli. When we breathe these tiny air sacs fill with air and then empty.

- The **lungs** are two thin-walled elastic sacs lying in our chests, in the thoracic cavity. This is an airtight area with ribs at the back and front and the diaphragm below.
- The **pleural membranes** surround the lungs. They are slippery, double skins which keep the lungs moist. They also lubricate the outside of the lungs. The membranes slide against one another as our lungs expand and contract. This reduces friction with the surrounding ribs and diaphragm.

- The **diaphragm** is a sheet of muscle which separates the thoracic cavity from the rest of the body. It is very important for breathing.
- The **intercostal muscles** are found between the ribs and they control rib movement. They are very important for breathing.

How do we breathe?

Breathing is the first stage in supplying oxygen to our body cells. Breathing is also called external or pulmonary respiration.

When breathing in (inspiration):

- The intercostal muscles contract, lifting the ribs upwards and outwards. The chest expands
- The diaphragm contracts. It pulls down and flattens out the floor of the rib cage. The chest expands some more

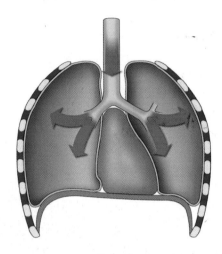

- The lungs increase in size as the chest expands. This is because their outside surface is stuck to the chest wall
- The pressure inside our lungs falls as they expand. The higher pressure of air outside means air is now sucked into the lungs through the nose and mouth.

When breathing out (expiration):

- The intercostal muscles relax. The ribs move downwards and inwards under their own weight. The chest gets smaller
- The diaphragm relaxes. It is pushed back into a domed position by the organs underneath it. The chest gets even smaller

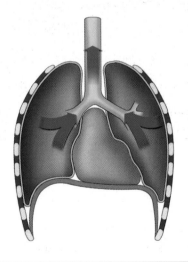

- The lungs decrease in size as the chest gets smaller. They are squeezed by the ribs and diaphragm
- The pressure inside the lungs increases as they get smaller. The air pressure outside is now lower than in our lungs. Air is forced out of the lungs through the nose and mouth.

Our breathing and sport

When the body is at rest the movements of the diaphragm alone are enough for breathing. Breathing is automatic. As soon as we start physical activity we use our intercostal muscles to increase the depth of breathing.

We breathe in and out about 16 times a minute at rest. We take in about 0.5 litres of air in each breath. If we exercise very hard, breathing rate can increase to 50 times a minute and the amount of air taken in can exceed 2.5 litres in each breath. Therefore the amount of air breathed in can increase from 8 litres to 125 litres a minute.

Some players have used nasal strips which they claim help them to breathe better whilst they are playing. Training can certainly improve breathing (see Chapter 4).

How do we get oxygen to our working muscles?

The respiratory system needs two stages to supply oxygen to the working muscles and all the other body cells.

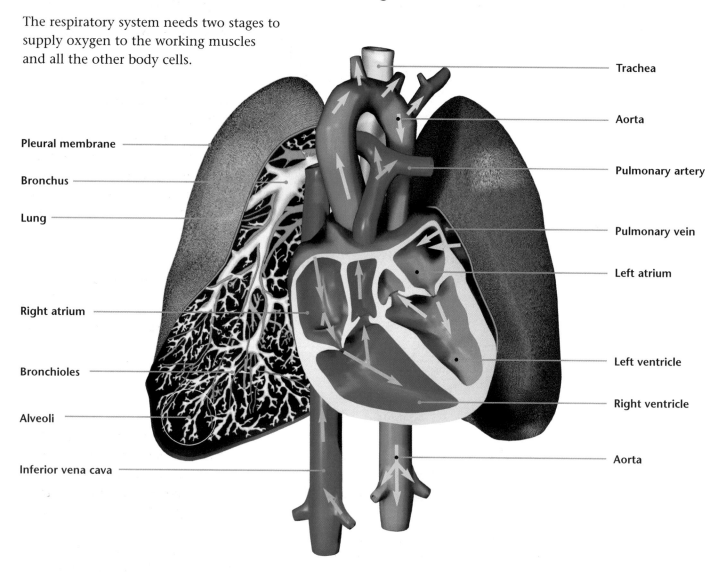

Trachea

Aorta

Pulmonary artery

Pulmonary vein

Left atrium

Left ventricle

Right ventricle

Aorta

Pleural membrane

Bronchus

Lung

Right atrium

Bronchioles

Alveoli

Inferior vena cava

Stage 1

This is called **external** (or **pulmonary**) **respiration**. We know it as breathing. It includes:

- getting air into and out of the lungs
- exchanging oxygen and carbon dioxide in the lungs
- getting oxygen into the bloodstream.

External (or pulmonary) respiration

- The air we breathe in passes through our trachea, into our bronchi, and through our bronchi into our bronchioles. The bronchioles end in tiny air sacs called alveoli.

- There is direct contact between the walls of the alveoli and the capillaries. The capillaries contain deoxygenated blood that has been brought to the lungs in the pulmonary artery.

- The haemoglobin in the blood of the capillaries takes up oxygen from the alveoli.

- Carbon dioxide is exchanged for the oxygen and is breathed out.

- The oxygenated blood is carried in the pulmonary veins to the left side of the heart.

- The oxygenated blood is then pumped through our aorta to muscles and other body cells.

- After exchanging oxygen for carbon dioxide and other waste products in our cells, the deoxygenated blood returns to the heart in our veins.

- In the alveoli the carbon dioxide is exchanged once again for oxygen and breathed out.

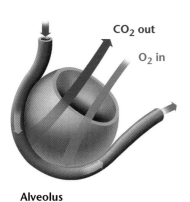

Alveolus

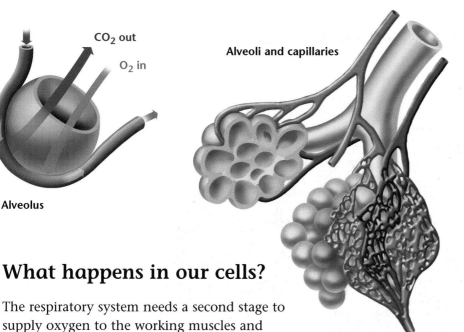

Alveoli and capillaries

What happens in our cells?

The respiratory system needs a second stage to supply oxygen to the working muscles and other body cells.

Stage 2

This is called **internal** (or **cell**) **respiration**. It includes:

- getting oxygen into the body cells
- exchanging oxygen and carbon dioxide in the cells
- removing carbon dioxide and waste

Internal (or cell) respiration

- The heart pumps the oxygenated blood around the body in the arteries. The oxygen is carried by the haemoglobin in the red blood cells.

- The arteries get smaller and smaller, becoming arterioles. These end in a network of capillaries which cover every part of the body cells.

- The capillaries are tiny, with walls only one cell thick. It is easy for oxygen and nutrients such as glucose to escape through these walls into the cells.

- At the same time carbon dioxide and other waste products such as water move from the cells to the capillaries. The blood has now lost its oxygen.

- The capillaries join up with small veins called venules. These carry deoxygenated blood to the veins.

- Blood returns to the heart in the veins.

- In this process we use oxygen to release the energy from glucose inside our body cells. This can be shown as:

$$\begin{array}{ccc} & & \text{energy} \\ \text{glucose} & & + \\ + & = & \text{carbon dioxide} \\ \text{oxygen} & & + \\ & & \text{water} \end{array}$$

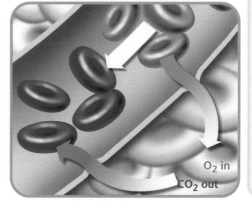

A capillary in a muscle

How does the air in our lungs change?

The air we breathe in (called inspired air) exchanges some of its oxygen for carbon dioxide in our lungs.

The air we breathe out (called expired air) therefore contains less oxygen and more carbon dioxide. It also has much more water vapour, which is also a waste product from our cells.

Inspired air		Expired air	
Nitrogen	79%	Nitrogen	79%
Oxygen	21%	Oxygen	16%
Carbon dioxide	0.04%	Carbon dioxide	4%

Our breathing control and sport

We breathe to supply our cells with oxygen. To play sport we need extra oxygen. The harder our muscles have to work, the more energy they will use up and therefore the more oxygen they will need.

Breathing can be increased whenever necessary. It is controlled by the respiratory centre in the brain. Carbon dioxide levels increase when we work hard. Carbon dioxide enters the bloodstream from the muscles. The respiratory centre checks this increased level of carbon dioxide and makes our body take more frequent and deeper breaths to help to get rid of the carbon dioxide through the lungs – and at the same time take in much-needed oxygen.

Extreme effort or anxiety can cause very fast breathing (called hyperventilation) due to the build up of carbon dioxide levels.

How much air can our lungs hold?

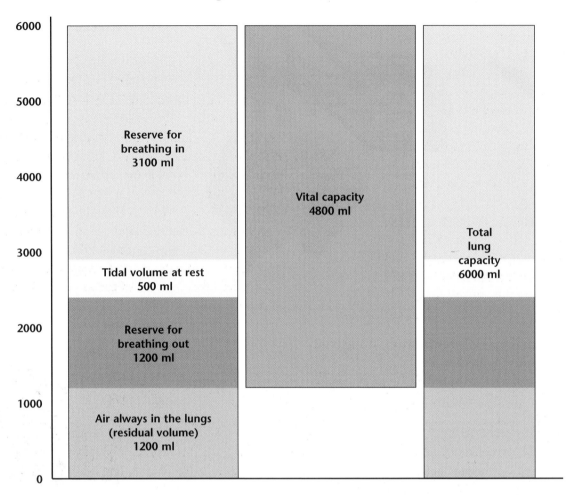

Respiratory rate is how many breaths we take in one minute.

Tidal volume is the amount of air we can take in or out with one breath. It can vary a lot. When resting, only about 0.5 litres of air moves in and out of our lungs with each breath. Not all of this reaches the alveoli: some remains in our nose and throat.

Minute volume is the amount of air we can breathe in in one minute. We can work it out using this formula:

minute volume = tidal volume x respiratory rate

If we start an activity the body will need more oxygen. We can supply it if we can increase our minute volume. We can do this by increasing our tidal volume or respiratory rate. To do this we can breathe more deeply, or increase our rate of breathing or do both.

Vital capacity is the largest amount of air that we can force out of our lungs after breathing in as deeply as possible. It is our maximum tidal volume and is usually about 4.8 litres in adults.

Residual volume is the amount of air left in the lungs after breathing out as hard as possible. We need some air in our lungs to prevent them collapsing. It is usually about 1.2 litres.

Total lung capacity is vital capacity added to residual volume.

Total lung capacity (6.0 l)	=	vital capacity (4.8 l)	+	residual volume (1.2 l)

Can lung capacity affect sporting success?

Lung capacity can differ with age, sex, body type and stamina (aerobic fitness). Just because you have a large lung capacity does not mean you will have stamina.

Two athletes could have exactly the same lung capacity but have totally different levels of fitness. The fitter athlete will be able to make much greater use of the oxygen that is inhaled through his or her lungs. We would say that the fitter athlete has a better maximum aerobic capacity, written as VO_2 max (see Chapter 2).

Our lungs are relatively delicate and can be harmed by a wide range of everyday pollutants. Car exhaust fumes, chemical insecticides and cigarettes are all harmful to even healthy lungs. People who suffer from asthma have to be particularly careful about the air that they breathe.

Oxygen and sport

We need energy for all our sports. To create this energy we need glucose and oxygen. The digestive system supplies the glucose to the working muscles. The respiratory and circulatory systems work together to supply oxygen to the working muscles. They also remove carbon dioxide and other waste products.

During strenuous sporting activity we produce a lot of carbon dioxide. Carbon dioxide reduces our ability to carry oxygen in the blood. We need to remove carbon dioxide as quickly as possible

Our success in getting extra oxygen to the working muscles and the removal of carbon dioxide depends on our stamina (aerobic capacity).

What happens to our respiratory system when we exercise?

When we exercise, more oxygen is needed by our working muscles and more carbon dioxide must be removed. This can be done by:

- increasing rate of breathing
- increasing depth of breathing, up to the vital capacity
- increasing the blood flow through the lungs
- increasing the oxygen taken up and used by the body.

Oxygen used during exercise can be up to 20 times a person's normal oxygen uptake. The maximum amount of oxygen a person can take up and use within a minute is the VO_2max. This may be, for example, 5.5 litres per minute for an endurance athlete.

Breathing changes during exercise:

Adult	Resting	During exercise
tidal volume	0.5 litres	2.5 litres
respiratory rate	12 breaths per minute	30 breaths per minute
minute volume	6 litres a minute	75 litres a minute

Our respiratory system and sport

The respiratory system is important for health and sporting performance. It is more important for some sports than for others. For example, in archery, snooker and shot putt competitions the efficiency of the respiratory system is not important. However, in swimming, running, cycling, major team games and most other sports performance will be affected by the efficiency of the respiratory system. As sportspeople we should avoid activities which reduce the efficiency of our respiratory system such as smoking cigarettes.

Examination-type questions: Our respiratory system

There are 12 marks for each question.

1 (a) During normal breathing in, what happens to:
(i) the ribs
(ii) the diaphragm? *(2 marks)*

(b) Which two gases are exchanged in the alveoli? *(2 marks)*

(c) List the two main ways in which our breathing changes when we exercise. *(2 marks)*

(d) Explain how the oxygen in the air is taken to our working muscles. *(6 marks)*

2 (a) Expired air contains about 79% nitrogen. What is the percentage of
(i) oxygen
(ii) carbon dioxide? *(2 marks)*

(b) Why are our intercostal muscles important for breathing? *(2 marks)*

(c) Explain why there is more carbon dioxide in the air we breathe out than in the air we breathe in. *(2 marks)*

(d) Describe what happens when we breathe out by referring to our ribs, diaphragm, intercostal muscles, size of lungs, pressure inside and outside lungs. *(6 marks)*

3 (a) Air enters the body through the nose and mouth. Name the two different pipes air passes along before it reaches the alveoli. *(2 marks)*

(b) What are the pleural membranes, and why are they important for breathing? *(2 marks)*

(c) What is meant by:
(i) vital capacity
(ii) residual volume? *(2 marks)*

(d) Explain why an efficient respiratory system is vital for some sportspeople. *(6 marks)*

4 (a) What part does blood haemoglobin play in respiration? *(2 marks)*

(b) The respiratory system adapts when we exercise.
Name two changes that occur. *(2 marks)*

(c) Why is the level of carbon dioxide in the blood important for breathing? *(2 marks)*

(d) Explain what is meant by tidal volume, minute volume and respiratory rate. Why is this knowledge important for sportspeople? *(6 marks)*

Answers are given in the World of Sport Examined Teacher Resource and Student Workbook.

Our hormonal system

The hormonal system (also called our endocrine system) works closely with the nervous system. Together they control the way our body systems work together. The nervous system acts quickly and usually has short-term effects on our bodies. The hormonal system can work quickly but often works more slowly and has longer-lasting effects.

The hormonal system is made up of a number of glands that make hormones. Hormones are the chemical messengers of our body. They are sent directly into the bloodstream when they are needed.

- The **pituitary gland** is the control centre of our hormonal system. It produces many hormones, some of which in turn control other hormonal glands.

- The **thyroid** controls the speed at which oxygen and food products are used to produce energy.

- The **pancreas** helps digestion. It also produces insulin, which controls the amount of sugar in the blood.

- The **ovaries** are found in the female. They control the development of secondary sexual characteristics through the production of oestrogen.

- The **adrenal glands** produce adrenaline and prepare the body for instant action. Adrenaline has the effect of increasing heart rate and of using up more oxygen in the cells to release more energy. It also moves blood away from areas such as the digestive system to the working muscles.

- **Testes** are in the male. They control the development of secondary sexual characteristics through the production of testosterone. This hormone is important for the development of muscle and has been used illegally to improve performance (see Chapter 6).

Our hormonal system and sport

We use many hormones when we take part in physical activity. They affect our body by:

- increasing heart rate
- increasing the rate at which the body works
- increasing the use of glucose in the muscles
- increasing the amount of glucose carried in the blood
- moving blood to the working skeletal muscles from other areas
- increasing blood pressure
- increasing breathing rate
- controlling fluid levels and preventing loss of water.

Our digestive system

Our bodies need a constant supply of food as fuel to remain healthy and active. Our digestive system breaks our food down small enough to pass into the bloodstream.

It also changes food into the basic nutrients we need for building new tissues, repairing damaged tissues and for producing energy.

Our digestive system and sport

The digestive system needs large amounts of blood to deal with food. As we exercise our active muscles need more blood. The amount of blood going to the digestive system is therefore reduced. This slows down digestion. We may also feel uncomfortable exercising with a full stomach. We should avoid eating a meal for at least two hours before exercise.

- Digestion starts in the mouth, where food is first ground up and mixed by the action of the teeth. It can then be swallowed easily.

- Food is moistened by saliva, which begins to turn starch into sugar.

- Food is pushed down the gullet (oesophagus) by a wave-like muscular movement.

- In the stomach food is churned about and mixed with gastric juices, which break down protein to form simple materials. The stomach acts as a storage tank.

- The food moves in small amounts into the first part of the small intestine (duodenum). Enzymes break it down into more simple substances.

- Digestion finishes in the second part of the small intestine. The remaining nutrients are taken into the blood system.

- The waste food passes into the large intestine (colon), where most of the water and any more nutrients are removed.

- The solidified remains leave the body through the anus. Waste fluids are taken to the kidneys. Here they are filtered and pass as urine to the bladder. The urine then leaves the body through the urethra.

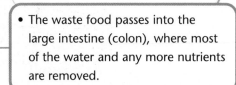

What are the immediate effects of exercise on our body systems?

We start to exercise

Our muscles work harder and use up more oxygen

The amount of carbon dioxide in our blood increases

Our brain detects this increase and releases adrenaline

Action by our heart

Our heart beats faster and stronger
(increased heart rate and stroke volume)

More blood pumped to our lungs
(increased cardiac output)
• to collect oxygen
• to remove carbon dioxide

More blood pumped to our muscles
(increased cardiac output)
• to deliver oxygen
• to remove carbon dioxide

Action by our lungs

Our lungs breathe faster and deeper
(increased tidal volume)

Increased exchange of gases
• more oxygen taken into our blood
• more carbon dioxide removed from
our blood

As a result:

• Blood pressure rises but blood vessels then expand to reduce the pressure

• Body temperature rises, but surface blood vessels expand to reduce heat
quickly through the skin, and sweating increases, producing water on the
skin which evaporates and cools us

• Blood flow is redirected away from parts of the body not involved in
excercise such as the digestive system, towards our working muscles

What are the health benefits of an active lifestyle?

We have seen how our bodies respond to exercise. When we exercise regularly our bodies adapt and our body systems become more efficient. Training for sport brings about specific changes in body systems.

Exercise is good for us. It is essential for all of us, whatever our age, gender, race, religion or ability. There are many benefits of regular exercise and an active lifestyle. The physical changes in our bodies bring with them improvements in the quality of our lives.

Physical benefits

- **Stronger muscles**. Our muscles can work harder and for longer. Our ligaments, tendons and joints will therefore be injured less often.
- **Improved heart–lung system**. We can do more work before getting tired and we can recover more quickly. Our heart gets stronger and pumps more blood. Our lungs take in more air. We use oxygen more efficiently.
- **Better flexibility**. Our joints move more freely. This means there is less chance of injury and that our skills improve.
- **Posture improves**. Better muscle tone means that we can hold our bodies in position with less effort.
- **Better weight control**. We use up calories when we exercise. This helps us to balance our energy intake from food with the energy we use through activity.

Quality of life benefits

- **Improved health**. We have more energy for work, rest, play and emergencies. We also feel better.
- **Better appearance**. Exercise helps us to keep down our fat levels, delays ageing and makes us happier about our bodies.
- **We become more relaxed**. Regular exercise helps us to relax and rest. We are less stressed and sleep better.
- **Better social life**. We have opportunities to meet people with similar interests and can develop friendships.
- **Reduced risk of illness**. With stronger, fitter bodies, we are less likely to have heart attacks, lung disease, diabetes, brittle bones and arthritis. Blood pressure will be lower and we will build up less cholesterol.
- **Improved morale**. By following an active lifestyle we are likely to feel good about ourselves and live longer, healthier and more satisfying lives.

2 Energy in action

Our bodies need energy so that our muscles can contract and make the body work. Our muscles can use energy only when it is in the form of a chemical compound called adenosine triphosphate, ATP. Our muscles have only very small stores of this high-energy compound. As soon as it is used up we have to re-make it. We can do this using any one of our three energy systems: the creatine phosphate system, the lactic acid system or the aerobic system.

Creatine phosphate system
page 60

This is our immediate energy system. It can provide us with energy at once, much faster than the other systems. However, this energy lasts for a very short period of time only.

Lactic acid system
page 61

This is our short-term energy system. It can provide us with energy quite quickly for a limited period of time. However, waste products soon build up in the working muscles and the pain that follows makes us tired quickly.

Energy systems and sport
page 63

In sport these three energy systems work together to re-make the ATP our muscles need to work. In most sports we use all three energy systems at different times, depending on our energy needs.

Aerobic system
page 62

This is our long-term energy system. It can provide energy slowly, over a very long period of time. However, it always needs oxygen to work.

Creatine phosphate system

Our **creatine phosphate energy system** gives us immediate energy.

- Muscular contractions rely on the high-energy compound adenosine triphosphate (ATP), which is stored in our muscles. This means that energy is available instantly but will not last for long. The small stores of ATP in the muscles will give enough energy for just 5–8 seconds of hard work.

- We can re-make ATP as quickly as we use up our muscle stores of ATP. To do this we use another chemical compound called creatine phosphate, which is also stored in our muscles in small amounts. The extra energy we can gain from using up the creatine phosphate in our muscles will give us up to another 20 seconds of hard work.

The creatine phosphate system and sport

This system is very important when we need bursts of explosive speed. Sprinters, throwers and many team players need to develop this energy system. After a burst of activity we need to rest to allow our bodies to refill their creatine phosphate stores.

Food supplements containing creatine are taken by some sportspeople. They believe it will help improve their performance (see Chapter 6).

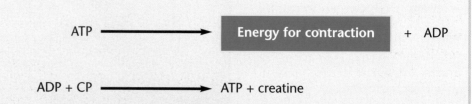

$$ATP \longrightarrow \text{Energy for contraction} + ADP$$

$$ADP + CP \longrightarrow ATP + creatine$$

Lactic acid system

Our **lactic acid energy system** gives us short-term energy.

- When we work very hard for more than about 10 seconds the energy supplies of ATP and creatine phosphate in our muscles are nearly used up. We breathe more quickly and deeply. This is to supply oxygen to the muscles to re-make our ATP so that we can continue with the activity. Unfortunately, it takes some time for the oxygen to get into our bloodstream and to reach the working muscles. In the meantime the lactic acid system uses **glycogen** to re-make ATP.

- We produce glycogen from the breakdown of carbohydrates in our food and store it in our muscles and in our liver. Glycogen is used to re-make ATP in our muscles. However, if there is not enough oxygen available at the same time then lactic acid will be formed as well as ATP. If lactic acid builds up in the muscle it makes muscular contractions painful and we become tired. Therefore we cannot use the lactic acid system for very long. The energy from the creatine phosphate and lactic acid systems will give a total of about one minute of hard work.

Oxygen debt

- When we use the creatine phosphate and lactic acid systems we produce an **oxygen deficit** – our muscles need more oxygen than they can get at the time.
- We continue the activity by using glycogen – and producing lactic acid.
- At the end of the exercise we need to rest and take in the extra oxygen we need. This makes up our oxygen deficit.
- The extra oxygen we have to take in at the end of the activity is called the **oxygen debt**.
- Taking in oxygen allows us to remove the lactic acid, replace the oxygen stores in our bodies and to build up ATP and creatine phosphate supplies.

The lactic acid system and sport

This system is very important for 100 m swimmers, 200 m runners and games players who need to keep up continuous short bursts of activity.

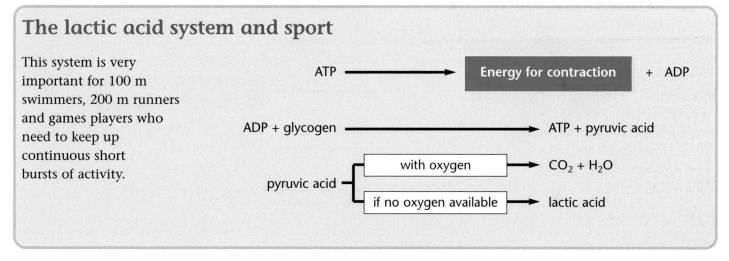

ATP $\longrightarrow$ Energy for contraction $+$ ADP

ADP + glycogen $\longrightarrow$ ATP + pyruvic acid

pyruvic acid $\Big\{$ with oxygen $\longrightarrow$ CO_2 + H_2O

if no oxygen available $\longrightarrow$ lactic acid

Aerobic system

Our **aerobic energy system** gives us long-term energy.

- We can use the aerobic system only when enough oxygen reaches the working muscles. Glycogen and oxygen together re-make the ATP. As enough oxygen is now available, lactic acid is not formed – the waste products are carbon dioxide and water, which do not cause tiredness. Therefore we can continue to use the aerobic system for a long time.

- We use our aerobic system for all light exercise, including most of our daily activities. It gives us energy much more slowly than either the creatine phosphate system or the lactic acid system. This energy comes from the breakdown of carbohydrates and fats. It gives us energy much too slowly for intensive activity. However, it can supply energy for a very long time.

The aerobic system and sport

This system is important for nearly all sportspeople. It is very important for those who need energy over a long period of time – such as runners, cyclists, swimmers and games players.

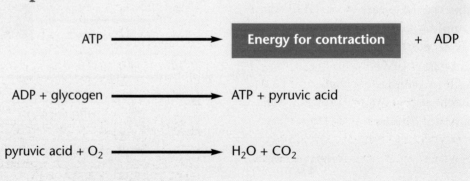

ATP $\longrightarrow$ **Energy for contraction** + ADP

ADP + glycogen $\longrightarrow$ ATP + pyruvic acid

pyruvic acid + O_2 $\longrightarrow$ H_2O + CO_2

Energy systems and sport

The energy we need for different sports varies a great deal.

- A shot putter uses one huge burst of energy lasting just a few seconds. The energy comes mainly from the creatine phosphate system – energy from the lactic acid and aerobic systems would take too long to arrive.

- A 100 m sprint swimmer needs a longer, but still quite short, burst of energy. The swim will take more than 8 seconds so the creatine phosphate supplies would be quickly exhausted. The aerobic system will not be able to supply oxygen fast enough. The swimmer will therefore rely on the lactic acid system to supply the energy needed. At the end of the swim there will be an oxygen deficit.

- A marathon runner needs a continuous supply of energy over a long period and has no need of the creatine phosphate or lactic acid energy systems. The runner will rely on a well developed aerobic system to send a steady stream of oxygen to the muscles over a long period of time.

- In many sports the three energy systems work together at different times to supply the particular type of energy needed. For example, a hockey player will need the creatine phosphate system when shooting for goal, the lactic acid system when repeatedly sprinting short distances and the aerobic system when jogging into position when the ball is out of play.

- Our creatine phosphate and lactic acid energy systems are anaerobic systems because they work without oxygen. In contrast, our aerobic system must have oxygen to work.

The energy system we need to use in sport depends on the kind of activity we are performing at any time

- To train our energy systems for our own particular sport we need to know the amount we use each energy system. We can then decide, together with our coach, which training is likely to improve performance. We will also need to think about **training thresholds** and **training zones**.

Sources of energy used for different sports

% aerobic	Events		Primary energy sources
0	weight lifting 200 m	100 m	
10	wrestling 100 m swim	basket ball 400m	Creatine phosphate and lactic acid system
20			
	tennis		
30		soccer	
40			
	800m		
50	boxing		Creatine phosphate, lactic acid and aerobic systems
60	rowing		
		1500m	
70			
		800m swim	
80	2 mile run		
			Aerobic system
90	skating 10km		
		cross country running	
100	jogging		

Training our energy systems

To train effectively we must know:
- our present level of fitness
- the amount of anaerobic training we need for our sport
- the amount of aerobic training we need for our sport.

We should use our maximum aerobic capacity (VO$_2$max) to work out our fitness level, but this needs scientific calculation. Fortunately there is a very close link between VO$_2$max and maximum heart rate (MHR).

So we can work out our MHR and use it instead of VO$_2$max to decide on our training zones.

Maximum heart rate can be estimated in the following way:

MHR (males) = 220 minus age
MHR (females) = 226 minus age

For example a 16-year-old male has a MHR of (220–16 =) 204 beats per minute. For a female of the same age the MHR would be 210 beats per minute.

The training triangle

The percentages of MHR which we give here are only approximate. Personal level of activity and fitness will cause differences. The less fit we are the lower our training thresholds will be.

Aerobic training zone

When we train in this zone we improve aerobic fitness. To achieve this we need to exercise above our **aerobic threshold** – we must keep our heart rate between 60 and 80% of our MHR. For a 16-year-old athlete heart rate ranges are:
- Male: 60–80% of 204 = 120–160 beats per minute
- Female: 60–80% of 210 = 125–170 beats per minute.

Anaerobic training zone

When we train in this zone we improve our anaerobic fitness. To achieve this we need to exercise above our **anaerobic threshold** – we must keep our heart rate above 80% of MHR. A 16-year-old male athlete must keep his heart rate above 80% of 204 (approximately 160 beats per minute); a female athlete of the same age must keep it above 170 beats per minute (80% of 210).

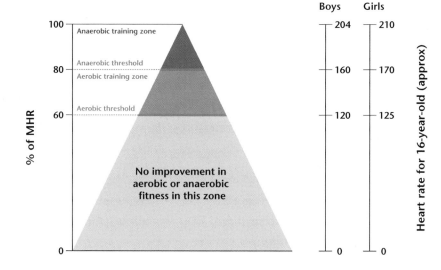

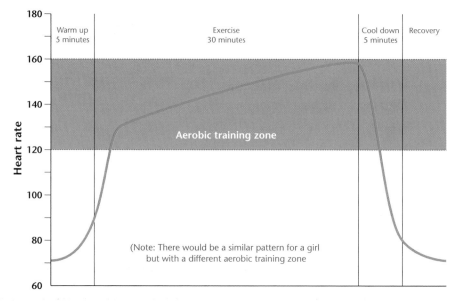

Heart rate for typical training session for 16-year-old boy

Examination-type questions: Energy in action

There are 12 marks for each question.

1 (a) Aerobic and anaerobic energy systems are different in their use of oxygen. Explain the differences. *(2 marks)*

(b) The lactic acid system is a short-term energy system. Describe these systems:
(i) creatine phosphate system
(ii) aerobic system. *(2 marks)*

(c) Give the formula for finding your maximum heart rate. *(2 marks)*

(d) Explain the aerobic energy system and describe when it is used in sport. *(6 marks)*

2 (a) Which of these activities is aerobic and which anaerobic?
(i) 100 m run
(ii) marathon run. *(2 marks)*

(b) List the two effects of a build up of lactic acid in the muscles. *(2 marks)*

(c) Oxygen is not needed in the creatine phosphate system. Explain why not. *(2 marks)*

(d) Explain when and why we sometimes produce an oxygen debt during exercise. *(6 marks)*

3 (a) Why is adenosine triphosphate important in the production of energy in the body? *(2 marks)*

(b) Name two athletic events for which the lactic acid energy system would be used. *(2 marks)*

(c) Glycogen is important for fitness.
(i) How is it produced in the body?
(ii) How is it used in the body? *(2 marks)*

(d) All three energy systems are used at different times in many games. For tennis, give examples of the use of the different energy systems. *(6 marks)*

4 (a) Which energy systems do we use for an activity needing
(i) a burst of explosive speed
(ii) energy over a long period of time? *(2 marks)*

(b) What is meant by VO_2max? *(2 marks)*

(c) Why can we not use the lactic acid system over a long period of time? *(2 marks)*

(d) Explain what is meant by the aerobic training zone and suggest how it might be used to improve aerobic fitness. *(6 marks)*

Answers are given in the World of Sport Examined Teacher Resource and Student Workbook.

3 Fitness for health and performance

Being fit is central to our health and to our sense of well-being. Health and fitness mean so much more that just the absence of illness. If we are healthy and fit then the physical, mental, cultural and social aspects of our lives are working together. Fitness is crucial to success in sport. It is essential for us to look at the particular demands of our sport and identify in what ways we need to develop our fitness.

Physical fitness consists of health-related fitness and sport-related fitness.

Health-related fitness

What is stamina?
page 70

What is flexibility?
page 72

What is body build?
page 74

What is strength?
page 77

Sport-related fitness

What is muscular power?
page 78

What is maximum strength?
page 77

What is muscular endurance?
page 79

What is speed?
page 80

What is agility?
page 81

What is coordination?
page 82

What is balance?
page 83

What is reaction time?
page 84

What is health-related fitness?

Health-related fitness is the minimum level of physical fitness that we all need in order to have good health. We need to be clear about what we mean by the terms good health and physical fitness.

What is good health?

If we are in good **health** then the physical, mental, cultural and social aspects of our lives are all working well together. We are able to lead a full and active life, combining work, recreation and social activities on a regular basis without becoming exhausted.

In order to have good health we should:

- eat sensibly
- take regular physical activity
- get regular rest and sleep
- limit intake of alcohol
- not smoke tobacco or take any other social drugs
- improve our ability to cope with stress.

Our health is to some extent affected by heredity. Problems such as high blood pressure and heart disease tend to run in families. If our parents and grandparents live a long and healthy life then we are likely to do so as well. However, we cannot assume that this will be the case. We should all adopt healthy lifestyles if we wish to maintain our health.

An active lifestyle helps to maintain health

What is physical fitness?

Physical fitness is the ability of the body to carry out everyday activities with little fatigue and with enough energy left for emergencies. Fitness means different things to different people. A man who is fit for his work as a taxi driver may be dangerously unfit for a game of squash. A marathon runner may be quite unfit for lifting weights.

Fitness is a blend of a number of physical qualities. We all need these qualities to a greater or lesser extent. There is a minimal level of fitness, which we all need to have good health. We call this health-related fitness.

To have enough fitness for good health we need: stamina, flexibility, body build and strength.

Stamina (or aerobic capacity)

Stamina is our ability to work for relatively long periods of time without becoming overtired.

Flexibility

Flexibility is the ability to move our joints through their full range of movement.

Body build

Body build is the capacity to carry the right amount of fat and muscle.

Strength

Strength is the ability of the muscles to carry out daily tasks. This involves maximum strength, muscular power and muscular endurance.

What is sport-related fitness?

Sport-related fitness is the level of physical fitness necessary to take on the demands of regular sporting activity. Although we may be fit from a health-related point of view we may not be fit for sport. There are many different kinds of sporting activities and each makes its own particular demands on the body. For example, the fitness required to be a table tennis player is totally different from the fitness demands of the triathlon.

To be successful in most sports it is important to have health-related fitness. It is also important to be as fit as possible in a number of additional areas: strength, speed, agility, coordination, balance and reaction time.

Strength

Maximum strength
This is part of strength. Maximum strength is the ability to use our muscles to apply maximum force to an immovable object.

Muscular power
This is also part of strength. Muscular power is the ability to contract muscles with speed and force in one explosive act.

Muscular endurance
This is a third part of strength. Muscular endurance is the ability to work the muscles very hard for a period of time.

Speed

Speed is the ability to move all or part of the body as quickly as possible.

Balance

Balance is the ability to maintain equilibrium when stationary or moving.

Agility

Agility is the ability to change the direction of the body at speed.

Reaction time

Reaction time is the ability to respond to a stimulus quickly.

Coordination

Coordination is the ability to carry out a series of movements smoothly and efficiently.

Different sports make different demands on our bodies

What is stamina (or aerobic capacity)?

- Stamina is the ability to work for relatively long periods of time without becoming tired. Stamina is also known as aerobic capacity or cardio-respiratory endurance.
- It is the ability of our heart and lung systems to cope with activity over a period of time.
- We need to keep our active muscles supplied with energy and to get rid of waste products during long periods of strenuous activity involving the whole body. Our ability to do this depends on the efficiency of our heart, lungs, and blood vessels.
- Our maximum stamina or aerobic capacity is also called our VO_2max. This is the maximum amount of oxygen that can be transported to, and used by, our working muscles during exercise.
- A person with a high VO_2max can use much more oxygen than other people. They can work their body at a higher rate for longer periods and will suffer less fatigue than people with a lower VO_2max.

How do we improve our stamina?

- By taking part regularly in any continuous exercise involving the whole body.
- The heart rate must be kept between 60 and 80% of the maximum heart rate for stamina to improve (see page 64).
- We should exercise at first for a minimum of 12 minutes, increasing this time to up to 40 minutes as we become fitter.
- To improve our stamina we should use continuous training (page 90) and interval training (page 91).

How do we measure our stamina?

We measure our stamina (or VO_2max) by finding out how much oxygen we can use in one minute of maximum exercise. There are complicated laboratory methods to do this but we can estimate VO_2max by using tests such as the NCF multistage fitness test, the Harvard step test or the Cooper 12-minute run.

Multistage fitness test (beep test)

To measure VO_2max we perform a number of 20-metre shuttle runs in time to beeps from a pre-recorded tape. After each minute the time interval between beeps gets shorter so our running speed has to increase. We keep going until we can no longer keep up with the speed set by the beeps. At this point we stop and record the level.

We can check our score with published tables and so work out our VO_2max. The test is easy to use and motivating, particularly if it is done with a group of people. It is the most widely used of all fitness tests.

Distance runners need an efficient cardio-respiratory system

British National Team Scores on MSFT

Sport	Male	Female
Basketball	11–5	9–6
Hockey	13–9	12–7
Rugby League	13–1	
Netball		9–7
Squash	13–13	

Harvard step test

There are a number of different versions of this test but this is the simplest one. Our resting pulse rate is taken before the test begins. We step on and off a 45 cm high bench at the rate of 30 times a minute for a period of 5 minutes. We must start with the same foot each time and we must also fully extend the leg at the top of the step.

At the end of the 5 minutes our speed of recovery is recorded. This is done by taking our pulse for 30 seconds at three different time intervals: 1 minute after the end of exercise, 2 minutes after the end of the exercise and 3 minutes after the end of the exercise.

The greater the aerobic capacity the lower the pulse rate will be at the end of the exercise. Also it will return to normal more quickly.

We can work out our fitness score using the following formula:

$$\text{Fitness score} = \frac{\text{duration of exercise in seconds (5 x 60 = 300)}}{2 \times (\text{pulse after 1 minute} + \text{pulse after 2 minutes} + \text{pulse after 3 minutes})} \times 100$$

Harvard step test

	Males 15–16 years	Females 15–16 years
High score	Above 90	Above 86
Above average	90–80	86–76
Average	79–65	75–61
Below average	64–55	60–50
Low score	Less than 55	Less than 50

Cooper 12-minute run

In this test we run as far in 12 minutes as we can around a marked area. The total distance we run is recorded. We can check our aerobic capacity using this chart.

Cooper 12-minute run

	Males 15–16 years	Females 15–16 years
High score	Above 2800 m	Above 2300 m
Above average	2799–2500 m	2299–2000 m
Average	2499–2300 m	1999–1900 m
Below average	2299–2200 m	1899–1800 m
Low score	Below 2200 m	Below 1800 m

Stamina and sport

Stamina is essential in all sporting activities lasting more than a few seconds. The better our stamina, the longer we can continue our activity, whether it is swimming, running, cycling or rowing.

What is flexibility?

- Flexibility is the ability to move our joints through their full range of movement.
- Flexibility is also known as mobility and suppleness. They all mean the range of limb movement around our joints.
- Flexibility is necessary to stay healthy and avoid injury.

How do we improve flexibility?

- We can improve our flexibility by stretching our muscles and tendons and by extending our ligaments and supporting tissues all beyond their normal range of movement.
- We should only overload our muscles whilst we feel comfortable.
- We must stretch the prime movers and then the antagonist muscles. This helps our muscles recover and adapt in a balanced way.
- The effects of flexibility exercises are very specific. We can, for example, be very flexible in our shoulders and yet show little flexibility in our lower limbs.
- Flexibility exercises, or stretching, should be part of all training programmes.
- A person's flexibility does not depend on their shape.

What are the different types of stretching?

There are four main types of stretching which can be used to improve flexibility. In each case we extend our limbs beyond their normal range and hold the position. How we get to the stretch position varies:

- static stretching – we use our own strength
- passive stretching – a partner or coach applies external force
- active stretching – we move rhythmically and under control to extend the stretch
- pnf stretching – we contract the muscle before stretching it.

Different sports demand varying degrees of flexibility

Flexibility and sport

All sports need a flexible body. Sports such as gymnastics and hurdling need a great deal of overall body flexibility. Other sports – for example, javelin and volleyball – need flexibility in particular parts of the body. Flexibility exercises should form a part of all training programmes as flexible joints are less likely to be injured when put under stress in sport.

How do we measure flexibility?

The tests used depend upon the joints that are being measured.

Sit and reach test

This test assesses the flexibility of the hamstrings.

Sit on the floor, legs straight, feet flat against the box, fingertips on the edge of the top plate. Bend the trunk and reach forward slowly and as far as possible, keeping the knees straight. Hold this position for 2 seconds. Measure the distance from the edge of the plate to the position reached by the fingertips. A person who can just reach their toes will score 0 cm.

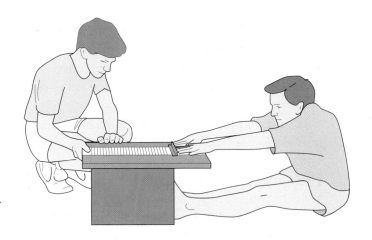

Sit and reach test

	Males 15–16 years	Females 15–16 years
High score	11 cm and above	16 cm and above
Above average	1–10 cm	11–15 cm
Average	0 cm	6–10 cm
Below average	-1 to -5 cm	1–5 cm
Low score	Less than -5 cm	Less than 1 cm

Shoulder hyperextension test

This test measures the ability to stretch the muscles of the chest and shoulders.

Lie face down on the floor with your arms stretched out in front. Hold a metre rule with your hands shoulder width apart. Raise your arms as high as possible, keeping your chin on the ground at all times and the stick parallel to the floor. Hold the highest position for three seconds. A partner measures the height reached.

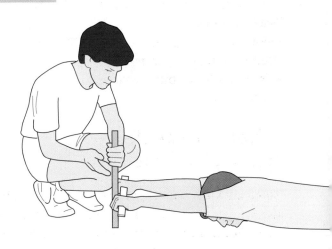

Shoulder hyperextension test

	Males 15–16 years	Females 15–16 years
High score	41 cm and above	46 cm and above
Above average	31–40 cm	36–45 cm
Average	21–30 cm	26–35 cm
Below average	11–20 cm	16–25 cm
Low score	0–10 cm	0–15 cm

Flexibility and strength

Sportspeople need a combination of flexibility and strength. Flexibility allows us to use our strength through a full range of movement. Strength is needed to stabilise joints and avoid injury.

What is body build?

Sporting success comes from a combination of ability and the right body build. Usually we find that top high-jumpers are tall and thin and gymnasts short and muscular. However, deciding what is the right body for each sport is complicated.

We need to carry the right amount of fat and muscle for our particular sport.

There are three main components of body build. These are:

- body type – a way of describing a person's physique based on muscularity, linearity and fatness
- body size – height compared to weight
- body composition – the percentage of bone, fat and muscle in the body.

Body type

There is a method of body typing called somatotyping. Three extremes of body types have been described – endomorphs, mesomorphs and ectomorphs.

These extreme body types are rare: we are all part endomorph, part mesomorph and part ectomorph.

Body type and sport

Most successful sportspeople are high in mesomorphy. They are suited to sport requiring explosive strength and power. Their muscular bulk also helps them in contact sports.

If we were high in endomorphy we could work to develop our strength and control our diet. Then we might be successful at sports needing power but only limited movement – such as weightlifting and wrestling.

If we were high in ectomorphy we could develop endurance and might be successful at long-distance running or cycling. By developing muscular strength we might also succeed in many non-contact sports. If we were tall then basketball and high jumping might suit us.

We can all be given a score (from 1 to 7) for each of these basic body types. For example: 2, 6, 3 means low endomorphy (2), high mesomorphy (6), low ectomorphy (3). In this way we can compare our body type with that of other people. Height is not important at all in working out body type.

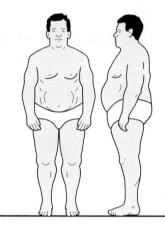

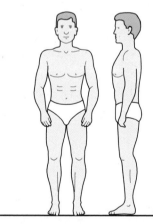

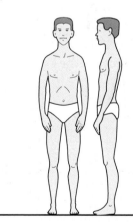

Endomorphs have:

- a pear-shaped body
- wide hips and wide shoulders
- a rounded head
- a lot of fat on the body, upper arms and thighs.

They are wider front to back rather than side to side.

Mesomorphs have:

- a wedge-shaped body
- wide shoulders and narrow hips
- a massive cubical head
- broad shoulders and heavily muscled arms and legs
- a minimum amount of fat.

They are narrow from front to back.

Ectomorphs have:

- narrow shoulders and hips
- a narrow chest and abdomen
- thin arms and legs
- a high forehead and receding chin
- little muscle and little fat.

They are thin and bony all round.

Body size

Height and weight are important factors in body size.

Body size and sport

The ideal body size for sport depends on the type of sport or the position we play in the game. For example, a height of 1.90 metres would be short for a top basketball player but very tall for a gymnast. Long-distance runners keep their weight down to reduce the load they have to carry. If we watch a game of rugby we can see a variety of heights and weights. Some sports – such as wrestling, boxing and weightlifting – have fixed weight categories. It is essential that these athletes control their diets to prevent rapid weight loss through crash dieting and consequent weakness.

Basketball players are at an advantage if they are tall. Gymnasts are usually small

Body composition

Scientists are able to work out how much of the body is fat. The rest of the body weight is called fat-free weight and includes bone, muscle, organs and connective tissue. A healthy adult male should be approximately 12–18% fat whilst a healthy adult female should be between 14 and 20% fat.

Body composition and sport

In most sports, the higher the percentage of a performer's body is fat, the poorer the performance. Therefore most sportspeople try to keep their body fat low and their fat-free weight – their muscle weight – high. However, long-distance runners must keep both their fat and non-fat weights as low as possible because they have to carry all extra weight during the race.

Standard height–weight tables give an ideal weight for a particular height. These tables are not helpful because they do not take into account our body composition. If we are overweight due to extra muscle this is not a problem but if we are overfat our sporting performance will suffer.

How do we improve our body build?

Our body type, body size and body composition depend to a large extent on heredity. However, we can make some changes to our body build.

Body type
Body type will be affected by any long-term change in the amount of fat and muscle in the body. It is clear that we cannot change our basic bone structure.

Body size
Body size will be affected by changing weight. A person's height will not change once he or she has reached physical maturity.

Body composition
Body composition can be changed a great deal. We can reduce the amount of fat and improve the proportion of lean muscle in our bodies through careful diet and exercise.

How do we measure our body build?

Body type
Somatotyping is too lengthy and complicated a procedure to do in college and school. However, we can look at our athletics team and put our athletes into approximate body types. The throwers tend towards endomorphy, the long-distance runners ectomorphy and the sprinters mesomorphy.

Body size
We can measure height and weight accurately.

Body composition
Working out accurately how much of a person's weight is fat and how much is fat free was once a very complicated procedure. However, today we can use modern testing equipment to accurately measure the amount of fat in the body. Alternatively, we can take skin fold measurements using a skin fold calliper and then refer to tables to estimate the body fat level.

Divers, like gymnasts, are often short in stature and mesomorphic in shape

What is strength?

For health-related fitness we describe strength as the ability of our muscles to carry out our daily tasks easily. For sport-related fitness it is more helpful to describe strength as the ability of a muscle or muscle group to apply force and overcome resistance.

Muscles work in a variety of ways. We will look at the three types of strength important for health and sport-related fitness. The three types of strength are:

- maximum strength – this is also called static strength
- muscular power – this is also called explosive strength
- muscular endurance – this is also called endurance strength

What is maximum strength?

Maximum strength, or static strength, is the maximum force than can be applied by a muscle group to an immovable object.

How do we improve our maximum strength?

We can improve our maximum strength by training with heavy weights (80–100% of our maximum) and a low number of repetitions. We must exercise through the full range of joint movement and work slowly when lifting (see page 93).

Maximum strength is improved by training with heavy weights

How do we measure our maximum strength?

We need to find out the maximum force that a muscle group can apply. We can use special dynamometers to measure maximum strength at a range of speeds and angles and when the muscles are lengthening or shortening. The machines can be set to make our limbs move in the same way which they move in our sport.

One repetition max test

We can attempt a one repetition max test using free weights or multigym equipment. We will be able to work up to the maximum weight we can lift just once by adding weights gradually. This is called our one repetition max. We must allow at least 2–3 minutes between each lift for recovery.

Handgrip dynamometer

We can use a hand grip dynamometer in school. In this test we squeeze the handle as hard as possible with our hand. This will give a reading of the strength of our hand grip.

Hand grip strength test

	Males 15–16 years	Females 15–16 years
High score	Above 56 kg	Above 37 kg
Above average	56–52 kg	37–34 kg
Average	51–48 kg	33–32 kg
Below average	47–43 kg	31–29 kg
Low score	Less than 43 kg	Less than 29 kg

What is muscular power?

Muscular power is the ability to contract the muscles with speed and force in one explosive act. Muscular power, or explosive strength, is the combination of strength and speed of movement. The energy for our muscular power comes from the anaerobic system.

How do we improve our muscular power?

We can improve muscular power by training with medium weights (60–80% of our maximum) but performing the repetitions at speed. Plyometrics training is also an excellent way of improving power (see page 94). As power is a combination of strength and speed it is also important to train both of these areas of fitness.

How do we measure our muscular power?

There are two simple ways to measure muscular power: the standing broad jump and the standing vertical jump.

Standing broad jump
Stand with your feet comfortably apart and your toes immediately behind the start line. Then bend your knees and jump forward as far as possible. Measure the distance from your rear heel back to the start line. You are allowed two attempts.

Standing vertical jump
Stand next to a wall and reach up with your arm nearest to the wall. Mark the highest point you can reach with the fingers of this arm. Both feet must remain flat on the floor at this stage. Chalk your finger tips and leap upwards, tapping your fingers against the wall at the highest point. The distance between the two marks gives a measure of how high you can leap from the ground from a stationary start. It takes into account your height and so is a fairer test than the standing broad jump.

Standing broad jump

	Males 15–16 years	Females 15–16 years
High score	Above 2 m	Above 1.65 m
Above average	2.00–1.86 m	1.65–1.56 m
Average	1.85–1.76 m	1.55–1.46 m
Below average	1.75–1.65 m	1.45–1.35 m
Low score	Less than 1.65 m	Less than 1.35 m

Standing vertical jump

	Males 15–16 years	Females 15–16 years
High score	Above 65 cm	Above 60 cm
Above average	65–56 cm	60–51 cm
Average	55–50 cm	50–41 cm
Below average	49–40 cm	40–35 cm
Low score	Less than 40 cm	Less than 35 cm

Muscular power is essential in basketball

What is muscular endurance?

Muscular endurance or endurance strength is also called anaerobic endurance. It is the ability of a single muscle or muscle group to work very hard for a limited period of time. It is the efficiency of the anaerobic system within the working muscles. This includes high-intensity, repetitive or even static exercise.

A person who has a high percentage of slow-twitch fibres will have an advantage in events involving muscular endurance. Muscular endurance is closely linked with muscular strength.

Downhill skiers develop muscular endurance

How do we improve our muscular endurance?

We can improve our muscular endurance by training with light weights (40–60% of our maximum). We need to do the exercises at speed and with a high number of repetitions (20–30).

How do we measure our muscular endurance?

We can perform repeated exercises such as press-ups or sit-ups for a given time or to exhaustion. Then we can compare our score either with those of others or with our own previous best.

The NCF abdominal curl test

This test measures the muscular endurance of our abdominal muscles. Complete as many abdominal curls as possible within a time limit of 30 seconds, performing each curl properly. Start flat on your back and sit up to 90°. Your arms must remain across the chest and only light pressure is allowed to hold your feet in place.

Press-up test

This test measures the muscular endurance of our chest and shoulder muscles. One way of carrying out this test is to complete as many press-ups as possible in 60 seconds. Girls can perform press-ups from the kneeling position.

Abdominal curl test – number of curls performed correctly in 30 seconds

	Males 15–16 years	Females 15–16 years
High score	Above 26	Above 23
Above average	26–25	23–21
Average	24–23	20–19
Below average	22–21	18–17
Low score	Below 21	Below 17

Strength and sport

Many sports demand a combination of maximum strength, muscular power and muscular endurance.

Maximum strength is very important in activities such as scrummaging in rugby, wrestling and tug-of-war. In these activities we have to hold our bodies in a steady position against an opposing force.

Muscular power is shown clearly in activities such as throwing and jumping when we try to move an object or ourselves as far and as fast as possible.

Muscular endurance can be seen in rowing, canoeing and other sporting activities where the same muscle groups work continuously with near-maximum effort.

What is speed?

Speed is the ability to move all or part of the body as quickly as possible.

For our bodies to achieve speed, we have to supply energy to our muscles very quickly. The muscles then have to contract in the shortest possible time. We use our anaerobic energy supply system for speed work. If we have a high percentage of fast-twitch fibres in our active muscles then we will have a natural advantage.

How do we improve our speed?

We cannot increase the percentage of fast-twitch fibres in our bodies but we can improve our speed in sport in other ways, such as:

- increasing strength through a programme of weight training and plyometrics. Stronger muscles will give more power and therefore more speed
- improving reaction time (see page 84)
- improving ability to change speed and direction when moving quickly (see page 81)
- improving the ability to cope with lactic acid (see page 105)
- improving skill in our sport. For example, a more efficient swimming stroke will create less water resistance and lower swim times.

Speed is an advantage in most sports

How do we measure our speed?

A person's speed can be measured simply by timing them over a measured distance; for example 50 metres. We can measure reaction time, speed off the mark, time to reach top speed and deceleration times as part of a training programme.

50 m Speed test (in seconds)

	Males 15–16 years	Females 15–16 years
High score	Faster than 7.2 s	Faster than 7.8 s
Above average	7.2–7.8 s	7.8–8.4 s
Average	7.9–8.4 s	8.5–9.0 s
Below average	8.5–9.0 s	9.1–9.6 s
Low score	Slower than 9.1 s	Slower than 9.7 s

Speed and sport

Speed is important in sports that require a great deal of effort over a very short period of time. Sprinters, speed skaters and sprint cyclists all need to develop their speed. It is also important in many team games, when a sudden change of pace and direction can bring success.

What is agility?

Agility is the ability to change the direction of the body at speed. It is a combination of speed, balance, power and coordination.

How do we improve our agility?

We can improve our agility by training. We develop agility by rehearsing the movements made in our sport. This is done at full speed and under conditions similar to those in a competitive situation. We must also improve our speed, balance, power and coordination as all of these fitness aspects affect our agility.

How do we measure our agility?

An expert watching us play our particular sport can make a very good assessment of our agility. We can assess our general agility using a test such as the Illinois agility run.

Illinois agility run

A course is set up as shown in the diagram. Lie face down on the floor at the starting line. When told to start, leap to your feet and complete the course in the shortest possible time.

Top tennis players display excellent agility

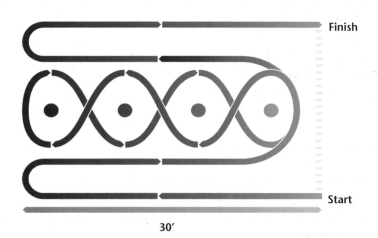

Finish

Start

30'

Agility and sport

We need agility for all games and most other sports. Gymnasts, basketball players and skiers all need specific agility if they are to be successful. Only in static activities such as archery and shooting will agility be of no importance.

Illinois agility run (in seconds)

	Males 15–16 years	Females 15–16 years
High score	Faster than 15.9 s	Faster than 17.5 s
Above average	15.9–16.7 s	17.5–18.6 s
Average	16.8–18.6 s	18.7–22.4 s
Below average	18.7–18.8 s	22.4–23.4 s
Low score	Slower than 18.8 s	Slower than 23.4 s

What is coordination?

Coordination is the ability to carry out a series of movements smoothly and efficiently. This will happen if the nervous and muscular systems work well together.

How do we improve our coordination?

Coordination improves with practice. Very many of the toys we played with when young helped to develop our hand–eye, foot–eye and whole-body coordination. Early PE lessons further developed our coordination through gymnastics and playing with balls, hoops and skipping ropes. Coordination improves with good coaching and regular practice.

Good coordination is essential for skilful performance

How do we measure our coordination?

An expert watching us play our particular sport can make a very good assessment of our coordination. We can assess our hand–eye coordination using a test such as the alternate hand wall toss test.

The alternate hand wall toss test
Stand two metres away from a smooth wall. Throw a tennis ball from your right hand against the wall and catch it in your left hand. Then throw it with your left hand and catch it with your right. Do this as quickly as possible for 30 seconds.

Juggling test
An enjoyable way to test our coordination is to try juggling with first two and then three balls. Some people are able to achieve the three ball juggling much more quickly than others.

Coordination and sport

Good coordination is essential for skilful performance. Sport is full of examples of good coordination, from triple somersaults to saving penalties. We become only too aware of poor coordination when we try to learn a new sporting skill.

Alternate hand wall toss test

	15–16 years
High score	Above 35
Above average	35–30
Average	29–25
Below average	24–20
Low score	Below 20

What is balance?

- Static balance is the ability to maintain our *equilibrium* when stationary.
- Dynamic balance is the ability to maintain our equilibrium when moving.

Maintaining equilibrium means keeping the centre of gravity over the area of support. If we do not keep our equilibrium we will fall over. We maintain our balance through the coordinated actions of our eyes, our ears and the proprioceptive organs in our joints.

How do we improve our balance?

We can improve the balance needed in particular sports by developing the appropriate skills through practice and training. We can then put these skills to the test under the stress of competitive situations.

How do we measure our balance?

- Dynamic balance is best measured by an expert watching us play our particular sport.
- Static balance can be measured in a number of ways. The stork stand described below is a test of static balance.

Windsurfers need good dynamic balance

The stork stand

Stand comfortably on both feet and place your hands on your hips. Then lift one leg and place the toes against the knee of the other leg. On command, raise the heel and stand on your toes, balancing for as long as possible without letting either the heel touch the floor or the other foot move away from the knee. Time your balance in seconds.

The stork stand (in seconds)

	15–16 years
High score	Above 49 s
Above average	40–49 s
Average	26–39 s
Below average	11–25 s
Low score	Below 10 s

Balance and sport

Static balance is shown in activities such as gymnastics. Dynamic balance is important in most sports. Snowboarders and surfers must have very good dynamic balance. They move very fast over uneven surfaces and must constantly adjust their positions.

What is reaction time?

Reaction time is the ability to respond to a stimulus quickly. A reaction can be simple, or it can involve choice.

- Simple reaction time is the delay between the stimulus and our action – for example, between the gun going off in a sprint race and our first movement.
- Choice reaction time is the time delay between the stimulus and an action which involves making a choice – for example, when we receive a ball from our opponent in a tennis match.

In both of these cases we have to react quickly. However, in the second case we will have to decide where and how to hit the ball. These decisions will depend on where the ball is about to land, in which direction our opponent is moving and many other factors. We are involved in making choices. The more skilled and experienced a tennis player is, the more likely he or she will be to make the right choice and the most appropriate type of return.

Games players need to react quickly

How do we improve our reaction time?

Simple reaction time

It is not possible to improve our simple reaction time through training. A person's speed of reaction to a single stimulus is due mainly to the efficiency of their nervous system. If we are lucky, our sensory and motor nerves will be capable of transmitting messages very speedily. Therefore our muscles will get the message from our brain to contract very quickly.

Choice reaction time

We can improve our choice reaction time a great deal through practice and experience. In a game like hockey the player will be receiving stimuli from:

- eyes – about the position of the ball, other players and goal
- ears – from players, spectators and referee
- kinaesthetic sense – about our body position and our options to pass, kick etc.
  Skilled players can reduce choice reaction time by focusing on important information. They can anticipate the action of other players and the movement of the ball. We gain this skill mainly through training and experience.

Movement time

Movement time is the time that we take to move once the decision to move has been made. If we have a high percentage of fast-twitch fibres then we will be able to respond faster than people with a high percentage of slow-twitch fibres. We can improve movement time by improving our muscular power.

How do we measure our reaction time?

A number of computer programmes are available to measure reaction time. They all ask for a response as quickly as possible to a stimulus such as a sound or a visual cue. Some measure simple reaction times by only asking for one response to a single stimulus. Others measure choice reaction time by giving a variety or responses, only one of which is correct.

Reaction time and sport

Simple reaction time is very important in activities such as the 100 metre sprint on the track or in the pool. Choice reaction time is important in all games where we have to respond rapidly and effectively to the movements of other players, a ball or both. However, movement time is critical in all sports and is most easily improved through training.

Examination-type questions: Fitness for health and performance

There are 12 marks for each question.

1 (a) What is sport-related fitness? *(2 marks)*

  (b) Body build is one of the components of health-related fitness. Name two other components. *(2 marks)*

  (c) Suggest two ways of measuring stamina. *(2 marks)*

  (d) Describe each of the three basic somatotypes (mesomorph, endomorph and ectomorph). *(6 marks)*

2 (a) Name the following sport-related fitness factors:
  (i)   ability to move the body quickly
  (ii) ability to react quickly to a stimulus. *(2 marks)*

  (b) Using weights, how might we improve
  (i)   maximum strength
  (ii) muscular endurance? *(2 marks)*

  (c) Suggest two sports for which balance is very important. *(2 marks)*

  (d) Choose three factors of sport-related fitness and explain why they are important in badminton. *(6 marks)*

3 (a) Suggest one way to improve
  (i)   stamina
  (ii) muscular power. *(2 marks)*

  (b) Give two ways of measuring flexibility. *(2 marks)*

  (c) Name one sport that needs maximum strength and one that needs muscular power. *(2 marks)*

  (d) Explain why the fitness needs of a snowboarder and a long-distance cyclist are different. *(6 marks)*

4 (a) What is the difference between simple and choice reaction time? *(2 marks)*

  (b) What is meant by
  (i)   body size
  (ii) body composition? *(2 marks)*

  (c) What do we measure using
  (i)   stork stand
  (ii) standing vertical jump? *(2 marks)*

  (d) Explain the difference between good health and physical fitness. *(6 marks)*

Answers are given in the World of Sport Examined Teacher Resource and Student Workbook.

4 Training for success

To be successful at sport, we need our energy systems and sporting skills at their highest possible level. We can reach these high levels by training. Training is a regular programme of exercise to improve performance.

There are many different methods of training and ways of organising a training programme. We must be sure the training programme is right for our sport and our levels of fitness and skill.

Principles of training (SPORT)
page 88

- **S**pecificity
- **P**rogression
- **O**verload
- **R**eversibility
- **T**edium

Training methods
page 90

- Continuous training
- Fartlek training
- Interval training
- Circuit training
- Weight training
- Plyometric training
- Flexibility training

Planning our training programme – periods
page 96

- Pre-season
- Peak season
- Off season

Planning our training programme (FITT)
page 96

- Frequency
- Intensity
- Time
- Type

Planning our training session – phases
page 97

- Warm up
- Fitness
- Skills
- Warm down

Types of training programme
page 98

Our training programme must be right for our own level of fitness, level of skill and the demands of our particular sport.

Other considerations
page 103

- Age and training
- Gender and training

Long-term effects of training
page 105

- Aerobic
- Anaerobic
- Resistance

Principles of training

We need to train to improve our fitness. For steady progress and to avoid injury we should follow the SPORT principles:

- **Specificity**
- **Progression**
- **Overload**
- **Reversibility**
- **Tedium**

What do we mean by specificity?

Every type of exercise has a particular effect on the body. The type of training we choose must be right for the type of improvement we want to see. If we want to improve the strength of our arms then running will not help: we must use strength-training exercises that work our arms. We must always use a training programme that puts regular stress on the muscle groups or body system that we want to develop. Our training programme must be designed to suit the needs of our sport.

- Sprinters include a lot of speed work in their training. This helps their fast-twitch muscle fibres to develop.
- Endurance athletes need to develop their slow-twitch muscle fibres. They train over longer distances or for a longer time.
- Games players include both speed and endurance training in their programmes to develop both types of muscle fibres.

Progressive training will strengthen our muscles

What do we mean by progression?

The body takes time to adapt to more or harder exercise. We must build up the stress on our bodies in a gradual, or progressive, way – by lifting heavier weights or running further. If we build up the stress too quickly we risk injury or find the challenge too great and give up. If we build up the stress too slowly we may become disinterested or bored and give up.

The body needs time to recover and adapt to training. Our bones, ligaments and tendons may take longer to change than our muscles or other body systems. Our training thresholds tell us if we are training at the right level.

If we are unfit we can improve our fitness level quickly. The fitter we are the harder it is to improve.

What do we mean by overload?

To improve the fitness of our body systems we need to work them harder than normal. The body will then adapt to the extra stress and we will become fitter.

We can overload our bodies by training more often, by working harder or by spending more time on an exercise. For example, to improve our aerobic fitness by running, we could run more times a week, complete the run in a shorter time or increase the distance we run. Each one of these methods will overload the aerobic system. The aerobic system will gradually adapt to cope with the overload and we will become fitter.

What do we mean by reversibility?

Our bodies adapt to the stress of exercise by becoming fitter. In the same way, we quickly adapt to less exercise by losing fitness. If our muscles are not used they atrophy – that is, they waste away. We cannot store fitness for future use. It will disappear if we stop training. It takes only 3–4 weeks for our bodies to get out of condition.

We lose our aerobic fitness more easily than our anaerobic fitness because our muscles quickly lose much of their ability to use oxygen. Our anaerobic fitness is affected less by not training. If we follow a strength-training programme for 4 weeks, we will lose our gains in strength after about 12 weeks of inactivity.

What do we mean by tedium?

Our training programme must be varied to avoid tedium – boredom. By using a variety of different training methods we will keep our enthusiasm and motivation.

- We can follow a long work out with a short one, a hard session with a relaxed one or a high-speed session with a long slow one.
- We may be able to change where we train and when we train.
- We can avoid overuse injuries by varying the way we train. For example, shin splints can be avoided by running on grass rather than on hard roads.

High-level performance depends on systematic training

Overtraining

We train to improve our performance. Overtraining – that is, too much training – can be bad for our health. Our bodies need rest and sleep between training sessions. Overtraining can cause muscle soreness, joint pain, sleeping problems, loss of appetite and extreme tiredness. After injury or illness we must start training again only gradually.

Principles of training and sport

We all have some natural ability in sport. However, ability alone is not enough. To improve our sporting performance we must train. For training to be effective we must base it on the five principles of training:

- Specificity: train for our own particular sport.
- Progression: increase training gradually.
- Overload: work harder than normal.
- Reversibility: we lose fitness if we stop training.
- Tedium: make training interesting.

Training methods

There are many different training methods. They are all based on the different ways our body adapts to regular exercise and include: continuous training, fartlek training, interval training, circuit training, weight training, plyometric training and flexibility training

Continuous training

There are two types of continuous training:
- long, slow, distance training
- high-intensity continuous training.

Aerobics improves stamina

What is long, slow, distance training?
- Running, swimming, cycling, rowing, taking part in aerobics or doing any other whole-body activity
- Working at the same pace for between 30 minutes and two hours
- Being moderately active, working in the aerobic training zone at 60–80% of MHR

Why use long, slow, distance training?
- To improve stamina (aerobic capacity)
- To help improve health-related fitness
- To reduce amounts of body fat
- To maintain fitness in the off season

What is high-intensity continuous training?
- Running, swimming, cycling, rowing or doing any other whole-body activity
- Working for only a short period of time
- Working very hard at 80–95% MHR – close to our competition pace in our anaerobic training zone

Why use high-intensity continuous training?
- To improve anaerobic capacity
- To improve leg speed, leg strength and muscular endurance
- To prepare for competition during the peak season

Fartlek provides variety in a training programme

Fartlek training

What is fartlek training?
- The name comes from the Swedish for 'speed play': it involves many changes of speed
- Walking, running, cycling or skiing at different speeds and intensities
- Working for a minimum of 30 minutes
- Varying the type of country over which we travel

Why use fartlek training?
- To improve aerobic and anaerobic fitness, depending on how we train
- To help games players who need both aerobic and anaerobic fitness.
- To enjoy moving quickly but within our own ability

Interval training

What is interval training?
- Any training using alternating periods of very hard exercise and rest
- Rest periods are essential for recovery
- Rest periods enable us to train for a longer period of time
- We can vary:
  - the time or distance of each exercise
  - the amount of effort (intensity) we put into each period of exercise
  - the length of time we rest between each period of exercise
  - the type of activity we take part in during each period of rest
  - the number of exercise and recovery periods in training sessions
- For example, an interval training session on the track could involve six 200 metre runs in 30 seconds with 90 seconds rest between each.

Why use interval training?
- To improve anaerobic and aerobic fitness, depending on how we exercise. Our aerobic fitness will improve if we train for a long period at 60–80% of MHR. Our anaerobic fitness will improve if we train over a short period at 80–95% MHR. Using this high-quality speed training we will need rests of 2–3 minutes but it will develop our ability to work when we are tired
- To improve the performance of games players. Recovery is faster if we exercise lightly during our rest periods, and this is what happens in a game

Circuit training

What is circuit training?

- Performing a series of exercises or activities in a special order, called a circuit
- A circuit usually involves 6–10 exercises or activities, which take place at stations
- Circuits should be designed to avoid working the same muscle groups at stations that follow one another
- The circuits should be designed to include exercises to work opposing muscles around a joint
- As our fitness improves we can make the circuit more difficult by increasing:
  - the number of stations
  - the time we spend at each station
  - the number of repetitions at each station
  - the number of complete circuits

Why use circuit training?

- To improve aerobic or anaerobic fitness by designing a circuit with this in mind. High numbers of repetitions will improve aerobic fitness
- A great variety of exercises can be included in a circuit. This makes it extremely adaptable for the needs of different sports
- To improve sporting performance. Circuits can be designed for our particular sport. For example, if we need leg power then our circuit should contain a number of exercises to develop leg power
- We can construct a skills circuit for games players. Exercises are replaced by short skills practices – for example, passing a ball against a wall.

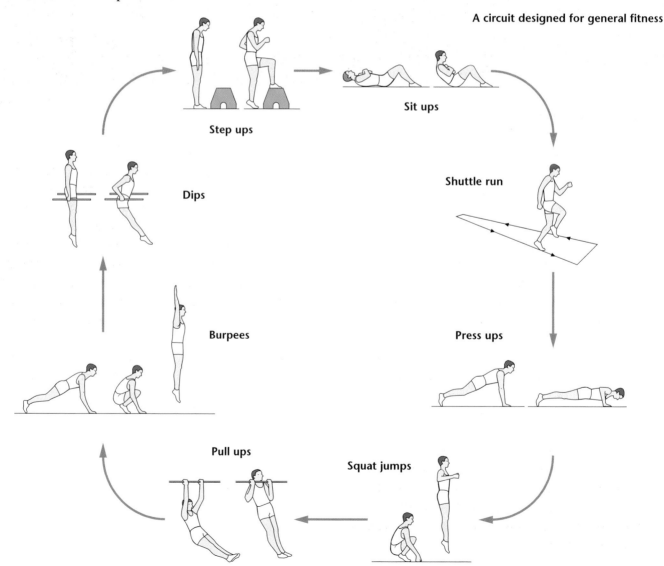

A circuit designed for general fitness

Step ups   Sit ups   Shuttle run   Press ups   Squat jumps   Pull ups   Burpees   Dips

Weight training improves strength

Weight training

What is weight training?
- Using weights as a form of resistance training (either free weights or weights in machines)
- Gradually increasing the weight lifted
- Lifting weights in sets. A set is a number of the same exercises performed one after each other
- We can overload our muscles safely over a sensible period of time
- Any weight training programme can take account of our current state of fitness

Guidelines:
- aim for at least three training sessions a week
- make sure you are thoroughly warmed up before starting
- breathe in when you lift the weight and out as it is lowered
- never hold your breath as this could make you faint
- increase the weights as your muscles grow stronger
- decide which muscle groups are important for your sport and choose exercises to develop them
- work the different muscle groups in turn, to give time for recovery

Why use weight training?
- To improve sporting performance by designing a programme for our own particular sport
- To improve muscular strength – that is, maximum strength, muscular power or muscular endurance
- Maximum strength is improved using at least three sets of six repetitions at near-maximum weight
- Muscular endurance is improved using at least three sets of 20–30 repetitions. The weight should be 40–60% of the weight which we can lift just once (our one repetition maximum, 1 RM)
- Muscular power is improved by at least three sets of 10–15 repetitions. We should do these at speed, using 60–80% of our 1 RM

Plyometric training

What is plyometric training?
- A series of explosive movements designed to improve muscular power (explosive strength)
- Movements include bounds, hops, jumps (onto and off boxes) leaps, skips, press-ups with claps, throwing and catching a medicine ball
- The muscles can be stretched before they contract. This stores up elastic energy. When they next contract, they will produce extra power.
  For example, in a vertical jump:
  - bend at the knees, which stretches the thigh muscles
  - immediately contract these muscles as you jump upwards
  - this movement converts the stretch into an elastic recoil
  - the extra power enables you to jump higher.
- Plyometric training puts great stress on the muscles and joints

- Always warm up thoroughly first
- Take great care, particularly beginners
- Start on grass (if outdoors) or on mats if indoors

Why use plyometric training?
- To improve muscular power by training the muscles to contract more strongly
- To improve sports performance by designing a programme to improve muscular power for a particular sport

Plyometric training

Flexibility training

What is flexibility training?

- Using a series of exercises to improve flexibility – the range of movement at a joint
- Stretching and moving the joint just beyond its point of resistance
- The joint is made more flexible by stretching the tendons and ligaments surrounding the joint
- Warm up thoroughly and stay warm whilst stretching
- We can use a variety of stretching exercises involving static, passive, active and PNF stretching

Why use flexibility training?

- To improve flexibility and therefore performance. Good flexibility is important for most sports
- To design a programme which will improve flexibility for our own particular sport
- To reduce joint injury by increasing the range of movement at a joint
- To allow us to use our strength through a full range of movement

Flexible joints aid performance and help prevent injury

Static stretching

We extend our limbs beyond their normal range. We hold the position for at least 10 seconds. After a few seconds rest we repeat the stretch. We should continue this for at least five repetitions of 10 seconds. We try to build up the time we hold the stretch.

Active stretching

We extend a movement beyond our normal limit and repeat this rhythmically over a period of 20 seconds. It is very important that the muscles are warmed up before active stretching is started. We should perform active stretches slowly at first, and must never bob or bounce.

Passive stretching

We improve flexibility of our joints by using a partner to apply external force. He or she moves the limb being exercised to its end position and keeps it there for a few seconds. It is most important that this type of stretching is carried out carefully to avoid injury.

PNF stretching

PNF (proprioceptive neuromuscular facilitation) stretches use the fact that muscles are most relaxed (and therefore can most easily be stretched) immediately after contraction. We first contract the muscle as hard as possible. We then stretch it fully and hold the stretch for a few seconds. We then relax the muscle briefly before repeating.

How do we plan our training programme?

Training should follow the FITT principles

We need to train to improve our fitness. When planning a fitness programme, we should follow the FITT principles: frequency, intensity, time, type.

Frequency: how often we train
- We should train at least three times a week to improve our fitness
- The body needs time to recover from each training session
- We should spread these sessions out over the week

Intensity: how hard we train
- We will only get fitter if we work our body systems hard enough to make them adapt
- We must start at the right intensity, depending on our current fitness
- We must understand and use our training thresholds

Time: how long we train
- To improve aerobic fitness our training sessions should last longer and our working heart rate level should rise
- Each session must last at least 20 minutes to see any real benefit

Type: what kind of training we do
- We should analyse our particular sport to know the fitness and skills we need
- The training programme should include types of activity to develop these skills and fitness

How do we plan our training programme for a year?

If we take part in competitive sport we always want to be at our best at the time of our most important competition. This is called peaking. Our training programmes will vary with type of sport and level of competition. We therefore need to plan well ahead. Dividing a training programme into different parts is called periodisation. For example, for some sports we could talk about three main periods: pre-season, peak season and off season.

Pre-season
- Focus on fitness for the particular sport
- Concentrate on muscular endurance, power and speed work
- Develop the techniques, skills and strategies for the particular sport

Peak season
- Emphasise speed
- Practise skills at high speed and in competitive situations
- Extra fitness sessions might be needed if we do not compete enough

Off season
- Following the competitive season a period of active rest is needed at first
- Maintain a high level of general fitness through moderate activity
- Develop muscular strength, flexibility and aerobic fitness
- Develop our sports skills

How do we plan individual training sessions?

To avoid injury and to get the most out of our training we should divide each session into four phases: warm up, fitness training, skill development and warm down.

Warm up

The warm up should include:

- gentle exercise for the whole body, such as light jogging. This gradually increases heart rate, breathing and blood supply to the muscles. It warms up our muscles and prepares us mentally for the session
- gentle stretching, to prepare muscles, ligaments and joints
- practising techniques and skills to be used in the session.

Fitness training

- Our fitness activities will depend on the demands of our sport
- We can design fitness activities to develop skill as well
- If training is too intense at the start of the session we may be too tired to practise our skills well later
- However, games players need to practise their games skills when they are tired.

Coaches play an important role in training

Skill is developed in training

Skill development

- The techniques and skills we need to develop will depend on our particular sport
- We may need to work in pairs, in small groups and in teams as well as on our own
- We may play small sided and modified games

Warm down

- We should always finish the session with a period of lighter exercise
- We should avoid going from hard exercise immediately to rest
- Light exercise shortens recovery time by helping to remove carbon dioxide, lactic acid and other waste products
- Light exercise makes sure that the blood continues to circulate well and prevents it pooling in the skeletal muscles, which may lower blood pressure and cause dizziness
- While the muscles are thoroughly warm, flexibility exercises can be carried out with less chance of injury through over-stretching
- Light exercise will prevent muscle soreness and stiffness

How do we design a training programme?

The training programmes for an elderly, recreational golfer and a young, competitive triple jumper would be very different.

We must design our training programme for:
- a particular sport
- a specific level of ability
- an individual sportsperson or group of sportspeople at a similar level of ability.

Training programmes are sport specific

Before planning the programme we must find out about:
- the sport (skill requirements)
- the type of fitness needed (body build, strength, stamina, flexibility, power, muscular endurance, speed, agility, coordination, balance, reaction time)
- the sportsperson's background (age, health, fitness level, experience, sporting ability, motivation)
- the principles of training (SPORT: specificity, progression, overload, reversibility, tedium and FITT: frequency, intensity, time, type)
- the types of training available (continuous, fartlek, interval, circuit, weight, plyometric)
- the training year for the sport (pre-season, peak season, off season).

Training case studies

Name:	James Towner
Age:	18
Sport:	Triathlon
Experience:	County U19 Swimming Champion 2000
	50 m, 100 m and 200 m Breaststroke
	District U20 Triathlon Event Winner 2000

James trains for the triathlon in addition to his training for the swimming season.
The triathlon season begins as the swimming season ends. He only has a two-
week break from training and during this time he surfs and swims for fun.
The programme is a summary of his training for triathlon in the year 2000.

Off season: November–March

The focus in this period is to develop strength and stamina. The different sessions will take place in the morning and afternoon/evening. The swimming sessions will often feature interval training. Gym work is weight training for whole body.

Monday	13 km run (hard); 90 minute swim approx. 5 km (easy) or gym work
Tuesday	32 km cycle (easy); 2 hour swim approx. 6 km (hard)
Wednesday	16 km run (easy); gym (strength); 1 hour swim (easy)
Thursday	13 km run (hard); 32 km cycle (easy)
Friday	16–20 km run (easy); 1 hour swim approx. 3.5 km (hard)
Saturday	55–65 km cycle (hard); gym (strength)
Sunday	Rest day

Pre-season: March–June

During this period James seeks to add speed to his stamina and strength by doing faster, powerful work.

Monday	10 km run (hard); 90 min. swim (easy)
Tuesday	40 km cycle (hard); 2 hour swim (easy)
Wednesday	13 km run (easy); gym (power); 1 hour swim (hard)
Thursday	Hill reps running (hard); 32 km cycle (easy)
Friday	13 km run (easy); 1 hour swim (hard)
Saturday	24–32 km cycle (easy); gym (endurance)
Sunday	Rest day

Peak season: July–October

In the peak season competitions may occur once every two weeks. James will select key competitions and will aim to be in top condition and peak for these. Much of the training during this period is designed to sharpen his performance.

Monday	16 km cycle (hard); 8 km run (medium)
Tuesday	2 km swim; 16 km cycle (easy)
Wednesday	5 km run (striding); 90 minute swim (easy)
Thursday	10 km run (easy); light gym session
Friday	Short swim
Saturday	Race day
Sunday	Recovery day; short swim

Training case studies

Name:	John Piercy
Age:	21
Sport:	Football
Experience:	U18 England – European Championships
	U20 England – World Cup
	Professional: Tottenham Hotspur – Premiership,
	Worthington Cup

John is a professional sportsman. His training programme is designed for him and he must achieve his targets. For example, he must report for pre-season training within a weight limit set by the club.

Off season: end May–beginning July

The off season lasts for 6 weeks. The first 2 weeks are a complete rest. Then 2 weeks of this programme will be followed by 2 weeks of harder work in preparation for pre-season training. The focus in this period is to maintain general fitness and flexibility.

Monday	10 min run (easy), 20 min stretch, 10 min run (easy)
Tuesday	60 min swim (easy), gym (light weights)
Wednesday	15 min run out, 20 min stretch, return run in faster time
Thursday	60 min swim (easy), gym (light weights)
Friday	Rest day
Saturday	10 min run (easy), 20 min stretch, 10 min run (easy)
Sunday	Rest day

Pre-season: July

This is the first week of pre-season training. In the second week every day begins with ball work, which is very hard physical work. The afternoons are spent working on speed (fast footwork) and strength (with heavy weights) The third week features the first pre-season games.

Daily session Monday to Friday	
Morning:	five 15 min runs, five 20 min stretches with 100 sit ups and press ups, 5 hill sprints
Afternoon:	Light ball work – dribbling, side foot passing etc
Saturday	5-a-side tournament, progressive intervals around pitch to finish
Sunday	Rest day

Peak season: August–end May

In the peak season matches may take place twice a week. Speed and strength work continues until Christmas, but after that most time between matches is spent recovering and working on tactics or set pieces.

Monday	Shooting, keep-ball
Tuesday	7-a-side, easy warm up. Set pieces, shooting
Wednesday	Meet in hotel, sleep 2 hours, meal, team talk, match, warm down
Thursday	Rest day
Friday	Shooting, keep-ball. Leave at midday for away match
Saturday	Easy morning, lunch, team talk, match, warm down
Sunday	Rest day

Training case studies

Name: Nicola Willis

Age: 15

Sport: Gymnastics

Experience: U12, Junior and Senior National Squad member

England and GB International

Training is based around competitions, not seasons.

Off season

Monday, Tuesday, Wednesday, Thursday, Friday – 3.5 hours
- 15 min warm up: pulse raising, stretching.
- 30 min conditioning: exercises for upper body, middle body and lower body plus 5 kg free weight exercises
- 30 min each: vault – into pit, bars, beam, floor – tumble track (learning new moves and practising old moves)
- 30 min conditioning and stretching
- 15 min cool down

Saturday – 4 hours
- 30 min ballet.
- Remainder of training as above.

Sunday – rest

Pre-competition

Five weeks before competition, build up to routines.

Monday to Saturday
- 3.5 hours working on routines
- Week 1 and 2: practise moves contained in routine
- Week 3: practise half routines
- Week 4: practise complete routines – five routines on each piece
- Week 5: practise complete routines and trial competitions.

Competition - Back to off season + 1 hour conditioning daily.

Conditioning exercises:

- Leg lifts x 30
- V-sits x 30
- Rocks in dish position x 30
- Leg bounces x 30
- Curl ups x 30

- Straddle up to handstands x 10
- Pike up to handstand x 10
- Press ups x 30
- Exercises with free weights
- Stamina

Training case studies

Name:	Steve Bish
Age:	25
Sport:	Badminton
Experience:	Full-time badminton player
	England International
	Regular player in German badminton league

Off season: June–September
The period June–July is used for strength and stamina building as competitive play does not begin until September.

Off season: June–July
During August/early September training is geared towards speed work, court work and tournament preparation.

Monday	30 min run; 30 s x 10 shadow badminton; upper body weights, stretching
Tuesday	1 h steady cycle; circuit training (general exercises); plyometrics; 30 min shot practice; stretching
Wednesday	Match play; 45 min run; leg weights; stretching
Thursday	Hill sprints – 10 x 30 m x 5; shadow badminton 10 x 1 min x 3; 20 min jog; shot practice and corner work (hard); stretching
Friday	Rest day
Saturday	30 min run; 20 min bike; 20 min rowing; on court corner work, 1 min on, 1 min off x 10
Sunday	Match play – morning. Rest

Off season: August–early September
During the tournament season (September–May) training is based around peaking for competition, maintaining fitness levels, speed and quality court practice.

Monday	Sprints – 10 x 20 m x 4; Court work – 30 s max; longer rest (1 h); stretching
Tuesday	Shadow badminton (15 s work/rest) x 10; run (20 min); shot practice (1 h); match play – singles (1 h); stretching
Wednesday	Hill sprints – 6 x 20 m x 3; footwork to music (20 min); fast feet; multi shuttle-smashing/lunging (1 h); stretching
Thursday	Plyometrics; shadow 15 s work/rest x 10; matchplay, 2 h
Friday	20 min run; shot practice; light weights; pyramid sprints; stretching
Saturday	Rest day
Sunday	Singles routines (1 h); circuit

Tournament season: September–May
During the season tournaments, county matches or German league club matches take place most weekends. A free weekend may involve a rest one day and some relaxed play and a gym session on the other. If there is a break in competitive play, training will intensify over the weeks.

Monday	Multi-shuttle hitting (1h); shot practice (drop/net); fast feet
Tuesday	Shadow play – 30 s on/off x 10; Corner work – 1min work/1min rest – hard (1 h)
Wednesday	Light weights; sprints – 10 x 20 m x 10; 5 min skipping/fast feet; matchplay – tactics analysis 2 h; individual shot play
Thursday	Shot practice; footwork to music; 15 min jog; matchplay
Friday	Stretching; mental preparation
Saturday	Tournament
Sunday	Tournament

Age and training

Childhood and adolescence

We grow very quickly in the first two years of our lives. Our rate of growth then slows down until we reach puberty, when we grow very rapidly – with girls reaching their full height at about 16.5 years and boys reaching theirs at about 18 years.

Our performance changes as we grow older

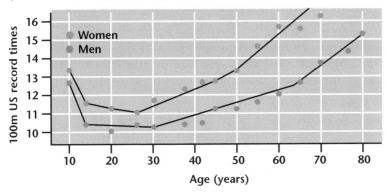

If we exercise regularly during childhood and adolescence, we are likely to establish a healthy pattern of activity for the rest of our lives. Exercise also helps our bones to develop fully.

Balance, agility and coordination improve as the nervous system grows. As their body systems develop children come to have much more control over their movements. Their performance in most sports improves as they approach physical maturity. However, in some sports, for example women's gymnastics, a mature body may be a disadvantage.

Training can improve the strength, aerobic capacity and anaerobic capacity of young sportspeople, but training programmes must be designed for specific age groups. During childhood, strength can be increased by careful resistance training. However, we must be careful not to damage the growth areas at the end of our long bones by, for example, heavy weight training, before the bones are fully formed.

Physical maturity and beyond

Sports records suggest we are in our prime for most sports during our twenties. After this age, our physical strength and endurance decline by about 1–2% a year.
From our mid-twenties:
- MHR decreases at about the rate of one beat per minute per year
- arteries gradually lose their elasticity. This increases our blood pressure and reduces the blood flow to our working muscles
- maximum stroke volume, heart output and vital capacity all steadily decrease. These changes mean that less oxygen is carried to our working muscles and our $\dot{V}O_2$ max decreases
- maximum strength decreases because our muscles reduce in size
- muscle fibres change to slow-twitch rather than fast-twitch
- body fat builds up steadily over the years, leading to increased weight. We exercise less, eat more and are unable to make use of fat for energy so easily.

This steady decline in physical ability is due mainly to a reduced amount of regular aerobic activity. We can slow down the effects of ageing on our cardiovascular and muscular systems by continuing to exercise.

Gender differences and training

Boys and girls mature at a similar rate until they are about 9 or 10 years old. They have similar body shapes and similar amounts of bone, muscle and fat. Sporting competition between the sexes is quite fair at this stage.

Body size and shape

At puberty, boys develop larger bones and there is a big increase in their muscle size due to the release of the hormone testosterone, an anabolic (growth-producing) steroid. Adolescent boys are larger and more muscular than girls.

The release of oestrogen in girls results in breast development, broadening of the hips and increase in body fat. Women have more fat in the hips and lower body whilst men carry more fat in the abdomen and upper body.

Women have narrower shoulders, broader hips and smaller chest diameter than men.

Women need wide hips for childbearing. As a result their legs are in a less mechanically efficient position for running.

However, none of these differences need affect the training programmes for girls and women.

Strength

Women are generally weaker than men. However, when their body size is taken into account, the differences are not at all significant. Men are much stronger in the upper body than women. None of these differences need affect the training programmes for girls and women. When women train with weights, it is body tone which is increased rather than body size. Weight training helps a man's muscles become larger and stronger because of his high levels of testosterone.

Stamina (aerobic capacity)

Up to the age of 10, girls and boys have the same oxygen-carrying capacity. The capacity of boys continues to develop throughout puberty but girls stop improving after the age of 12. The best male competitors in endurance events are better than the best females by at least 30%. The differences are due to women having smaller lungs and hearts and a smaller amount of blood. Women also have up to 30% less haemoglobin in their blood. This means that less oxygen will get to their working muscles. None of these differences need affect the training programmes for girls and women. However it is important that women take sufficient iron in their diet, as they lose iron in blood during menstruation.

The differences in times and distances achieved in sport by men and women are becoming smaller. It is vital that women have equal opportunity to take part in sporting activities and are given every encouragement to do so.

Long-term effects of training

If we follow a well planned, long-term training programme we will change our body systems. These changes will depend on the type of training we have carried out. The long-term effects of aerobic, anaerobic and resistance training will be different.

What are the long-term effects of aerobic training?

As aerobic training needs a constant supply of oxygen, the effects are mainly to do with the way the body maintains this supply.

On our heart

- The heart chambers become larger, with thicker and stronger muscular walls
- The heart empties its chambers more completely
- Stroke volume increases – and can be double that of an untrained person
- The heart beats more slowly when at rest
- The heart copes well with hard work
- The heartbeat will return to its resting rate more quickly than an untrained heart

On our blood and arteries

- Arteries become larger and more elastic, reducing the risk of hardening of the arteries
- Blood pressure is reduced
- Blood volume increases
- Capillaries increase in number
- We have more red blood cells and haemoglobin to carry more oxygen
- There are lower levels of fat in the blood
- We can cope with more lactic acid during exercise

On our muscles

- Aerobic energy systems become more efficient
- Slow-twitch muscle fibres increase in size

On our tendons, ligaments and bones

- Tendons become stronger
  - Ligaments become more flexible through stretching
  - Bones become stronger as more calcium is produced
- The cartilage layer at the ends of the bones becomes thicker and a better shock absorber

On our body fat

- We use more fat and less carbohydrate as fuel for exercise
  - This is helpful because we have good supplies of fat

On our lungs

- The rib muscles and diaphragm grow stronger
  - The volume of air we take in at each breath increases
  - Breathing is more efficient
  - We can continue breathing deeply for longer
- The number of alveoli increases
- The number of capillaries around the alveoli increases
- More oxygen gets into the bloodstream and more carbon dioxide gets out
- We can increase our $\dot{V}O_2$max by as much as 20%;
- The increased amount of oxygen going to the working muscles helps to reduce the effects of fatigue

What are the long-term effects of anaerobic training?

Most of the long-term training effects will take place in our muscles. This is because our muscles have to work without oxygen during anaerobic training. Actual changes include:

- our muscles hypertrophy – they become larger as the individual muscle fibres grow thicker
- the heart walls increase in thickness
- anaerobic threshold increases, enabling us to work harder and longer before becoming tired
- we can cope with lactic acid better
- recovery rate after exercise is quicker because removal of lactic acid is faster
- fast-twitch muscle fibres increase in size and become better able to cope with lactic acid before becoming tired
- muscle cells store greater amounts of ATP, creatine phosphate and glycogen
- the chemical reactions in our muscle that produce energy increase in quantity, speed and efficiency.

Sprint cyclists learn to cope with their oxygen debt

What are the long-term effects of weight training?

Our muscles work very hard during weight training. The effects are mainly to do with the way our muscles adapt to harder work.

- Muscles hypertrophy
- Our muscles contract more quickly and more strongly
- Fast-twitch muscle fibres increase in size
- Ligaments and tendons become stronger
- Muscle cells store greater amounts of ATP, creatine phosphate and glycogen
- Muscles adapt to the amount of work they have to do
- Maximum strength (static strength) increases when we lift very heavy weights for very few repetitions
- Muscular power (explosive strength) increases when we lift heavy weights for a number of fast repetitions
- Muscular endurance (endurance strength) increases when we lift light weights for many repetitions
- Our muscles atrophy – they become smaller and weaker – when they become inactive, for example due to injury.

Weight lifting develops great strength

Examination-type questions: Training for success

There are 12 marks for each question.

1 (a) Name two principles of training. *(2 marks)*

(b) Which training methods are described here:
   (i)   using jumps, leaps and hops;
   (ii) using a variety of activities, speeds and distances. *(2 marks)*

(c) Explain why it is important to warm up before playing sport. *(2 marks)*

(d) Our body adapts to different types of training.
   Give six long-term effects of aerobic training. *(6 marks)*

2 (a) There are four FITT training programme principles. What is meant by:
   (i)   frequency?
   (ii) intensity? *(2 marks)*

(b) Describe circuit training. *(2 marks)*

(c) Give two reasons for using flexibility training. *(2 marks)*

(d) We can divide our training year into pre-season, peak season and off season.
   Explain what this means. *(6 marks)*

3 (a) Which training principles are described here?
   (i)   We must work harder than normal.
   (ii) We must increase our training gradually. *(2 marks)*

(b) Why use interval training? *(2 marks)*

(c) Suggest the type of weights and the repetitions that should be used to
   improve muscular endurance. *(2 marks)*

(d) Explain the factors you would take into account when designing an
   individual training programme for a sportsperson. *(6 marks)*

4 (a) Give two benefits of weight training. *(2 marks)*

(b) Name two training methods that would improve stamina. *(2 marks)*

(c) All training sessions for games will include a warm up and fitness
   development. Which two other phases should also be included? *(2 marks)*

(d) Explain how you would apply three of the principles of training to
   hockey training. *(6 marks)*

Answers are given in the World of Sport Examined Teacher Resource and Student Workbook.

5 Skill in sport

When we watch top sportspeople in action, we see them perform their skills smoothly and with great control. They are exciting to watch because they seem to make difficult actions seem very easy. What we do not see are the hours of practice that take place over many years and which have enabled them to become highly skilful. As sportspeople we need to know how we learn our skills, how we perform them and how we could improve them.

What is skill?
page 110

We see skill in every performance. It is a pattern of movement. Techniques are only part of skill. We need a basic amount of natural ability in order to develop techniques and skills. We also need adequate health-related fitness together with our own sports-related fitness. There are many different types of skills. We usually classify them as open or closed.

How do we learn skills?
page 112

We all have the ability to perform skills but we must learn to be skilful. There are three phases of skill learning which we must pass through to become skilled. These are called the cognitive, associative and autonomous phases.
Certain things help us to learn skills. These are:
• guidance
• practice
• feedback
• experience.

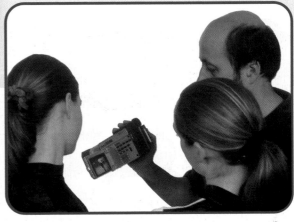

How do we perform skills?
page 114

Our ability to be skilful depends on how efficient our brains are at processing information. The brain must deal with:
• input
• decision making
• output
• feedback.
Other factors affecting sports performance are:
• personality
• motivation
• arousal
• anxiety
• aggression
• goals.
Putting our skills into action involves strategies and tactics.

How do we analyse our performance?
page 122

We analyse our performance in order to improve next time. Individual performance can be analysed by looking at a performer's:
• techniques and skills
• decision-making ability
• strategies and tactics
• fitness level.
Team performance can be analysed by looking at:
• individual performance
• support for other players in the team in attack and defence
• relationships with other team members.
As players we should think of Planning, Performing and Evaluating (PPE) continuously during a performance.

How do we improve our performance?
page 124

We must train to improve our performance. Training sessions must be well planned and should include:
• warm up
• fitness
• skills
• games (if appropriate)
• warm down.
Coaching will improve performance. Practice must always be of good quality and a good coach will plan training sessions to match the performer's ability and experience. He or she will know how to motivate a sportperson to perform well.

What is skill?

Skill is the learned ability to choose and perform the right techniques at the right time, effectively, consistently and efficiently within a competitive game or activity.

We all have some **ability**. It is part of our make up as a person. We inherit ability from our parents. However, we are not born with skill. We have to learn to be skilful.

What is the difference between a technique and a skill?

- Skill refers to a standard of performance. It is essential to all sports performances. Sportspeople use their skill to achieve their objectives – for example, scoring a goal, completing a trampoline routine or winning a race.

- **Techniques** are the basic movements in sports. A volley in football is a technique; so is a handstand in gymnastics or a smash in badminton. In sport we usually select a number of different techniques and combine them into a pattern of movement. This is what we call skill.

- Skill is a pattern of movement that we have learned and can perform when we choose. An example is the skilled basketball player who is able to put together the techniques of shooting, passing and dribbling at the right times in the game. He is usually successful in his play and always seems to have plenty of time.

- We can think of skill in sport as being a combination of physical and mental qualities. The badminton player needs a variety of techniques – a range of different strokes. She also needs to know what her opponent is doing now, and what she is likely to do next. She must decide which stroke to use and where to hit the shuttlecock. The skilful performer has the mental strength to do this even when under intense pressure.

- Decision making is a very important part of skill. By learning techniques and practising hard within the game situation decision making becomes easier and the player becomes more skilful.

Top-class basketball players train for many hours to develop their skills

What types of skill are there?

There are very many different sports and an amazing variety of different skills. Some people describe skills such as running as basic and more complicated skills, such as the spike in volleyball, as complex.

Open and closed skills

Dividing skills into open and closed skills is a way of comparing the skills used in different sports. We look at how the sporting environment affects the skills of the sport. The environment includes such things as weather, surfaces and players on both sides.

- **Open skills** are used in games like lacrosse, which take place outside with many players. This gives the games a lot of uncertainty. For example, each player must take account of his opponents, his own team players and such things as the speed of the ball, the surface of the pitch and the weather. In other words, you need open skills where you cannot control what will happen next.
- **Closed skills** are used in a fixed environment where the performer has the situation under control. For example, a vault in gymnastics, where the equipment is fixed and there are no influences from other people or the weather, uses closed skills. We use closed skills when we can control what happens next.

However, we usually classify skills as being open or closed. We can place them on a continuum from 'open' at one end to 'closed' at the other.

A skill continuum

We can place skills on a line (called a continuum) which goes from 'open' at one end to 'closed' at the other.

- **Judo** is placed towards the 'open' end because the player must react to his opponent – he cannot control what will happen next. However, the surface for competition is always the same, there are no other players to consider and the weather has no effect. In this sense judo is not as 'open' as lacrosse.
- **Archery** is nearer to the 'closed' end of the continuum because the whole action is learned and repeated for competition. However, wind strength and direction will affect the flight of the arrow, so it is not a completely closed skill.
- **High jump** could be put near to the middle of the continuum. The jump itself is a closed skill, but the run up must take account of the weather, runway surface and height of the bar.

Some open sports will also use closed skills. For example, squash and netball are open sports, but when players take a free serve or shot they are in control, so it is a closed skill.

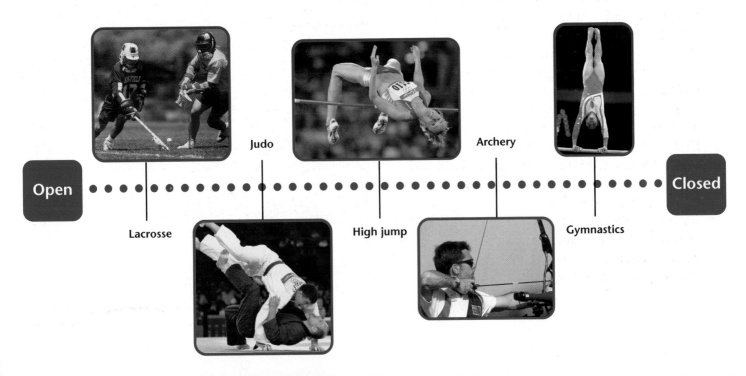

Open · Closed

Judo   Archery

Lacrosse   High jump   Gymnastics

How do we learn skills?

We can split the complex process of skill learning into three different periods called phases: the **cognitive** phase, the **associative** phase and the **autonomous** phase. The phases are not completely separate, but they help us to understand how we learn skills. This helps the learning process.

The cognitive phase – beginners understand the movement clearly

During this phase we are beginners. We need to understand what we have to do. We need a clear mental picture of the movements we have to make. We think carefully about technique and may talk our way through it. We will often make major errors such as missing the ball completely. We find it hard to correct our own actions. At this stage of learning we need our teachers to give us:

- clear demonstrations
- simple instructions
- short periods for practising
- praise for the correct action. They must emphasise the technique not the outcome.

The associative phase – improvers practise and get a feel for the skill

During this phase we have learnt the technique so we concentrate on practising the skill. Our performance improves a lot. We make fewer errors and begin to analyse our movements and make corrections. We start to use **internal feedback** from our senses as well as **external feedback** from our teacher. Some sportspeople do not move beyond this phase.

The autonomous phase – experts perform the skill automatically

We can now perform our techniques almost automatically and can give more attention to making decisions about strategies and tactics. As an example, in this phase a squash player can now focus on where to play the next shot, rather than the shot itself. We are skilled and use our techniques at the right time and in the right place. We can often detect and deal with our own errors. Our coach helps us with the fine detail of the skill, with tactics and with mental preparation.

Skill learning and sport

Knowing about the different phases helps a coach to plan training activities that match the development of each player or performer. This helps the learning process. A lack of understanding may lead to unreasonable expectations of beginners. This may create pressure and tension – which, in turn, affects performance and slows the learning process.

What helps us to learn skills?

We learn techniques and skills by practising.
Our learning is affected by:

- the guidance we are given
- the type of practice we use
- the feedback we get
- what experience we have.

We need guidance when learning skills

Guidance

Guidance is given to us in three ways.
- Visual – demonstrations give us a good idea of what we hope to do
- Verbal – explanations must be brief and focus on the most important points
- Manual – support will keep us safe and give us confidence

All guidance must be easily understood and linked to our phase of skill learning.

Practice

Skill can be taught as a whole or broken down into parts. This is called **whole** or **part practice**. If all of the parts of the action take place at the same time we usually practise them as a whole – for example, cycling. Skills that use a number of techniques are usually practised in parts at first – for example, the basketball lay-up shot, which involves footwork with the bounce, the pick up, the jump and the shot itself.

Massed practice means using long active sessions without rests. An example is a gymnast who might spend an hour repeating the same vault.

Distributed (or **spaced**) **practice** means having rests between shorter practice periods. For example, a gymnast might have three sessions of vaulting practice in an hour, with other activities in between. Long practice sessions can lead to tiredness and boredom, which may be dangerous for difficult activities.

Feedback

Feedback is vital information about our performances. If it comes from our own senses it is called internal feedback. We can also receive external feedback by watching videos of ourselves, listening to our coach or being given our score.

Experience

We might have built up the basic movement patterns of some skills in the past when we played similar sports. For example, a person who has played tennis usually finds some **transfer** to squash when first learning the game. Teachers can help by pointing out the similarities. Sometimes negative transfer can interfere with learning a similar but different skill.

How do we perform skills?

The **information-processing model** of skill performance uses the idea that the brain works like a computer. The process has four stages:

1 **Input** – our senses tell us what is happening
2 **Decision making** – our brain decides what to do
3 **Output** – our body carries out the action
4 **Feedback** – we find out whether or not we have been successful

Input

Receiving information

During this stage our brain gets information from our senses. For example, in basketball our eyes tell our brain the positions of the ball and the other players. Our ears tell our brain what the coach is saying. Messages come from our joints and inner ear to tell our brain about our movements and body position.

Selecting information

We must choose, very quickly, the pieces of information that are important. Our **selective attention** allows us to focus only upon the right information – for example, the gun in a sprint start. We become better at shutting out information that we do not need as we become more experienced in our sport.

Selection of information is important as we have **limited channel capacity**. This means that our brain can deal with only a limited amount of information at a time. If we are dealing with one piece of information and a second arrives, it is delayed. This delay can be seen in the fake shot – a player moves to block the fake shot because he is dealing with the first piece of information and is then too late to deal with the actual movement.

Decision making

At this stage we must make sense of what is happening using our memory and perception. We can then decide on an action and form a plan for the next movement.

Perception is the way we use experience to sort out the information we receive. Skilled performers use their perception to anticipate what will happen next. For example, an experienced batsman can work out the sort of 'ball' to expect from the bowler's run up and delivery.

Memory and experience help us to make sense of the information we receive. They help us to decide what new action to take. Our memory has two parts: short-term and long-term. When practising passing we keep our last attempt in short-term memory to help improve the next attempt. Anything important is transferred to long-term memory – for example, some almost automatic movements such as cycling.

Output – taking action

This is the stage when we react to the situation. Our central nervous system sends messages to our muscles, which then contract. Movement is a complex process. Our muscles must work at the right time, in the correct order and with the right amount of force.

Input – our senses tell us what is happening

Decision making – our brain decides what to do

Output – our body carries out the action

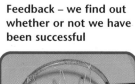

Feedback – we find out whether or not we have been successful

Feedback

Feedback is vital information about our performances. By using feedback we are able to analyse and improve our performances. We receive feedback from two sources.

Internal feedback comes to us from our senses. The **proprioceptors** in our joints tell us how the movement felt and our eyes tell us whether or not we were successful.

External feedback comes to us, for example, by watching ourselves on video, listening to our coach or being given our score. There are two forms of external feedback. These are:

- **knowledge of results**, which tells us the outcome of our performance. We know whether or not we scored the goal, how many points we were given or our position in the race
- **knowledge of performance**. This is about how well we performed rather than the result. This is partly internal as skilled performers will know how good their performance felt. By talking to our coach we can find out about the standard of our performance.

Winning is the most obvious type of feedback

Feedback and sport

Feedback is essential for skill learning. Improvement depends on knowledge of performance or knowledge of results. Coaches must take care to give the right kind and amount of feedback at the right time if they are to get the best from their performers. The feedback given will mainly depend upon the ability and experience of the performers.

- **What feedback to give?** Beginners need only a small amount of verbal, or visual feedback. They find it difficult to use internal feelings about their performance and they cannot handle a great deal of detailed information. More experienced performers get the 'feel' of successful movements. They can then rely more on internal feedback backed up by their coach's observations.
- **How much feedback should be given?** Too much information can lead to confusion, especially for beginners. The coach should focus on specific movements and provide precise feedback only about those movements. Comments should be made at key moments, but should not be made after every attempt. Games players will often be trying to do the right thing, and will know when they have made a mistake.

- **When is feedback given?** Coaches should always allow a little time for performers to process their internal feedback. The coach should also check that the performer understood what she was trying to do. Perhaps she did not understand earlier instructions, or she might have been trying something else.

Feedback needs to motivate as well as correct a performer. Coaches must make positive comments before giving advice to correct performance.

What other factors affect our sports performance?

Successful coaching requires knowledge of the players' personality and the demands of their sport. Coaches have to know when to calm players down and when to 'psych' them up. This is not always easy when dealing with a team, which contains different personality types.

The three main factors that affect our sports performance are closely linked. They are:
* **personality** – our character and temperament
* **motivation** – our determination to achieve success
* **arousal** – the intensity of our motivation.

Our best performances are only possible when we, along with our coach, match our motivation level to our personality and achieve an optimum level of arousal.

Different sports attract different types of personality

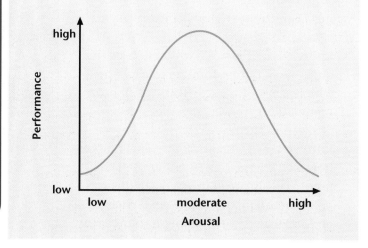

Inverted U theory

How does personality affect performance?

Some researchers have described personalities called **extroverts** and **introverts**. In simple terms, we can say that extroverts are socially outgoing whilst introverts are shy in social situations. Research suggests that, although there are many exceptions to the rule, extroverts and introverts prefer the following types of sports.

Extroverts prefer	Introverts prefer
team sports	individual sports
activities involving the whole body	activities involving fine physical skills
activities involving much movement	activities with limited movement
plenty of activity and uncertainty	routine and repetitive sports

Extroverts seem to need high arousal levels to perform well. Introverts perform better at lower arousal levels.

What is motivation?

Motivation is the driving force which makes us do something. There are two different types of motivation:
* **Intrinsic (or self) motivation** comes from our own inner drives. We may play for fun, for the satisfaction of performing well, for the pride in winning or for the enjoyment of taking part with others.
* **Extrinsic motivation** comes from rewards and outside pressures. We may play to win trophies, to please other people who are important to us or to avoid letting our team down.

Most motivation in sport is a mixture of both types. We may play for the school team for enjoyment and to win trophies. It is intrinsic motivation that will keep us interested in sport when extrinsic rewards have gone.

What is arousal in sport?

In a sporting situation the intensity of our motivation is called **arousal**. The link between arousal and performance can be explained using the 'inverted U theory'. This theory suggests that our best performances come when we are moderately aroused. If our arousal level is not high enough we may feel bored and we will perform badly. If our arousal is too high we may become anxious and worried. This creates tension, which makes our performance less effective.

How do we cope with anxiety in sport?

It is natural to feel anxious about performance before competition. However, we must manage our level of anxiety, or stress, in order to perform to the best of our ability. Before performing we can help to do this by:

- thinking positively – telling ourselves that we *are* good enough and *will* do well
- using mental rehearsal – picturing ourselves carrying out successful movements and practising them in our mind
- relaxing – using controlled breathing and gentle movements.

  Our coach can also help us to cope with anxiety by giving verbal reassurance – talking calmly to us and focusing upon our success.

What types of aggression do we see in sport?

In sport we might compete against opponents, standards of performance or the natural environment. The amount of **aggression** involved varies with the type and level of the sport.

We see a range of aggression in sport.

- **Direct aggression** is a part of boxing, judo, rugby and many other sports. We have to be very aggressive to be successful in these sports. However, we must compete within the strict rules of the sport. Some sports require a limited amount of physical aggression. For example, players must be aggressive in hockey, football and basketball, but the amount of physical contact is limited by the rules of these games.
- **Indirect aggression** is used in sports such as volleyball and tennis. We hit the ball towards our opponents and the ball does the scoring rather than the player. The aggression is still aimed at the opponent, but it is directed through the ball. Aggressive players may find it difficult to mix both delicate and fierce shots.
- **Object aggression** is seen in some sports where an object, not the opponent, receives the aggression. For example, a golfer may hit the ball aggressively, but this does not guarantee success.
- Some sports involve no aggression. For example, in ice skating, trampolining and archery there is no advantage in being aggressive.

NO AGGRESSION

INDIRECT AGGRESSION

DIRECT AGGRESSION

Setting goals

Achieving goals is very rewarding

Why should we set goals to improve performance?

Many of us have long-term ambitions in sport. One ambition, or **goal**, might be to run a mile in under 5 minutes. We would call this a **long-term goal**. To achieve this we need to meet **short-term goals** along the way. Short-term goals would include achieving quicker and quicker times as a result of training regularly.

Setting goals is an excellent way to motivate a person to work hard. It also helps to reduce anxiety because we know that we are not expected to achieve everything at once. By giving a performer confidence in this way, goals help performance.

What types of goals can we set?

The type of goals we choose and the way we set them are important. We cannot win all the time in sport. It is important for us to focus on our achievements, whatever happens when we compete. There are two types of sporting goals:

- **outcome goals** are linked to the result of a competition – for example, winning a trophy or a league
- **performance goals** are concerned with the standard of performance compared with previous ones – for example, getting a better time for a race.

We have more control over our performance goals than over our outcome goals. We can, for example, improve our best time but still not win the race. It is better, therefore, for us to set performance goals as these give a better chance of success. Success in turn can increase confidence and motivation.

How should we set goals?

The National Coaching Foundation (NCF) has found a way to write performance goals.

S pecific	• goals should be as specific as possible to focus attention
M easurable	• they should assess progress against a standard
A ccepted	• they should be accepted by the performer and the coach
R ealistic	• they should be challenging, but within the performer's capacity
T ime phased	• there should be a specific date for completion
E xciting	• they should challenge, inspire and reward the performer
R ecorded	• they should be written down by the performer and coach to evaluate progress, provide feedback and motivate performers

Here is an example of a **SMARTER** performance goal in volleyball:

S pecific	• to receive serve and make a controlled underarm pass to the setter
M easurable	• one set of ten repetitions
A ccepted	• yes
R ealistic	• 70% success rate (7 out of 10)
T ime phased	• achieved consistently by 31 December
E xciting	• yes, especially with varied servers
R ecorded	• in performer and coach training diary

Goal setting and sport

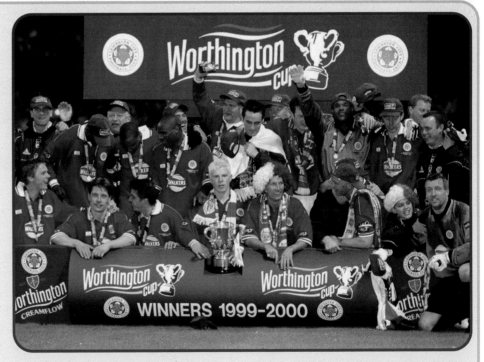

Sporting performance is usually a team effort involving the performer, the coach, other club members and the people who support the performer (such as their parents). It is important that everyone who is involved has the same goals. In an individual sport the coach and the performer need to agree upon the goals and share them with the others. If this does not happen it is very easy for confusion, and possibly conflict, to arise. This leads to anxiety, lack of motivation and poor performance.

In a team sport the goals need to be shared by all of the team members. When this is not the case conflict on the field of play and in the changing rooms will affect performance. We sometimes see teams in different sports who seem to play beyond their potential. The usual explanation is that they have great team spirit. This is another way of saying that the coach and players had set and agreed their goals and that they were all motivated to achieve them.

Putting skills into action

Tactical skill is the ability to choose the right plan of action when performing. Different types of sport require us to use different **strategies** and **tactics**.

In order to develop our tactical skill we need to understand the needs of our sport.

Planning a race is very important

What are strategies and tactics in sport?

- **Strategies** are plans that we think out in advance of the sporting competition. They are methods of putting us in the best position to defeat our opponents.
- **Tactics** are what we use to put our strategies into action. Tactics can also be worked out in advance of the sporting competition, but they will often need to be adapted to the real situation during competition. Tactics involve planning and teamwork.

Strategies and tactics will be very different for different types of games. For example, rugby involves large numbers of players, a variety of set plays and an opportunity for individuals to respond to many different situations. It gives many choices to players, such as kicking, passing or running with the ball. By contrast, in a judo competition there is only one opponent to concentrate on and there are a limited number of attacking moves to make or defend.

Children at the cognitive and associative phases of learning (see page 112) will not be able to cope with strategies. They need only simple tactics such as 'pass the ball to a player who is free'. It is the skilful players at the autonomous phase who are able to give time and attention to strategies and tactics.

What sort of strategies and tactics are used in sport?

Strategies and tactics become more important as the level of competition increases.
When developing a strategy the coach will focus on:
- teamwork
- the game plan
- team **formations**
- set plays.

Setting the strategy from a restart

Teamwork

A successful team will have good teamwork. This means that all members of the team will understand the agreed strategy. They will also put the tactics for each game into practice by working as a unit. Managers, coaches and captains have important roles to play in teamwork. The motivation to work hard for each other has to be developed through training and team-building activities.

Game plan

In some matches and competitions, players and teams talk of a 'game plan'. This is the set of tactics for use in one particular game. The game plan will be based on the team's strengths and the weaknesses of the opposition.

Formations

Teams can use different formations – that is, the players can take up different positions on the field of play. Some sports have rules limiting where the players can move during the game. For example in netball these restrictions present certain problems to be solved. In basketball there are few restrictions on the positions of players so teams can be more flexible. The formations in football are discussed endlessly.

Restarts and set plays

All games have restarts. In net games these are the serves, in other games they are free hits, throw ins, corners, scrums, etc. These restarts give the team an opportunity to have free possession of the ball. At these times many teams use set plays which they practise during training.

How do we develop strategies and tactics?

We need to know:
- our own strengths and weaknesses
- the strengths and weaknesses of our opponents
- our level of fitness
- the importance of the competition
- any important environmental factors.

How are strategies and tactics put into practice?

In a net game, such as tennis, a player might have considered all of the above factors and decided a **strategy** – to move the opponent around the court in order to get her out of position and to tire her. This will then allow the player to play a winning shot or force an error. The **tactic** she uses to achieve this might be to serve wide on both sides of the court and to come in to the net quickly. In the game she might find that these tactics are not working because her opponent is returning serve very well. In this case she will have to decide whether or not to continue with the same tactic or change it – perhaps to stay at the baseline, but to play disguised drop shots to draw the opponent forward and then lob or pass the ball beyond her. Our tactics must be flexible to respond to the situations we meet during a game.

How do we analyse our performance?

Most of the time coaches have to carry out live observation. They watch a player in action and then make comments about the quality of the performance. Many coaches today use technology such as videos to help them analyse performance.

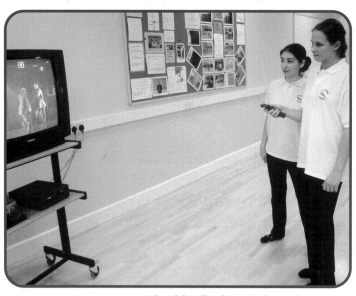

Visual feedback can help performance

How do we analyse a specific technique?

- We must know what the correct technique looks like. We might use books, photographs, video or an expert performer to build an image of excellent performance.
- We must break down the technique into a number of parts. We can then look at each part in turn as the performer repeats the technique a number of times.

For example, in the overhead clear in badminton a player might look separately at:
- movement into position
- foot placement
- body position under the shuttlecock
- arm and racket preparation
- hitting action
- follow through.

How do we analyse a competitive individual performance?

We must focus on six factors: techniques, skills, decision making, fitness, strategies and tactics

Analysis of techniques and skills
By looking at his action we can see if poor technique or skill is preventing our player from carrying out his tactics.

Decision-making ability
A good performer will show good decision making within the game. If a player is anticipating his opponent's moves and selecting successful moves of his own then his performance will be good.
We must analyse the decisions made by the player. This is vital if he is losing and needs our help to suggest better tactics.

Knowledge of strategies and tactics
We must know the strategies and tactics that a performer is attempting to use before we can analyse the performance as a whole. We can then look at how effective they are within the game. If they are not effective we must look for reasons why.

Level of fitness
In most sports fitness affects performance. Unfit people get tired quickly and their performance suffers. We must check that the player is fit for the sport and the level of competition.

How do we analyse a competitive team performance?

We must look at:
- the factors of an individual performance
- the part played by each player in the team effort, such as support for other players in attack or defence
- the attitude of players towards each other, such as supportive or critical relationships.

What is the player's role in analysing performance?

Players and their coaches spend a lot of time preparing for their next performance. They analyse past performances and plan strategies and tactics for the competition. However, all this preparation is wasted if the player does not play well. It is very important that players, at all levels, stay focused throughout their performance.

A good coach will ask her players to ask 'What if?' throughout their play. Players should think about what is happening and what might happen next. The coach wants them to be aware of the 'plan, perform, evaluate' (PPE) process. We all use this process as we play competitive sport.

PPE and sport

The PPE process is repeated over and over again during a match. The most skilful players can plan, perform and evaluate very quickly. They will make many more good decisions than players who are less skilful. The key to success in competitive sport is anticipating what your opponent is likely to do. You also need to be able to adapt to the new situations that arise. Teachers and coaches analyse players' ability all the time.

What do we mean by PPE?

Planning – what we are trying to do

Each time a player does something in the game, for example makes a run off the ball in football, he should know what he is trying to do. The player should also have an idea of what will happen as a result. This means he has a plan.

Performing – what we actually do

The moment the player moves into action he is performing. The performance may be successful or unsuccessful.

Evaluating – considering our performance

The next time that the player is in a similar situation in the game, he will have a chance to repeat the action.

- If it was successful he is likely to try it again
- If it was unsuccessful, but he thinks that the plan was good, he might try to perform it better the next time
- If it was unsuccessful and it was not a good plan he will not repeat it.

How do we improve our performance?

Training for sport can begin at an early age

The objective of every training session is to improve performance. Our analysis of performance will provide a focus for our training sessions. Each session must be well planned. The teacher or coach must guide us through techniques and into skills. We must also develop our strategies and tactics in preparation for competition. Our fitness will have to be maintained or improved.

A training session for games players must include:

- a warm up
- fitness training
- skills practice
- games
- a warm down.

Warm up and warm down

These are essential parts of a training session and must be linked closely to the sporting activity. Full details are given in Chapter 4.

Fitness training

Fitness training should be part of all training sessions. It can be included in skills practices (pressure drills), but should not exhaust players so that they cannot concentrate on their skills. Regular fitness testing provides valuable feedback to coaches and players. Players must take responsibility for their own personal fitness. This includes eating and drinking sensibly and getting plenty of rest (see chapters 3 and 4).

Guided practice improves skill

Skills practice

Skills practices in sport are drills used to teach techniques and skills. A drill is a movement or number of movements that are repeated until they can be performed easily. We may practise techniques individually even if we are training for a team game. Small groups might also practise their skills separately from the rest of the team – for example, the defenders in a hockey team might work on defending crosses. We often link a series of techniques into a skilled movement that mirrors the game situation. This is important because skill practices should be like the real game.

Once technique has been learned, skills can be practised unopposed, with passive opposition, with active opposition and under pressure.

Unopposed

- In basketball, the jump shot can be practised by the shooter alone. In the game the shot is used to clear the defender but at first the techniques are more easily learned without the pressure of an opponent.
- Volleyball team organisation often takes some time to learn initially. At first it is best practised with the coach feeding the ball rather than within the game itself, when the opposition will be trying to win.

Passive opposition

Learning to tackle in rugby is made far easier if the player with the ball stands still! This is known as passive opposition. Learning to keep control of a ball whilst dribbling in and out of a line of opponents is also helped when the opponents are not trying to steal it from you. Passive opposition drills are often used with beginners.

Active opposition

Once the technique of tackling is learned the opposition can simulate the real game by running with the ball and trying to dodge the tackler. This is known as active opposition. A common example of active opposition in football and hockey is the 3v1 possession drill in a grid square. The player in the middle has to try to get the ball.

Pressure training

Pressure training should be used only when the performers have good technique. Pressure can be applied in two ways.

- The performer works very hard for a period of time. This combines skill and fitness work. As the performer tires his or her skill level will drop. The practice will increase fitness levels and help the performer to play when tired.
- The performer is forced to react very quickly. For example, in basketball the jump shooter receives the ball from a player who is between him and the basket. As he receives it the defender attempts to block the shot. The pressure to receive the ball, prepare and execute the shot in a short period of time is similar to the game situation.

Games

We need to transfer our skills from the practice situation into the game situation. We also need to try to put our strategies to work and to practise our tactics.

- **Modified games** give each player plenty of action and lots of time with the ball, for example five-a-side hockey.
- **Conditioned games** have rule changes that focus on a particular skill or tactic. For example, two-touch football can develop good control and passing, but it also encourages support for the player with the ball. Conditioning the game can extend to providing areas of the pitch where the player with the ball cannot be tackled. Once the habit of looking to create width in attack has been learned the players will try to do it in 'normal' games.

The use of games within training sessions also helps us to assess our strengths, find our weaknesses and plan future sessions.

Coaching to improve performance

The time that we spend practising will not always lead to skill improvement: success relies upon good-quality practice. This is a result of good coaching. PE teachers and coaches have different roles but they have all been taught to coach.

PE lessons develop the pupils' skills

What are the roles of PE teachers and coaches?

The PE teacher's central task is to educate all the pupils in his or her lesson using a variety of physical activities. PE teachers:
- introduce children to the basic techniques of sport
- develop skill in all their pupils during lessons
- coach and develop excellence in interested pupils after school
- help young people move smoothly from school to sports clubs
- try to develop pupils' competence in a range of physical activities
- give knowledge and understanding about sporting performance
- aim to develop a positive attitude towards an active lifestyle.

The coach's central task is to improve the performance of the sportspeople in his or her group. Coaches:
- specialise in one sport
- have a deep knowledge of their sport
- work with both beginners and internationals
- know the best ways to develop techniques, skills and fitness
- understand the needs of sportspeople and motivate them
- plan programmes and training sessions
- need to be aware of the problems of competitive sport, such as drug misuse
- analyse performance and check progress.

How do coaches plan to improve performance?

Coaches must know their players and plan programmes that match their level of ability and experience. A good coach will understand the personality of each player and will know how best to motivate every individual in the squad.

Analysis of performance plays a large part in helping a coach to prepare training sessions. It provides specific information that enables him or her to select activities and drills to suit the needs of the players.

How do coaches improve different types of skill?

Closed skills are relatively easy to train. In gymnastics and archery, for example, competition is very similar to training. Closed skills within 'open' games can be simulated very simply. For example, bowling the ball in cricket, taking penalties in football or taking a free throw in basketball are closed skills within 'open' activities. In all of these activities the coach has to try to create the pressure that a player may feel within a competitive situation if the player is to be fully match prepared. This can be done by:

- setting 'closed' drills when the player is tired
- creating pressure by rewarding success, or punishing failure (in the sporting sense, of doing an extra run)
- simulating the match with recorded crowd noise
- creating pressure by having team mates talking at, and trying to put off, the performer.

Open skills are performed within open activities where it is difficult to predict what will happen next. Coaches need to provide their performers with as wide a variety of experiences as possible so that they can practise their skills and techniques in many different situations.

If we are to perform skilfully and develop tactical understanding our coach needs to allow us to make our own decisions during game play. The best coaches know when to advise and when to let their players take control for themselves.

Officials and sport

The official's central task is to enable sportspeople to take part in sport fairly and safely. Administrators organise events, but officials control the sporting action. Officials:

- have excellent knowledge of the sport and its rules
- apply rules firmly and fairly
- need to be patient, good with people (and have a sense of humour!)
- look after the safety of all those involved
- may need to be in good physical condition.

We should always respect officials and never take them for granted, because without them our sport would not exist.

Officials need to be good with players!

Information and communication technology (ICT) in coaching

Good coaches have always used their eyes to analyse performance. This is a very difficult task because of the speed of most sporting movements.

We are now able to analyse performance better by using recent developments in ICT to help us become better coaches. Coaches can now collect and analyse information about performance in the following ways:

Technical information

Coaches can obtain technical information from a wide variety of sources. Books and videos containing examples of technique and tactics are available in many shops. The Internet now enables coaches throughout the world to share their ideas. We can find examples of good training and the latest research within minutes by searching the 'net'.

Recording performance

Coaches can use digital camcorders to record a performance. They can then watch it again at both normal speed and in slow motion. This is immediate visual feedback. We can also compare our actions with those of top performers. This helps us to identify, for example, differences in arm action, leg action, body position, speed of movement.

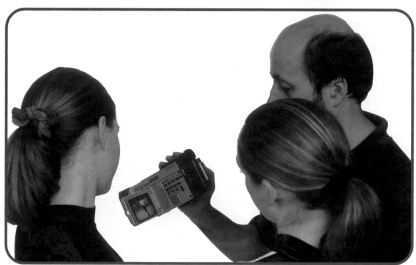

Today in schools ICT is used to help improve performance

Statistical analysis

We can use statistics to measure the effectiveness of players. We can record our performance in many ways – for example, the number of shots, tackles and interceptions. We can then use a computer to sort and analyse this information for immediate use. These statistics can be used to work out a player's strengths and weaknesses. In a similar way we can determine the strengths and weaknesses of our opponents and plan appropriate strategies and tactics.

Fitness monitoring and analysis equipment

Coaches can now use a range of general fitness testing equipment directly linked to computers. Sophisticated software can describe current levels of weakness and will suggest how areas of weakness can be improved upon. Specialised fitness and technical analysis machines are now available for many sports – rowing machines for example.

Tactics boards

Tactics boards enable a coach to explain tactical ideas and player positions. Computers can now be used to show these ideas more clearly – during training, at pre-match meetings and even during breaks in the game. These explanations ensure that every player is clear about his or her specific role.

Examination-type questions: Skill in sport

There are 12 marks for each question.

1 (a) What do we mean by motivation in sport? *(2 marks)*

(b) Suggest two sports that extroverts are likely to enjoy. *(2 marks)*

(c) Give examples of two different sorts of aggression seen in sport. *(2 marks)*

(d) Explain how you would break down a badminton serve in order to analyse it. *(6 marks)*

2 (a) Guidance helps us to learn skills.
Name two other factors that help us to learn skills. *(2 marks)*

(b) How might a sportsperson's performance be affected by
(i) too much arousal?
(ii) too little arousal? *(2 marks)*

(c) Give an example of
(i) an outcome goal
(ii) a performance goal *(2 marks)*

(d) Explain what is meant by planning, performing and evaluating by referring to one sport. *(6 marks)*

3 (a) Explain the difference between open and closed skills. *(2 marks)*

(b) Give an example of
(i) internal feedback
(ii) external feedback *(2 marks)*

(c) What is the difference between a skill and a technique? *(2 marks)*

(d) Suggest three types of skills practice which we could use in a training session. Give examples for each from one particular sport *(6 marks)*

4 (a) There are three phases of skill learning, called cognitive, associative and autonomous. Describe two of these phases. *(2 marks)*

(b) Explain the difference between strategies and tactics in sport. *(2 marks)*

(c) In the information-processing model of skill performance what is meant by
(i) input
(ii) output? *(2 marks)*

(d) How do we analyse a competitive individual performance? *(6 marks)*

Answers are given in the World of Sport Examined Teacher Resource and Student Workbook.

6 Care of our bodies

Our sporting performance is influenced by many factors, including our ability and our training programme. However, we must have a healthy lifestyle if we are to perform to our potential.

We also know that following a healthy lifestyle when we are young will slow the ageing process and reduce the risk of an early death from disease.

Social drugs
page140

We need to understand that many drugs that are part of our social scene are not helpful to sportspeople. Drinking large amounts of alcohol is harmful to our health. Drinking alcohol also affects sporting performance. Smoking is harmful to health and sporting performance.

Sensible eating
page 132

We need to know about the food types and why they are important. We need to know about what makes a healthy diet. Poor nutrition can affect our sports performance.

Food for sport
page 138

We need to know what sports foods contain and how effective they are. Food is energy and we need to know how we can use that energy for sporting success. We should understand the effects of eating before, during and after activity. Many products are claimed to improve our sports performance. Some products can aid performance, but they must be used within good general eating habits.

Good health is our own responsibility. We can
control many of the factors that affect our health
such as lifestyle and diet. We must not neglect our
bodies or abuse them by smoking, taking non-
prescribed drugs or drinking unwise levels of alcohol.

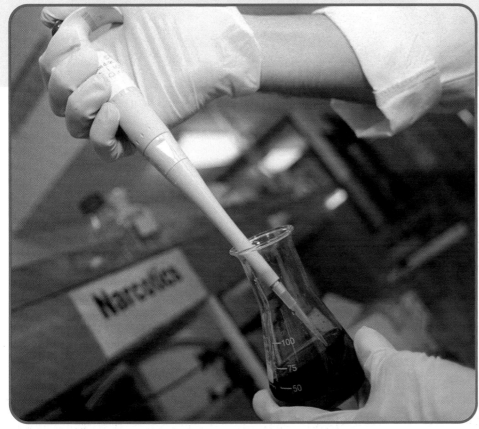

Performance-enhancing drugs
page 144

We need to know about the use of
drugs in sport, including:
- why some sportspeople
  use drugs
- which drugs are banned
- why they are banned
- how we test for drugs
- who makes the rules about drugs.

The right lifestyle
page 150

We need to give ourselves enough
time to sleep and rest. We should
also stick to basic rules of personal
hygiene in order to care for our
bodies. The right lifestyle will keep
us healthy and help us achieve
sporting success.

Sensible eating

To be healthy and successful in sport, we need to know about the food types, what makes a healthy diet and how food can provide us with the right energy.

Why do we need food?

We need food for:
- energy
- repair
- growth
- good health.

We get energy from food for our muscles to work. Food contains the basic materials needed for growth and repair. We need many different nutrients for good health and a balanced and varied diet will provide them.

What is a balanced diet?

A balanced diet contains seven essential components:
- carbohydrates
- fats
- proteins
- vitamins
- minerals
- fibre
- water.

We should limit the amounts of the three main food types which supply energy. The Department of Health recommends that a healthy diet should contain:
- 50–60% carbohydrates (mainly from starch and natural sugars)
- 25–30% fat (mainly from unsaturated fat)
- 10–15% protein (mainly from lean meat, fish, poultry and plants)
  We should also:
- decrease the amount of salt that we eat
- increase the amounts of fibre, calcium and vitamin C that we eat.

We need carbohydrates and fats to give us energy for sport

What are carbohydrates?

Carbohydrates are broken down in the body into different sugars. There are two types of carbohydrate:

1 **Sugars** (simple carbohydrates). We find sugars in:

- fruits
- honey
- jam
- sweets
- cakes
- biscuits
- beer
- table sugar.

Highly processed food, such as sweets, will give us a quick supply of energy but no other nutrients. Biscuits and cakes often contain a lot of fat.

2 **Starches** (complex carbohydrates). We find starches in:

- vegetables
- bread
- rice and cereals
- pasta.

It is better to take most carbohydrates in the form of starches rather than sugars.

Why are carbohydrates important?

Carbohydrates give us the energy we need for our working muscles. We can also get energy from fats and proteins, but not as quickly or as efficiently as we can from carbohydrates. Large amounts of carbohydrates are stored as glycogen in the liver and muscles. Small amounts are stored as glucose in the blood. Intense exercise quickly uses up these stores so active sportspeople need plenty of carbohydrates in their diet. We store any extra carbohydrates as fat around our bodies.

What are fats?

Fats are broken down in the body into saturated and unsaturated fatty acids. There are two types of fats:

1 **Saturated fats**. We find saturated fats in animal products, and foods made from them.
   These include:

   - milk
   - meat
   - cheese
   - cream
   - butter
   - cakes
   - biscuits
   - chocolate.

   Saturated fats can raise our cholesterol levels.

2 **Unsaturated fats**. We find unsaturated fats in:

   - fish
   - corn
   - nuts
   - soya beans.

What are proteins?

Proteins are broken down in our bodies, into amino acids. There are two types of amino acids:

1 **Non-essential amino acids**. For our bodies to function properly, we need 21 different amino acids. We can make 13 of these, which are called non-essential.

2 **Essential amino acids**. These are the 8 amino acids that we have to take from our food because we cannot make them ourselves. We find them in both animal and plant foods.
   We find proteins in:

   - fish
   - meat
   - poultry
   - eggs
   - cheese
   - milk
   - cereals
   - beans
   - peas
   - nuts.

Proteins from animal products contain all of the essential amino acids. However, plant proteins (with the exception of soya beans) lack some essential amino acids.

Why are fats important?

Fats give us energy, although much more slowly than carbohydrates. Fats need extra oxygen supplies to provide that energy. Fats are our main source of energy when we are resting or asleep. Fats keep the skin in good condition, help to keep us warm and protect our vital organs. Extra fat is stored just under the skin. This extra weight will not help sportspeople. Too much fat can lead to obesity and high **cholesterol** levels.

Cholesterol is a fat-like substance found in our blood. It is present in some foods, especially fatty animal products. Cholesterol not needed by the body builds up on the artery walls and can cause circulatory and heart problems.

Fats give us energy for sport more slowly than carbohydrates

Why are proteins important?

Much of our body's tissue is made up of protein, including our skin, bones and muscles. Proteins are needed for the repair, growth and efficient working of our tissues. Protein is only rarely used as an energy source when no carbohydrate or fat is available. Excess proteins cannot be stored in the body.

What are vitamins?

Vitamins enable our bodies to work normally and efficiently.
Our bodies cannot make vitamins so we must take them in in
our food. There are two types of vitamin:

1 **Water-soluble vitamins.** These are the Vitamin B group and
   C vitamins. They cannot be stored in our bodies – any excess
   is removed. Our daily diet must include foods that contain
   these vitamins, such as those shown in the table.

Vitamin	Name	Contained in:
B_1	Thiamin	Cereals, whole-grain bread, yeast, milk, potatoes, fish, sunflower seed
B_2	Riboflavin	Cereals, liver, kidneys, green leafy vegetables, peas, peanuts
B_3	Niacin	Poultry, beef, fish, peas, peanuts, beans, eggs, brown rice.
B_6	Pyridoxine	Yeast, bananas, fish, peanuts, beans, spinach
B_{12}	Cobalamin	Liver, kidney, yoghurt, milk, beef, chicken, egg
C	Ascorbic acid	Most fruits and vegetables. High concentrations in citrus fruits

Sources of water-soluble vitamins

We need these vitamins in small regular amounts. They are water soluble so
they are 'washed' out of foods during cooking. Because of this fruit and
vegetables containing these vitamins should be cooked as little as possible.

2 **Fat-soluble vitamins.** These are vitamins A, D, E and K.
   They can be stored in our bodies.

Sources of fat-soluble vitamins

Vitamin	Name	Contained in:
A	Retinol	Deep orange or yellow fruits and vegetables, dark green vegetables, liver, cod liver oil, dairy products
D	Calciferol	Oily fish (mackerel, salmon, tuna) liver, cod liver oil, butter, eggs
E	Tocopherol	Beans, nuts, seeds, green leafy vegetables, egg yolk, cod liver oil
K	Phytomenadione	Green leafy vegetables, wheat germ, peas, beans, beef liver, milk, egg yolk

Why are vitamins important?

Vitamins regulate the chemical reactions of
our bodies. They help in the growth and
repair of body tissues, in the working of our
muscles and in the release of energy from
food. Vitamins all have their own functions,
as shown in the table.

Vitamin	Function
A	Good vision and healthy skin
B	Energy production, stress reduction
C	Fighting viruses, keeping skin and gums healthy, healing wounds
D	Helps to build bones and teeth
E	Protects cells, helps immune system, aids growth
K	Helps form blood clots

Functions of the vitamins

What are minerals?

We cannot make minerals so we must take them in from our food. They enable the body to work normally and efficiently. Minerals are found in a variety of foods.

Sources of minerals in a wide variety of foods

Mineral	Contained in:
Calcium	Milk, sardines and salmon with bones, vegetables, beans
Iodine	Iodised salt, saltwater fish, milk
Iron	Spinach, dark green vegetables, liver, red meat, beans, peas, nuts
Potassium	Bananas, dried fruit, meat, vegetables, sunflower seeds
Sodium	Table salt, soy sauce, preserved meat, crisps, canned foods

We need small but regular amounts of minerals, and they can all be provided by a balanced diet. Too much of some minerals can be harmful – for example, too much sodium (in the form of salt) can increase blood pressure.

Why are minerals important?

Minerals all have their own function in helping the body to work well.

Functions of minerals

Mineral	Function
Calcium	Strengthens bones, helps blood to clot, strengthens muscles
Iodine	Helps the thyroid gland to promote normal growth and energy production
Iron	Aids production of red blood cells, creates good skin tone, prevents fatigue, helps resistance to disease
Potassium	Aids muscle contraction, promotes healthy skin, maintains normal blood pressure
Sodium	Maintains body fluid levels, aids muscle contractions

What is fibre?

Fibre is also called roughage or dietary fibre. Fibre is the part of a plant that we cannot digest. It does not contain any nutrients. Fibre is found on the outside of seeds, in vegetables, fruits and nuts.

Why is fibre important?

Fibre adds bulk to our food. This helps the food move through our digestive system and prevents constipation. Fibre is also involved in food absorption. It slows down the release of sugars from food so that we get a more even release of energy. Dietary fibre adds bulk without adding extra kilojoules. Eating a high-fibre diet can help us to lose weight if we need to. A high level of fibre helps to maintain good health.

Why is water important?

Water is essential for living. It comes from the fluids we drink and the food we eat. We lose water in our sweat, urine, faeces and in the air we breathe out. About two-thirds of our body weight is made up of water. It is the main component of blood and cells. As part of the blood it carries nutrients, blood cells and waste products around the body.

Water in the blood also helps to control body temperature by absorbing heat produced during exercise. This heat is then carried to the skin where it is lost to the air. Water as sweat helps to cool the body when it evaporates on the surface of the skin. Heat is also lost in the water vapour in the air that we breathe out. Loss of water can lead to dehydration and **heatstroke**.

We must replace fluid lost when playing in the sun

We need energy for all our sporting activities

Why do we need energy?

We need energy to make our bodies work.
There are two main purposes:

1 Energy to keep our body systems going. We call this amount of energy our **basal metabolic rate (BMR)**. It is the amount of energy we need to keep alive and healthy. BMR is affected by our age, sex, body size and body composition.

2 Energy for our activities. This is known as our **physical activity level (PAL)**. We use energy for all of our everyday activities – walking, housework, gardening etc. If we take part in sport we will use a lot more energy (depending on the type of sport and how much exercise is involved). A person's age, sex, work, health and lifestyle will all affect their PAL.

Remember that:

BMR + PAL = our total energy needs

How is energy measured?

Energy is measured in kilocalories (kCal) or kilojoules (kJ). One kilocalorie is the equivalent of 4.2 kJ. All food contains an energy value, which is usually calculated as the number of kilojoules per gram of food. Exercise is measured as the number of kilojoules used per hour.

How much energy is in our food?

The amount of energy in a food depends on the amount of carbohydrates, fats and proteins it contains. It is greatly affected by the way the food is cooked. You can see from the table that potatoes contain 3 kJ per gram when boiled, but 15 kJ per gram when served as chips. A baked potato may contain fewer calories than the butter that you spread on it!

Food	kJ per gram
Butter	31
Crisps	23
Milk chocolate	22
Sausage roll	21
White sugar	16.5
Chips	15
White bread	10
Boiled eggs	6.2
Boiled rice	5.8
Low-fat yoghurt (fruit)	3.8
Boiled potatoes	3
Milk (semi-skimmed)	1.9
Fizzy soft drink	1.5
Apple	1.4

How much energy do we need?

We need to match the amount of energy in the food we eat with the amount of energy our body needs.
* We will lose weight if our body needs more energy than our diet is providing.
* We will put on weight if our body needs less energy than our diet is providing.

The energy equation

The link between diet, energy and weight is quite straightforward. The diagrams show the effects of an imbalance between the number of kilojoules taken in and burned up each day.

Experts have calculated the energy needs for growth and body maintenance:
* an average 15-year-old male needs to eat about 11500 kJ per day
* an average 15-year-old female needs to eat about 8800 kJ per day.

Weight stays constant
Kilojoules taken in each day equals kilojoules burned up each day

Weight gained
Kilojoules taken in each day is greater than kilojoules burned up each day

Weight lost
Kilojoules taken in each day is less than kilojoules burned up each day

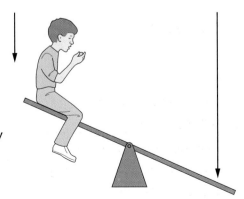

How much energy do we use when taking part in activity?

The amount of energy people use depends upon the intensity of the activity they are doing.

Activity	Energy used per hour (kJ)
Marathon running	4158
Basketball	3360
Brisk jogging	2520
Disco dancing	2100
Badminton	1848
Golf	1428
Cycling moderately	1260
Gardening	1260
Cleaning	798
Studying	420
Watching TV	378
Sleeping	252

There are many books – and websites – that will give you detailed information about a range of activities.

What is obesity?

If a person's weight is more than 20% greater than the standard weight for his or her height they are **obese**. **Obesity** often leads to heart, circulation and other health problems. Being overweight can affect sports performance and increases the risk of health problems.

What are anorexia and bulimia?

Sufferers of **anorexia** do not allow themselves to eat, and often think they are overweight. People with **bulimia** eat a lot of food, but get rid of it, usually by vomiting. Both conditions lead to extreme weight loss. These are medical conditions. Sufferers need urgent medical help.

Food for sport

We should eat our main meal at least 3 hours before competing

How do we get enough energy for sport?

When we work hard, the energy we use comes from our stores of **glycogen**. Glycogen is made from carbohydrates and fats. However, our stores of glycogen are limited. We need to eat extra carbohydrates, which build supplies of glycogen, to have enough energy for endurance activities. We call this **carbohydrate** ('carbo') **loading**. An athlete carbo loads by reducing his or her level of exercise for at least three days before competition while at the same time increasing the amount of carbohydrate in his or her diet.

When we work aerobically – using oxygen – we can get energy from our fatty acids. Fatty acids are found in fat stores around our bodies. At low activity levels our bodies use a mixture of carbohydrates and fats. Endurance training teaches our bodies to use more fat during exercise. This helps our limited supplies of carbohydrates to last longer.

We use proteins as an energy supply only rarely, when we have no other energy sources.

How should we eat for sport?

We need to look at how we eat before, during and after exercise.

Eating before exercise
We should:

- eat our main meal at least 3–4 hours, and our snack meal at least 1–2 hours, before exercise, to give us time for digestion
- include starches such as bread, cereal and fruit, to give a slow, steady release of energy
- avoid simple sugars (sweets) because they increase our insulin level, which in turn reduces our blood glucose and make us feel tired
- avoid foods high in fat and protein as they take longer to digest
- include plenty of fluids to avoid dehydration.

Eating during exercise
We should:

- continue to drink water, not waiting until we feel thirsty but taking small sips regularly
- drink a glucose-based sports drink if the activity lasts for more than an hour.

Eating after exercise
We should:

- eat foods rich in carbohydrate within an hour of exercising, even if we do not feel hungry, to restore our glycogen stores quickly
- drink plenty of water to replace lost fluids.

Which sports foods will improve performance?

Food supplements for athletes are widely available and sports drinks are heavily advertised. **Creatine monohydrate** is becoming popular as it can help in the production of energy and in the recovery process. When we are trying to perform at our peak we are easily tempted to buy these products. However, we need to look at the scientific evidence and decide for ourselves if the products will help us.

Keeping fluid levels high is important during endurance events

Drinks

- We only need to drink plain water before and during activities lasting 60 minutes or less
- Sports drinks containing carbohydrates and **electrolytes** (sodium, potassium and magnesium compounds) can enable us to work hard for longer if our activity lasts more than 60 minutes
- Sports drinks can help after exercise as they help to restore lost fluids, energy and minerals
- Sports drinks provide useful nutrition during whole-day tournaments
- There is no need to buy sports drinks containing extra vitamins. We do not lose vitamins when we sweat and we can get all the vitamins we need from a balanced diet

Food and food supplements

- A high-carbohydrate diet will allow us to work hard for longer, but we must also train well in order to do this
- If we are training very hard our diet should consist of 65–70% carbohydrate
- We should not increase our fat consumption even if we are training very hard
- Extra protein in the diet does not help to make extra muscle – it is broken down and stored as fat or used for energy. Using correct training techniques is the only way to increase muscle size
- High-protein foods are difficult to digest and we should not eat them before training or competing
- Creatine is found in large quantities in red meat. Our bodies can make it from amino acids

Guidelines for using sports food

	Before exercise	During exercise	After exercise
Sports drink	500 ml one hour before exercise	150-300 ml per 20 minutes	750 ml per 500g of body weight lost
High-carbohydrate energy drink	500 ml 2–5 hours before exercise	Used as a carbohydrate loading regime, not during a race	Immediately after and at 1 hour intervals
Sports bar	One bar 2 hours before exercise	Not advisable, except for endurance events	1–2 bars immediately after exercise
Sport shake	500 ml 2–5 hours before exercise	Not recommended	Immediately after and with meals
Energy gel	One packet with fluid before exercise	To supply 30–60 g carbohydrate per hour, but fluid intake must be high	Immediately after and at 1 hour intervals

Social drugs

Drugs are chemical substances that can affect our bodies. Medical drugs are made to fight illness and disease. The use of banned drugs in sport is known as doping. As sportspeople we need to know about social drugs and performance-enhancing drugs.

What are social drugs?

When we play sport we often become part of a social group that meets after training and after competition. Adult sportspeople often meet in bars. Many sports clubs earn money from having a successful clubhouse bar. The drugs that are available within social situations are known as **social drugs**. Some are legal and are widely used. Other social drugs are illegal, but are still used by a number of people. Social drugs are usually taken to help people to relax or to give users an enjoyable experience. We need to know about each social drug and how social drugs can affect our sporting performance.

Sporting celebrations often include drinking large amounts of alcohol!

What are the different social drugs?

There are many different social drugs and each has a different effect.

The most common social drugs

Name of drug	Type of drug	General effect
Alcohol	Depressant	Slows down how our body works
Amphetamines	Stimulant	Speeds up the nervous system. Fights fatigue
Caffeine	Stimulant	Increases heart rate. Increases alertness
Cannabis	Depressant	Reduces worry but slows down responses
Cocaine	Stimulant	Speeds up the nervous system. Creates a feeling of well-being
Ecstasy	Stimulant	Increases confidence and sense of well-being
LSD	Hallucinogen	Changes the way that we see and understand things around us
Nicotine (tobacco)	Stimulant	Increases heart rate. Increases concentration level

Only alcohol, caffeine and nicotine are legal in the UK.

Performance-enhancing drugs

Some sportspeople try to gain an extra advantage by using banned drugs. This is illegal and sometimes harmful. We need to know how performance-enhancing drugs work and how they can affect our sporting performance.

What are the different performance-enhancing drugs?

Performance-enhancing drugs take many forms. They are all banned in sport. They are grouped into doping classes of drugs that have similar effects:

Performance-enhancing drugs were linked to the death of Tommy Simpson in 1967

Doping class	Examples	General effect
Anabolic agents	Nandrolone, testosterone, stanozolol, clenbuterol	Reduce recovery time so that we can train harder and for longer. Increase muscle bulk, strength and endurance when combined with regular exercise
Analgesics (narcotic)	Codeine, methadone, heroin	Pain-killing effect allows training and competing even when injured
Diuretics	Frusemide, probenecid	Produce rapid weight loss by the reduction of fluid levels in the body
Peptides, glycoprotein hormones and analogues	Human growth hormone (HGH), erythropoietin (EPO)	Decrease fat mass. Thought to improve performance Increases number of red blood cells, more oxygen can be carried to the muscles and endurance is improved
Stimulants	Amphetamines, cocaine, ephedrine	Speed up the nervous system, quickening reactions. Mask fatigue and reduce feelings of pain

Some drugs are restricted in certain sports, but are not completely banned. These include all the illegal social drugs and alcohol.

Other restricted drugs

Restricted drug	General effect
Beta blockers	Keep heart rate and blood pressure low. Reduce tremble in the hands
Corticosteroids	Reduce inflammation and pain, allowing us to perform
Local anaesthetics	Reduce pain, masking injury to allow us to perform

What other methods of enhancing performance are banned?

- **Blood doping** – see page 145
- **Changing samples**, or interfering with them in any way
- Using **masking agents** – taking other drugs to hide the use of a performance-enhancing drug

Social drugs and sport

How does drinking alcohol affect our sporting performance?

Alcohol has a number of effects on our sporting performance:

Reduced co-ordination, slower reaction time and poorer balance

These changes affect our movements and skills, especially where catching and balance is involved, and in sports needing steadiness such as archery, gymnastics and shooting.

Dehydration

Alcohol is a diuretic and increases urine production. This leads to water loss from the body. Dehydration seriously affects our performance in endurance events and all competitions on hot days.

Lower muscle glycogen levels and slower removal of lactic acid

Muscle glycogen is needed during endurance events. Lactic acid is produced during exercise and must be removed quickly. Therefore, drinking alcohol before any sport involving endurance will reduce performance. It will also take us longer to recover.

Rapid loss of heat

Alcohol causes the blood vessels in the skin to open up. We lose heat quickly through our skin, which reduces our body temperature although we feel warm. If we are in a cold environment hypothermia can develop.

Longer injury recovery time

We use RICE (see page 162) to reduce the blood flow to an injured area. Alcohol has the opposite effect. Recovery time will be increased. If we receive an injury during a match we should not drink alcohol afterwards.

Reduced size of arteries

Alcohol reduces the size of the arteries, so that less blood can flow along them. Our heart rate and blood pressure both increase.

Other effects

Alcohol also affects our:

- thinking, judgement, vision and hearing
- stomach (and can cause vomiting)
- liver, as it takes a long time to process
- weight, as it is very high in kilojoules.

How does smoking cigarettes affect our sporting performance?

Smoking also has many effects on sporting performance:

Reduced lung efficiency

The smoke damages the hairs lining the bronchial tubes. Dust is not removed from the air so our lungs become clogged and do not work efficiently. We need efficient lungs for all sports.

Reduced oxygen-carrying ability

Carbon monoxide is taken into our lungs in the smoke and passes into our blood. It attaches to red blood cells, reducing the amount of oxygen that the blood can carry. This affects endurance activities.

Reduced fitness level

Even if we train hard, our fitness level will be reduced because of the damage to our lungs and circulatory system caused by smoking.

Lowered resistance to illness

Smokers catch colds more often and take longer to recover from chest infections. Smoker's cough is a special hazard, as is bronchitis. Sportspeople need to keep well to train and compete.

Raised blood pressure

Nicotine causes the brain to release hormones. These hormones make the heart beat faster and the blood vessels in the skin to contract. This causes an increase in blood pressure and a feeling of being cold.

Other effects

Smoking also affects our:

- life expectancy – smokers are at much higher risk of cancer and cardiovascular disease
- social standing – we breathe harmful and unpleasant fumes on people around us. We also smell of stale tobacco
- senses of taste and smell, by reducing them
- appetite, by reducing it.

How do other social drugs affect our sporting performance?

Amphetamines

Amphetamines increase heart rate and blood pressure. They hide symptoms of fatigue and reduce feelings of pain. They are addictive and can cause anxiety and aggression.

Cocaine

Cocaine is a highly addictive stimulant. It encourages us to think that we are doing better than we are. This deception is not good in sport, when we need to know exactly how we are doing.

Cannabis

Cannabis, or marijuana, can result in lack of interest and poor judgement. It is smoked and this causes the same problems as cigarette smoking. It has no role to play in sport.

Ecstasy

Ecstasy is a stimulant with slight hallucinogenic properties. It is not useful in sport because it affects our perceptions. Our performance can also be affected during the day after we have used Ecstasy because of the negative effects of the 'comedown'.

LSD

LSD distorts reality and affects our ability to perceive situations and make decisions. The effects of LSD can often be felt long after the drug has been taken (flashbacks). This drug has no place in sport.

Caffeine

Caffeine, found in tea, coffee and many soft drinks, is a mild stimulant. It increases heart rate and blood pressure. This is not useful to endurance athletes.

Performance-enhancing drugs and sport

All performance-enhancing drugs and methods are banned throughout sport. Even nicotine and caffeine levels have to be below a prescribed limit in most sports.

How do anabolic agents affect our sporting performance?

Anabolic agents, or steroids, can be taken orally or by injection. They have positive effects upon performance because, when combined with extra exercise, they increase strength, muscle growth, body weight and endurance. They enable sportspeople to train more often and harder. However, they have serious side-effects.

Side-effects of anabolic drugs

Disadvantages for men	Disadvantages for women
Increased aggression	Increased aggression
Impotence	Development of male features
Kidney damage	Growth of facial hair
Baldness	Growth of body hair
Development of breasts	Irregular periods

How do narcotic analgesics affect our sporting performance?

Codeine, morphine, methadone and heroin are members of the opiate family. They have a positive effect on sporting performance by reducing the feeling of pain. By doing this they mask injury or illness and allow us to compete when really we should not.

The disadvantages of taking narcotic analgesics are that:
• injuries can be made much worse and even permanent
• they are highly addictive.

'Making the weight' is essential for most boxers

How do diuretics affect our sporting performance?

Diuretics are mainly used by sportspeople in events where they have to 'make the weight' to fit into a weight category. These events include horse racing, boxing, weight lifting and martial arts. The diuretic works by removing fluid from the body – as urine – so the result is rapid weight loss. They are also used to remove other drugs from the body to try to beat the drug testers.

The disadvantages of taking diuretics are that they often result in:

• dehydration   • headaches
• cramps   • nausea.
• dizziness

These conditions seriously affect our ability to play sport.

How do peptide and glycoprotein hormones and analogues affect our sporting performance?

These hormones are produced naturally by our bodies. Analogues are the same hormones produced artificially.

Erythropoietin (EPO) improves endurance by increasing the number of oxygen-carrying red blood cells. The disadvantages of using this type of drug are that it may:
- thicken the blood, so increasing the risk of a stroke and heart problems
- cause oily skin, acne and muscle tremors.

Human growth hormone (HGH) encourages muscle growth, increases the use of fat and improves our body's ability to cope with fatigue. The disadvantages of using this type of drug are that it may cause:
- abnormal growth, including enlargement of internal organs
- atherosclerosis and high blood pressure
- diabetes, arthritis and impotence.

All medallists at the Olympic Games are tested for drugs

How do stimulants affect our sporting performance?

Drugs such as amphetamines, ephedrine and cocaine can lead to an improvement in performance because they give us a lift, keeping us awake and competitive. They speed up reflexes and reduce feelings of fatigue.

The disadvantages of using stimulants are that they:
- increase heart rate and blood pressure
- hide symptoms of fatigue, putting high levels of strain on our bodies – which can lead to death
- reduce feelings of pain, bringing the risk of making injuries worse
- can lead to acute anxiety and aggressiveness
- are addictive.

How does blood doping affect sporting performance?

Blood doping does not involve the use of drugs – blood is injected into the body to increase the number of red blood cells. Athletes usually inject their own blood, which has been removed earlier and stored, but it can come from another person. Blood doping makes the blood able to carry more oxygen to the working muscles. This increases aerobic endurance, which is an effect that can also be gained by training at altitude.

Blood doping has disadvantages that are very dangerous. These include:
- overloading the circulatory system, increasing blood pressure and causing difficulties for the heart
- kidney failure
- transmission of AIDS and other diseases by injecting another person's blood.

Which drugs are allowed subject to certain restrictions?

Some classes of drugs are subject to certain restrictions by the International Olympic Committee's (IOC's) medical commission.

Local anaesthetics

These reduce pain, but are allowed for medical reasons only. This might include a pain-killing injection for an athlete who is injured during the early stages of competition. Professional footballers are sometimes given a pain-killing injection so that they can play in an important match. This is not recommended as the injury may become more serious.

Corticosteroids

Corticosteroids are used as pain killers, to reduce inflammation and for treatment of asthma. Cortisone is a well known corticosteroid. Their use is now banned except for special cases. All details of treatment must be given to the IOC Medical Commission or the International Sports Federation.

Beta blockers

These are used to treat people with heart problems. They keep the heart rate and blood pressure low even during periods of stress. The IOC has banned their use in competitors in archery, shooting, biathlon, modern pentathlon, bobsleigh, diving, luge and ski jumping.

Cannabis/marijuana

Cannabis is controlled in motor sport and some major team games, including football.

Alcohol

Alcohol has been used by some sportspeople to reduce anxiety and shaking in events. Alcohol testing is carried out at the Olympic Games in fencing and in the shooting part of the modern pentathlon.

Andreea Raducan of Romania tested positive for drugs at Sydney 2000

How do sportspeople know which drugs are banned?

The list of banned and restricted drugs is regularly updated. It contains over 1000 substances. Sportspeople must check the list before taking any medicine because some drugs, which are contained in everyday medicines, are banned. These include:
- the stimulant ephedrine, which is an ingredient of many cold remedies
- the steroid clenbuterol, which is used in asthma treatments.

Nandrolone

Some drugs may also be found in food supplements. In recent years the steroid nandrolone has been found in the samples of a number of athletes, although they all claimed that they had never knowingly taken it. It is claimed that they may have produced the high levels of the steroid within their bodies as a result of using a food supplement that contains a chemical related to nandrolone. Some recent research appears to show that physical and mental stress can increase natural levels of nandrolone in the body.

How are sportspeople tested for drugs?

A number of sportspeople are tested during each competition. Many sports federations also test competitors during out-of-competition periods, when they are in training. Competitors can be selected for testing anytime and anywhere. Refusal to be tested is taken as a sign of guilt.

These guidelines for urine testing are followed in competitions and are very similar in out-of-competition testing. In addition to the urine test described below a new blood test was introduced at the Sydney 2000 Olympics.

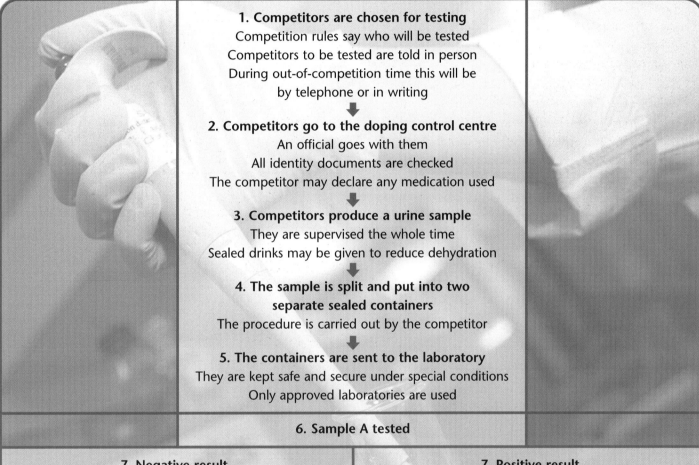

1. Competitors are chosen for testing
Competition rules say who will be tested
Competitors to be tested are told in person
During out-of-competition time this will be
by telephone or in writing

⬇

2. Competitors go to the doping control centre
An official goes with them
All identity documents are checked
The competitor may declare any medication used

⬇

3. Competitors produce a urine sample
They are supervised the whole time
Sealed drinks may be given to reduce dehydration

⬇

**4. The sample is split and put into two
separate sealed containers**
The procedure is carried out by the competitor

⬇

5. The containers are sent to the laboratory
They are kept safe and secure under special conditions
Only approved laboratories are used

6. Sample A tested

7. Negative result
No drugs found
No further action

⬇

8. Sample B is destroyed
The governing body is told
The competitor is told

7. Positive result
Drugs are found
The governing body is told
The competitor is told and suspended

⬇

8. The governing body of the sport investigates
The competitor is asked for an explanation
Sample B is tested if this is requested

⬇

9. A governing body hearing is arranged
The competitor presents his or her case
If the competitor is found guilty he/she will be
punished. The competitor may appeal

Why do sportspeople take performance-enhancing drugs?

- The desire to win is very high amongst competitive sportspeople. If they believe that a drug will help them to achieve their goal they may be tempted to use it.
- The temptation is even higher when success will lead to great financial rewards.
- The pressure to be successful – from the media and public as well as coaches and managers – can be very great.
- They believe that other competitors are using drugs and that without drugs they will have no chance of winning.
- Some sportspeople may use anabolic agents while they're being treated for injury to speed up the recovery process. Some sportspeople believe that such treatment is acceptable. Out-of-competition testing may catch them and lead to a ban.
- They believe they will not get caught and are prepared to cheat in order to win.

Why is doping not allowed?

The International Olympic Committee (IOC) does not allow doping for three main reasons:

1 To ensure that competition in sport is as fair as possible. Taking drugs to improve performance is a way of cheating
2 To protect the health of the sportspeople
3 To protect the wholesome image of sport

The drug rules – who decides?

Each sport has its own international sports federation (ISF) which controls its sport world-wide. The ISFs make their own rules about doping. In the case of Olympic sport, the sport must also follow the drug code of the IOC. Each governing body in a country has the responsibility for testing sportspeople in and out of competition. In Britain drug testing is co-ordinated at the London office of UKSport. National administrators in England, Northern Ireland, Scotland and Wales support the work.

Doping tests at the Olympics, Sydney 2000

The IOC changed its rules shortly before the 2000 Games. It wanted the Games to have the toughest ever drugs testing programme. In addition to the urine test a new blood test was used for the first time. It was designed to detect EPO and other known drugs. In the past some sportspeople had objected to testing on religious grounds but in Sydney competitors had to sign to say they accepted the IOC rules.

Before the Games started 40 athletes and officials from the Chinese team were withdrawn. During the Games a number of individual sportspeople were not allowed to compete because of positive test results before the games. Yet more were banned during the Games, including weightlifters and a star gymnast.

Mark Richardson tested positive for drugs in 2000 but maintains his innocence

What are the main issues in doping?

Drug takers are always one step ahead of drug testers

Some scientists support sportspeople wishing to cheat by taking drugs. They constantly design new varieties of drugs and new ways of disguising their use. Some new drugs, such as EPO and HGH, occur naturally in the body and are very difficult to detect. The drug testers have to try to keep up. They are also hampered when mistakes in drug testing are made and sportspeople claim damages in the courts.

Insufficient punishment

Competitors found guilty of doping are banned from competition in their sport. Bans are usually for a minimum of 2 years. Many then return to competition. Some people think bans should be for life. The sportsperson will also face loss of earnings from competition and sponsorship. The personal disgrace of being revealed as a cheat must also be accepted.

Legal difficulties in applying punishments

Some ISFs have found it difficult to apply punishments to known drug takers because sportspeople, for example in cycling, football and tennis, have claimed that their freedom to earn a living is being restricted. Lengthy court battles have been very expensive for the sports organisations. However, the IOC has fought to create an independent anti-doping agency. It has been agreed that doping disputes should be referred to the Court of Arbitration for Sport in Lausanne, Switzerland.

Some attitudes are changing

The Lancet, an English medical journal, said in 1998 that sportspeople are highly paid professional entertainers in an arena where 'fair play is becoming an old-fashioned idea'. It argues that it is difficult to tell the difference between drugs and scientifically prepared food. In the light of this *The Lancet* asks, 'Why should an adult competitor not be allowed to make an informed choice about a substance provided it is legally acquired?'

Ben Johnson paid a high price for taking drugs

The right lifestyle

We should keep ourselves healthy as part of our preparation for sport. We should also develop hygienic habits after taking part in sport. We must ensure we get enough sleep and rest.

What do we mean by hygiene?

Hygiene means the different ways we look after our body to keep it healthy.

Skin

We must keep look after our skin as it protects the body. Soap and warm water remove the dirt and sweat which encourage bacteria and lead to body odour. We should shower or bath daily and always after physical activity, remembering our towel, soap and shampoo.

Acne is a skin complaint caused by blocked grease glands. To reduce the problem we should keep our skin very clean, avoid make-up, eat fresh fruit and get plenty of sunlight.

Nails

Our nails should be kept clean and cut regularly to reduce injury from scratches in sport.

Hair

We must wash our hair regularly to keep it clean. Long hair can be a hazard in some sports and should be tied back.

Teeth

Our teeth must be kept clean and free from decay. We should avoid sugary foods and keep our gums healthy by eating foods that need chewing. Regular dental check-ups are essential.

Feet

Our footwear must fit well to avoid problems. We must wash our feet regularly and dry them carefully, always checking for:

- athlete's foot – a fungal infection between the toes. The skin can split, causing itching. We can treat it by drying our feet carefully and using anti-fungal powders
- verrucas – warts found on our feet, caused by a virus. They can be painful but can be treated with a special liquid.

Clothing

We should change and wash our clothes regularly. We should have a complete change of clean clothes for taking part in sport and wash them after each exercise session.

Does our pattern of rest and sleep affect our sporting performance?

Sleep

We will not be able to train or compete effectively if we don't get enough sleep. Most people need between 7 and 9 hours of sleep each night. If our patterns of sleep are disrupted then our sporting performance suffers. Our sleep patterns can be disturbed by drinking alcohol or caffeine, smoking or eating high-protein meals shortly before sleeping.

Rest

Rest is essential for us to recover, both physically and mentally, from the activities of the day. Rest is especially important for sportspeople who train and compete regularly.

Examination-type questions: Care of our bodies

There are 12 marks for each question.

1 (a) Give examples of two foods rich in carbohydrates.   *(2 marks)*

   (b) Why does smoking affect our sporting performance?   *(2 marks)*

   (c) Suggest two reasons why sportspeople might take steroids.   *(2 marks)*

   (d) List six important points of hygiene that are especially important
        for sportspeople.   *(6 marks)*

2 (a) Why are fats important in our diet?   *(2 marks)*

   (b) Name one food which contains
        (i)   vitamin C
        (ii) calcium.   *(2 marks)*

   (c) Give two sporting advantages of taking stimulants.   *(2 marks)*

   (d) Explain the link between the amount of food we eat, the amount of
        exercise we take and our weight.   *(6 marks)*

3 (a) Name two social drugs, apart from tobacco and alcohol.   *(2 marks)*

   (b) What is meant by blood doping?   *(2 marks)*

   (c) Suggest two rules about eating before exercise.   *(2 marks)*

   (d) There are seven components of a balanced diet. Water is one.
        Name the other six.   *(6 marks)*

4 (a) Suggest why the following drugs might be taken by sportspeople:
        (i)   diuretics
        (ii) analgesics.   *(2 marks)*

   (b) Explain why water intake is important for sportspeople.   *(2 marks)*

   (c) Give two reasons why doping is not allowed in sport.   *(2 marks)*

   (d) Describe the main points in the drug testing procedure.   *(6 marks)*

Answers are given in the World of Sport Examined Teachers Resource and Student Workbook.

7 Safety in sport

If we are to perform to the best of our ability we must avoid injury when training and competing. To do this we must plan to be safe and take every precaution to stay safe. The people who organise sport play an important part. If we do get injured, we must know how to recognise and treat the injury so that we recover quickly. Knowing when to return to training is also important because returning too soon can cause problems.

Reducing risk
page 156

As individuals taking part in sport we need to prepare ourselves properly, prepare our dress and equipment properly and take part with the right attitude.

Preparing ourselves properly

We need to look at our:

*   health and fitness
*   techniques and skills
*   training
*   warm up.

Preparing our dress and equipment properly

We need to make sure we have:

*   the right clothing and equipment
*   the right footwear
*   no jewellery.

Above all, our clothing needs to provide us with enough protection, and equipment needs to be safe.

Taking part with the right attitude

We need to:

*   obey the rules
*   respect our opponents and follow etiquette.

Planning for safety
page 154

When we organise sport for young people, we must take responsibility for their safety. We must ask:

*   what does the law say?
*   how must we prepare young people?
*   how can we arrange fair competitions?
*   how can we make sure that facilities and equipment are safe?
*   what safety precautions can we take?
*   what is the weather like?

We must also be ready for any emergencies that might occur.

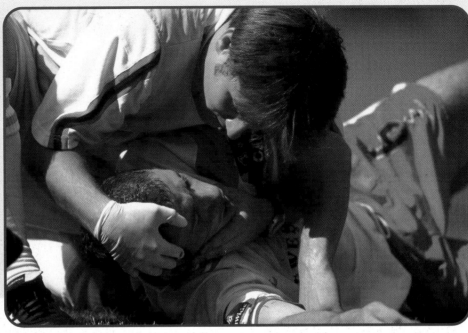

Causes of sports injuries
page 158

We need to know how sports injuries occur so that we can try to prevent them. We need to recognise that problems can be caused by:
- accidental injuries
- violence
- the environment
- overuse injuries
- chronic injuries.

Soft- and hard-tissue injuries
page 160

We need to know about a range of common sports injuries. We must be able to recognise:
- soft-tissue injuries
- hard-tissue injuries.

We need to know how to treat minor soft-tissue injuries.

Treatment of injuries
page 162

We need to know how to deal with more serious soft and hard-tissue injuries that might occur when we train or play sport. We need to know about RICE treatment and about avoiding HARM to reduce recovery time.

Emergency procedures
page 164

There are times when the situation or the injury are very dangerous. We need to know how to deal with such situations. We need to use the DRABC checklist when helping a badly injured person. We also need to know how to cope with a range of emergencies that might occur in sport.

Extreme conditions
page 168

Some activities take place in extremely hot or cold conditions. We need to know how to prevent these conditions from creating problems for performers. We also need to know how to treat performers who are injured by extreme conditions.

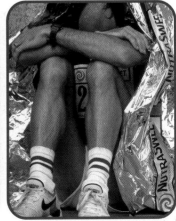

Planning for safety

All sport carries some risk of injury so we must always be prepared. When planning for safety, there are some important questions we need to ask and answer.

What does the law say?

The Health and Safety at Work Act 1974 says that employers must ensure the safety of the people who work for them and all other people involved. This means that local authorities, governing bodies and managers of sports facilities and outdoor activity centres must look after their teachers, pupils, instructors and members of the public using their facilities.

How must we prepare young people?

We must be sure that we have the right qualifications, knowledge and experience to teach, coach, train or instruct young people in an activity.

If we are responsible for young people we must exercise a 'duty of care'. This means that we must take all reasonable precautions to see that they are safe. We must:

- prepare them properly
- plan the activity carefully
- check we have the right group size
- make sure the facilities and equipment are safe
- supervise the activity well
- take safety precautions
- have first aid equipment ready
- explain emergency procedures.

How can we arrange fair competitions?

If we organise a competition for young people we must ask:

- Are they the same age?
- Are they of similar size and weight?
- Are they of the same sex?
- Do they have similar levels of skill?

We know that mixed-sex teams are fine in volleyball and badminton. However, rugby and football can be very dangerous if there are large differences between the body size and skill levels of the players involved.

How can we make sure that facilities and equipment are safe?

- Owners of sports facilities are responsible for the safe condition of their facilities
- Indoor facilities must be well maintained. Equipment should be stored safely and moved carefully
- The way we use and look after our outdoor playing surfaces will affect their condition. They are also affected a lot by the weather. If a player falls over when the pitch is hard and dry, he is likely to be injured. Equipment such as posts and nets should be in good condition. Synthetic surfaces can cause injuries to joints and ligaments because of the hardness of the surface, especially if people are not used to running on them.

What safety precautions can we take?

Large equipment

We all need to learn to use large pieces of equipment properly. Opening up trampolines, moving vaulting boxes and carrying goalposts are all dangerous activities if not done safely. Weight-training equipment must be used carefully. We must take special care when using free weights not attached to a machine. We must lift, carry, place and use all equipment in the safe manner we have been taught.

Landing areas

Purpose-built facilities have landing areas sunk into the floor to prevent injury during training. High jumpers and pole vaulters need special landing cushions. They should not attempt to jump if the landing area is too small, too thin, or has gaps between mats. Mats used in gymnastics must absorb impact and be non-slip so that they do not move when the gymnast lands on them.

Changing rooms

Wet floors and broken tiles in changing rooms and showers can be dangerous. Players should also beware of the risk of wearing boots with aluminium or nylon studs that slip on changing room floors.

Officials

All events need officials to organise and control the activities. They make sure that people play within the rules – for safety reasons as well as to ensure fair play. Organisers must ensure the safety of competitors and spectators.

Water

All water can be dangerous. Swimming pools need lifeguards, depth signs and rules about behaviour to keep them safe. People performing outdoor water-based activities such as sailing, canoeing and water skiing need to wear lifejackets, correct clothing, and follow training and safety precautions.

What is the weather like?

We can play most outdoor games safely in the rain and the wind, although it is usually not very enjoyable. However, when the surfaces are frozen injuries are likely and it is too dangerous to play. Cold weather need not stop us playing; we just need to wear the correct clothing.

If we are taking part in outdoor activities the weather will affect what we do.

Emergency procedures must be in place and explained to all. We must also consider the experience and ability of the group before starting some activities. It would be unsafe to take out inexperienced sailors in rough weather, although an advanced group might thoroughly enjoy the sail.

Reducing risk

All sporting activities carry some risk. We can reduce the risk and help to prevent injury by preparing properly for sport. We must prepare our dress and equipment properly and should take part with the right attitude.

Health and fitness

We must be in good health to take part in physical activities – we need **health-related fitness**. We must also be sure that our body has been trained to cope with the demands of our sport – we need **sport-related fitness**. Specific fitness for our sport will help prevent injuries. Tiredness and lack of sleep can reduce our skill, which, in turn, can lead to injury. Fatigue caused by the activity will also have this effect.

We should check that our diet and fluid intake are sufficient for our activity. We need enough fuel for the activity to delay the onset of fatigue. Eating should be completed 2–3 hours before the event so that the food has been digested.

Techniques and skills

We need the techniques and skills of our sport to perform well. We need to practise to perform difficult skills easily. When we have good skills we perform well, enjoy our sport and avoid injury. If, for example, a hockey player has not learned to tackle properly she is likely to injure herself and other players. We need to know our ability and how far we can go. A fit, skilful player will have the confidence which helps to avoid injuries.

Training

Although training for our sport is important it is possible to train too hard. If we train very hard and often, but do not give our bodies enough time to recover, we might find we are not improving. The signs of **overtraining** include such things as continuous tiredness and loss of interest in the sport. The best way to deal with this problem is to rest for some time and then restart training when the body has recovered.

Warm up and warm down

These are essential parts of each training session and competitive situation. They are important in preventing injury and should be closely related to the sport (see page 97).

The correct clothing and equipment

We should wear the correct clothing for the activity. We should check our clothing and equipment regularly to see that everything is in good order. Some sports have rules to make sure that protective equipment is worn. For example, hockey goalkeepers and school-age batters in cricket must wear helmets and other padding. Footballers must wear shinpads. For many sports, there are few rules about clothing, but players take sensible precautions.

Protective equipment must:
- properly protect the sportsperson
- allow freedom of movement
- permit air to flow around the body
- be comfortable
- be safe and reliable.

In very sunny conditions, players wear protection against harmful ultra violet rays. This includes sunglasses, hats, long-sleeved shirts and skin creams.

The right footwear

All sport shoes must support and protect the feet as well as be comfortable. Shoes must also grip the surface for which they are used and absorb impact when we are running or landing. This will reduce injury.

Cross-trainers are useful for moderate performers who play a number of sports, but top players will always choose shoes that are specially designed for their sport. They will also make sure that their shoes can provide maximum support and response to movement by tying the laces tightly when training and playing.

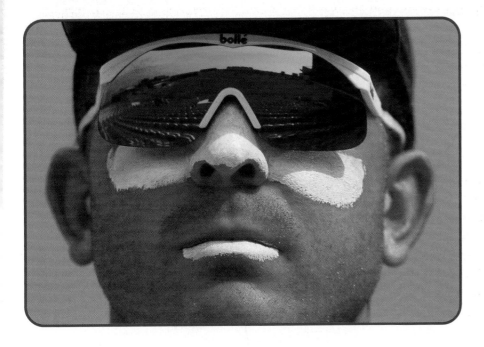

No jewellery

Players should remove as much jewellery as possible before playing sport. The risk of accidents due to jewellery will vary with the sport. For example, rings on fingers will be a much greater problem in judo than in shooting. People taking part in contact or combat sports should wear no jewellery at all.

Obey the rules

We need to know and understand the rules of our activity. Rules encourage good sporting behaviour, help games to flow and protect players from injury. Rules must be followed and players punished if they are broken. Injury causes pain and stops us from playing. In high-risk collision sports such as rugby, injuries will be part of the game. However, players who break rules and harm opponents must be dealt with severely. In recent years some players have been taken to court when their deliberate foul play has led to serious injury.

Respect opponents and follow etiquette

Etiquette means the special ways we are expected to behave in our sport. Etiquette is not a set of written rules, but has become part of each sport over a long period. Golf has many examples of etiquette. Tennis players will always shake hands at the net after a match and rugby players will clap their opponents off the pitch. Etiquette allows players to demonstrate fair play, sportsmanship, sporting spirit and respect for their opponents. In this way etiquette helps to reduce violence in sport.

Causes of sports injuries

In order to avoid sports injuries, we need to know what they are and why they happen.

A sports injury can be any damage caused to a sportsperson whilst in action. This will include such things as hypothermia brought on by cold weather conditions as well as broken bones and pulled muscles.

Some sports have a greater risk of injury than others – for instance, we are more likely to be injured when boxing than when taking part in archery. Knowing the risk can help to reduce it.

Causes of injury

There is a vast range of sports injuries which are caused in many different ways. Injuries can be classed as:

- accidental injuries (due to violence or the environment)
- over use injuries
- chronic injuries.

The force that causes accidental and over use injuries can be:

- internal – from within our bodies
- external – from outside our bodies.

Accidental injuries

Accidental injuries are those that surprise us by happening when we least expect them. They are caused by internal and external forces.

Internal forces are those created when our body works during exercise. When we perform at our highest level the extra strain on some body parts can cause damage. A sudden stretch or twist can strain or tear muscles, tendons or ligaments. These injuries may be caused by forgetting to warm up, by very sudden powerful movements or lack of skill. For example, sprinters can tear hamstrings in a race. Footballers often get a groin strain through stretching or knee ligament damage from twisting.

External forces come from outside our bodies. Direct contact, or violence, from another player is one external force. Another external force is the environment.

Violence

Injuries caused by violence are due to direct contact between players or equipment. Many sports have violent contact between opponents. Collisions may result in fractures, dislocations, sprains and bruises. They may also be caused by being hit by equipment such as balls, sticks or rackets. Breaking the rules can lead to violent injury.

The environment

The environment can lead to injury in two different ways.
- An injury may be due to the facilities – for example, you might trip and land heavily on the playing surface or collide with the goalposts.
- Alternatively, an injury may be due to weather conditions. Extreme heat can cause dehydration, heat exhaustion and then heatstroke. Extreme cold may lead to hypothermia.

Overuse injuries

Overuse injuries are caused by using a part of the body again and again over a long period of time. These injuries produce pain and inflammation.

Common overuse injuries include:
- 'tennis elbow' or 'golf elbow' – an inflamed elbow joint
- 'shin splints' – pain on the front of the shins
- 'cricketers' shoulder' – damage and inflammation to the front of the shoulder
- blisters and calluses – caused by gripping equipment very tightly during the activity.

The only cure for overuse injuries is rest.

Some of these injuries are caused by incorrect technique. When this is the case the action must be corrected to prevent the injury recurring.

Chronic injuries

All injuries must be treated at once. We need to give them time to heal. If we put an injury under stress before it is healed it will get worse. If this continues we will develop a **chronic injury**, which is difficult to heal. Chronic injuries can lead to permanent damage such as arthritis in joints.

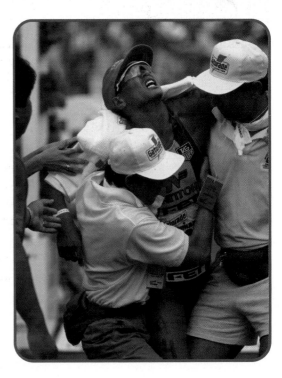

Soft- and hard-tissue injuries

What are soft-tissue injuries?

Soft-tissue injuries include damage to:
- muscles
- ligaments
- tendons
- cartilage

When **soft tissues** are injured they become inflamed. Treatment aims to reduce the swelling, prevent further damage and ease the pain.

A **sprain** happens when we over-stretch or tear a ligament. A sprain can be caused by a twist, or sudden wrench, for example a sprained ankle. In this case we must use RICE treatment. If the injury is severe we should treat it as a fracture.

A **strain** happens when we stretch or tear a muscle or tendon. This can be caused by a sudden stretch or extra muscular effort. In this case (for example a pulled muscle) we must use RICE treatment.

We have two cartilages between the bones of our knee joint which act as shock absorbers. They can be torn when the joint is twisted or pulled in an unusual way, for example during a tackle in football. If this happens we should seek medical advice.

How do we treat minor soft-tissue injuries?

We should deal with minor problems quickly and carefully. If we ignore them they may become more serious.

Skin damage
- Cuts: clean the cut with running water. Dab dry and cover using a dressing. Clean and dry the skin around the cut. Use an adhesive plaster over the dressing. Some lint-free dressings stick directly to the wound. These dressings are designed to remain in place until they fall off naturally.
- Grazes (also called abrasions): the top layer of skin has been scraped off because of friction with a rough surface. Treat it as a cut, but use a specialist non-stick dressing. Be careful to check that the wound is clean.
- Blisters: Damage to the skin by heat or friction can cause a bubble to form to protect the skin. Do not break the blister. Cover it with a specialist blister plaster that stays in place until it falls off naturally. This will ease pain and protect the area from further damage.

Other conditions
- Bruises: these are the result of damaged capillaries bleeding under the skin and are caused by impact. The skin changes colour, the area is painful and can swell. Treat by raising and supporting the bruised part. Put a cold compress (an ice pack) on the bruised area.
- Cramp: this is sudden painful muscle contraction. It can be caused by strenuous exercise or loss of fluid and salt through sweating. Treat by drinking fluid, stretching and massaging the muscle.
- Stitch: a sharp pain in the abdominal area caused by a cramp in the diaphragm. Treat by sitting down and resting. Light massage can also help.

What are hard-tissue injuries?

Injuries to **hard tissues** are injuries to bones.
These include:
- fractures
- dislocations.

Fractures

A fracture is a break in a bone. There are two types:
- a simple (closed) fracture – the bone stays under the skin
- a compound (open) fracture – the bone breaks through the skin.

   Complicated fractures also involve damage to nerves and muscles.
   All fractures are serious and need urgent medical treatment.

Stress fractures

These are small cracks in a bone. They are often an overuse injury.
They can be caused, for example, by too much running on hard
surfaces. The signs of a stress fracture are steadily increasing pain in a
particular part of a limb, swelling and tenderness. If this occurs the
player needs to:
- use ice to reduce inflammation
- get immediate rest
- keep fit by doing other activities
- check running action and footwear for problems
- run on softer surfaces after recovery.

Dislocations

A dislocation means that a bone at a joint is forced out of its normal
position. The ligaments around the joint may also be damaged. The
cause may have been a strong force wrenching the bone, such as a
rugby tackle. Treat all dislocations as if they are fractures.

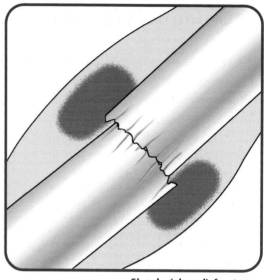

Simple (closed) fracture

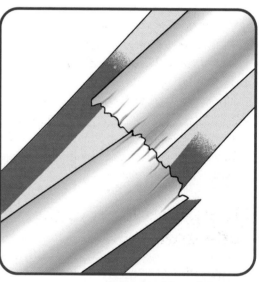

Compound (open) fracture

How do we treat bone and joint injuries?

Recognition:
- a recent blow or fall
- snapping sound of breaking bone or torn ligament
- difficulty in moving the limb normally
- pain made worse by movement
- severe 'sickening' pain (dislocation)
- tenderness at the site (fracture)
- deformity, that is the limb has an unusual shape
- swelling, bruising
- signs of shock.

   Some injuries are hard to diagnose. A sprained ankle
and a broken ankle are very similar. An early sign of a
break is that the casualty becomes pale and the skin is
clammy. This is a sign of shock that does not often
occur when the ankle is only sprained. If in doubt the
injury should be treated as a break.

Action:
- keep the casualty still, steady and comfortable
- support the injured part
- reassure the casualty
- send for medical help.

Treating soft-tissue injuries

The treatment known as **RICE** (Rest, Ice, Compression, Elevation) is a checklist to follow in the case of most soft-tissue injuries. These injuries include sprains, strains and impact injuries. We should treat such injuries as soon as possible after they occur to prevent them from becoming worse.

R • Rest
I • Ice
C • Compression
E • Elevation

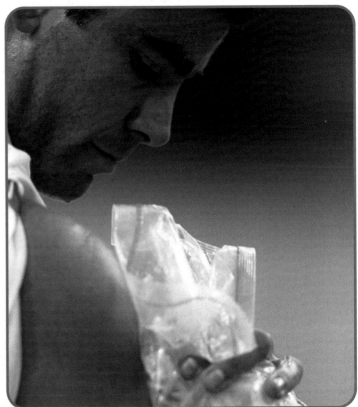

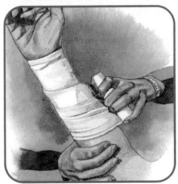

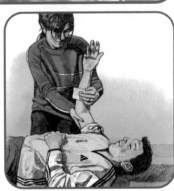

Rest

Reasons
- reduces internal bleeding
- prevents further injury.

Action
- stop your activity
- support the injury in a comfortable position.

Ice

Reasons
- reduces blood flow, pain and swelling.

Action
- put an ice pack on the injury, for 10–15 minutes every hour. Remove the ice pack after 15 minutes, or blood flow will increase to try to heat up the area.

Compression

Reasons
- reduces internal bleeding and swelling.

Action
- wrap a bandage firmly around the injured area. Do not stop the blood flow.

Elevation

Reasons
- reduces internal bleeding, swelling and throbbing.

Action
- raise the injury above the level of the heart.

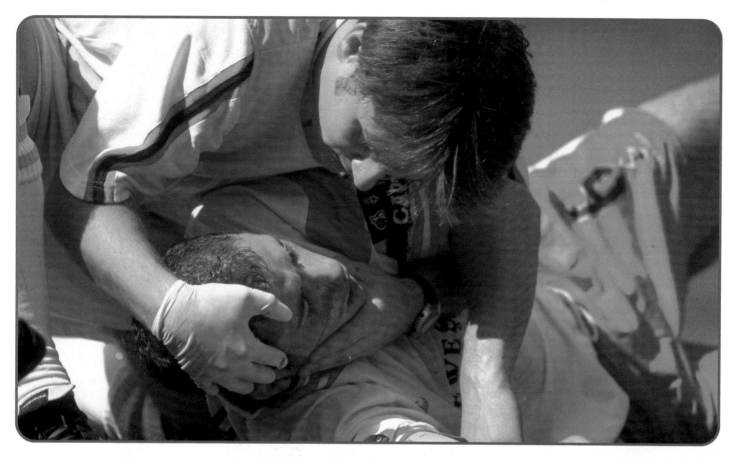

Returning to sport

All injuries need time to heal. We can reduce the time before we return to sport by acting quickly when we are first injured. We also need to continue to treat the injury properly throughout our recovery period. If we try to return to play too soon we can make the injury worse. There are three stages of treatment for sprains and strains.

The first 48 hours

Ice should be applied for 10–15 minutes every hour during this period.

Remember **HARM** – things to be avoided in the first 48 hours after an injury:

- do not use **heat** for 48 hours because it increases internal bleeding.
- do not drink **alcohol** because it increases the swelling
- do not **run** because the weight and impact causes further injury
- do not **massage** the injured area for 48 hours because it increases internal bleeding.

48–72 hours

Apply ice and heat alternately for 5 minute periods to increase blood flow to and from the injured area. This will encourage healing.

72 hours onwards

Use heat from baths, hot water bottles, etc. to increase blood flow and encourage healing. Most injuries will now be at the stage where some movement will help to speed up recovery. We should not try to move or play at full strength until we are sure we are able to do so.

This phase is called rehabilitation. It can last for between 10 days and 6 weeks. It has four stages:

1 Active movement – gentle movements that do not cause any pain. If movement is painful it should not be continued.
2 Passive stretching and active exercise – stretching and light endurance work that does not cause any pain.
3 Active strengthening – our muscles will have lost some strength during the period of injury. We should first train to improve endurance and only then develop power and speed.
4 Re-education – if we have no pain or swelling our muscles and joints need to be worked through their full range of movement. We can return to full training and then return to play.

Emergency procedures

Doctor ABC

Always get medical help if possible, but sometimes we have to deal with an emergency involving a serious injury. It is important that the first treatment is correct so we must not panic. Remember **DRABC** (Doctor ABC) to help focus on the key points. Follow the points in the right order.

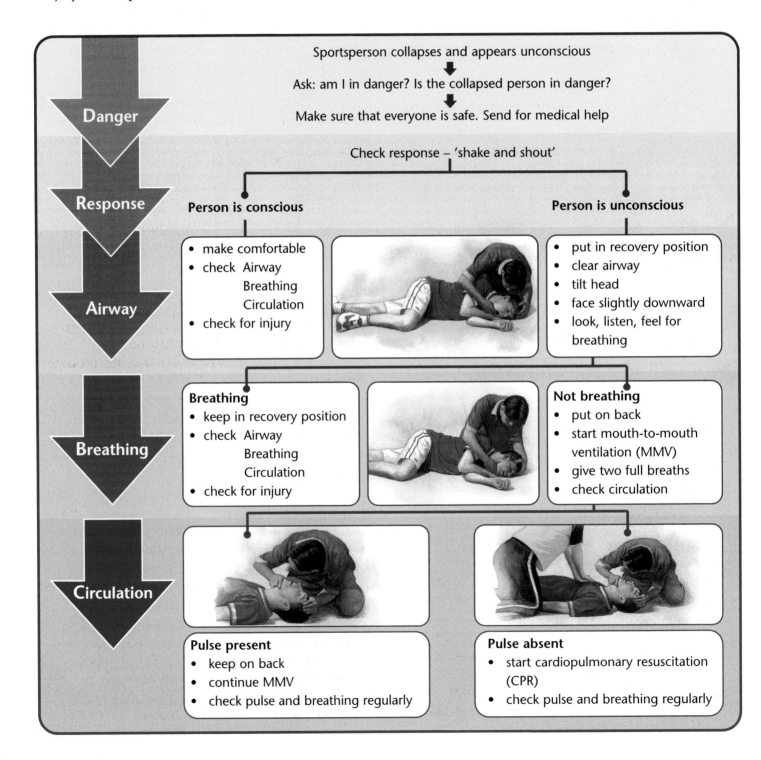

Sportsperson collapses and appears unconscious

⬇

Ask: am I in danger? Is the collapsed person in danger?

⬇

Make sure that everyone is safe. Send for medical help

Danger

Check response – 'shake and shout'

Response

Person is conscious

- make comfortable
- check Airway
         Breathing
         Circulation
- check for injury

Airway

Person is unconscious

- put in recovery position
- clear airway
- tilt head
- face slightly downward
- look, listen, feel for breathing

Breathing
- keep in recovery position
- check Airway
         Breathing
         Circulation
- check for injury

Breathing

Not breathing
- put on back
- start mouth-to-mouth ventilation (MMV)
- give two full breaths
- check circulation

Circulation

Pulse present
- keep on back
- continue MMV
- check pulse and breathing regularly

Pulse absent
- start cardiopulmonary resuscitation (CPR)
- check pulse and breathing regularly

Emergency treatment

When a sportsperson has stopped breathing we can breathe for them and help restart their breathing by increasing carbon dioxide levels in their blood. We do this by giving mouth-to-mouth ventilation (MMV). If their heart has stopped beating we can try to get it going again by giving cardiopulmonary resuscitation (CPR).

Mouth-to-mouth ventilation (MMV)

We should always try to send for medical help, but we can use MMV whilst waiting for help to arrive. There are seven actions that we should take:

1 With the person lying on his back open the airway by lifting the chin and tilting the head well back.
2 Clear the person's mouth and throat of any obstruction.
3 Check for breathing with your face close to the person's mouth. Look for chest movement. Listen for sounds of breathing. Feel his breath on your cheek.

4 If he is not breathing, pinch his nose. Take a deep breath. Seal your lips around his mouth. Blow into the mouth, and watch the chest rise. Take your mouth away and watch the chest fall back. Take another breath and repeat.
5 If his chest does not rise, check again for an obstruction in the mouth, check airway open, check firm seal around mouth.
6 Check the pulse before continuing. If there is no pulse, start chest compressions (see CPR).
7 If he has a pulse and his chest has risen, continue blowing into the mouth. Use ten breaths a minute and continue until breathing starts. Then put him into the recovery position.

Cardiopulmonary resuscitation (CPR)

If you are certain that a person has no pulse, use chest compressions to get his heart beating again whilst waiting for medical help to arrive. There are six actions that you should take:

1 Check for a pulse. If the heart has stopped, you will not be able to feel a pulse. The skin will be pale, the lips blue and the arms and legs will be limp.
2 Place the person on his back and use your fingers to find the point where the ribs meet the breastbone. Put your middle finger over this point and your index finger higher up on the breastbone.

3 Put the heel of your other hand on the breastbone, just above your index finger. This is the spot where pressure should be applied.
4 Move the heel of your other hand over the top of this hand. Interlock your fingers.
5 Lean over the person with your arms straight. Press down firmly to press in the breastbone about 4–5 cm. Then rock backwards to release the pressure. Keep your hands in place. Repeat at a rate of about 100 compressions a minute.
6 Check his pulse rate regularly. Stop compressions as soon as a pulse returns.

MMV and CPR

If you are alone with a person who has no pulse and no breathing you need to take the following five actions:
1 Open his airway. Give two breaths using MMV
2 Give 15 chest compressions (CPR)
3 Give two breaths (MMV)
4 Give 15 chest compressions (CPR)
5 Continue until help arrives – keep checking breathing and pulse.
If you have help you can share the work.

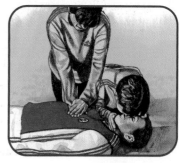

How do we treat serious injuries?

We expect help whenever we are injured whilst playing sport, and we also expect the helpers to know what they are doing. Every sports club should have a qualified first aider at every match and training session. We can all become qualified quite easily and should take the opportunity to do so. The St John Ambulance Brigade and The Red Cross organise first aid courses. With a little training we may be able to provide life-saving help in an emergency.

There are a number of serious injuries and conditions that need prompt action. We should know what to look for, and how to act if we face another person who is seriously injured.

The recovery position

Always use the recovery position for an unconscious person who is breathing.

We may need to alter the position slightly if she has injuries, but we can roll her towards us and into the basic recovery position by doing the following:

- Tilt her head well back. This prevents her tongue blocking her throat
- Keep her neck and back in a straight line
- Keep her hip and knee both bent at 90°. This keeps the body safe, stable and comfortable.
- Use her hand to support her head, which should be slightly lower than the rest of her body. This allows fluids to drain from her mouth.

Remember to:
- check pulse and breathing regularly
- send for medical help.

Concussion

A person may lose consciousness after a violent blow to the head. When he recovers he may suffer from concussion. Sometimes there is a delay between the injury and losing consciousness. This is a sure sign of concussion.

If we suspect that a person has concussion we should check for dizziness or sickness. He may also have a headache. People suffering from concussion often cannot remember what has happened.

Always put someone with concussion in the recovery position and check their breathing and pulse regularly.

Any sportsperson who is knocked unconscious must not continue with their activity until medical advice has been obtained. Many sports will not allow a player who has suffered concussion to play again for a period of time to prevent further injury to the brain.

Shock

Serious injuries of many types may cause shock, as well as a heart attack. If you suspect that a person is suffering from shock you should check for:

- a rapid pulse
- paleness
- cold clammy skin
- light-headedness
- nausea (feeling sick)
- thirst.

Eventually the person may become restless, anxious and aggressive, may yawn and gasp for air. She may even become unconscious.

Treat shock by removing or treating the cause, if possible, then:

- lie the injured person down, with head low and feet high to assist blood flow to the brain
- give room and air, loosen tight clothing to assist breathing and increase oxygen intake
- keep her warm.
- send for medical help
- give reassurance
- keep checking for pulse and breathing.

Serious external bleeding

Massive bleeding is frightening. Remember DRABC to help stay calm. After sending for medical help, or if we are alone, we should aim to control the bleeding and prevent shock. We should reassure the person constantly and treat the wound.

- Cover the wound with a clean pad and apply pressure with the hand, or squeeze the sides of the wound together with the fingers
- Lie the person down.
- Raise the wound (e.g. leg or arm) above heart level, taking care in case there is a fracture. If the wound continues to bleed, add extra pads and bandage over the wound.
- If bleeding continues, find a pressure point and apply pressure. Pressure points are found where an artery is close to the bone, for example in the groin and under the biceps.

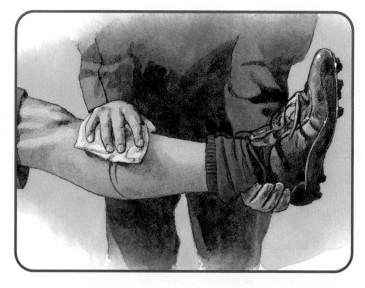

Take care to release the pressure within 10 minutes to prevent permanent damage. *Never* use a tourniquet – a tight bandage some way away from the wound.

Dealing with extreme conditions

Extreme sports are becoming very popular. These, and many mainstream sports, take place in very cold or very hot conditions. Such conditions can create very serious problems for sportspeople. There are three common but dangerous conditions that we should be able to recognise and treat. They are **hypothermia**, **heat exhaustion** and **heatstroke**.

Heat exhaustion

Heat exhaustion develops during activity in hot conditions. It is caused by **dehydration** – that is, loss of fluid and salt from the body due to excessive sweating.

Signs of heat exhaustion
- headaches, light-headedness
- feeling sick
- sweating
- pale clammy skin
- muscle cramps
- rapid weakening pulse and breathing.

Treatment of heat exhaustion
Send for help and then:
- lie her down in a cool place
- raise and support her legs
- give her plenty of water and sips of weak salty water
- if she is unconscious put her in the recovery position.

Hypothermia

Hypothermia can be caused by being outdoors in the cold and wind, or being in very cold water. The internal body temperature becomes dangerously low.

Signs of hypothermia
- shivering
- cold, pale dry skin
- slow, shallow breathing and slow weakening pulse
- feeling confused and lacking energy.

Treatment of hypothermia
If someone is suffering from hypothermia, send for help and then:
- insulate him with extra clothing and cover his head to keep in heat
- move him to a sheltered place and protect him from the ground and weather
- use a survival bag, if you have one
- give him hot drinks if he is conscious
- check his pulse and breathing regularly.

Heatstroke

The body becomes dangerously overheated after being in the heat for a long time.

Signs of heatstroke
- headaches
- dizziness, restlessness, confusion
- hot, flushed, dry skin
- very high body temperature
- a full bounding pulse.

Treatment of heatstroke
Send for help and then:
- move him to a cool place
- remove outer clothing
- cool his body with wet towels
- cool his body with a cold, wet sheet
- if he is unconscious put him in the recovery position.
  Careful planning and proper training, together with the right clothing and equipment, can help to prevent all of these dangerous conditions.

Examination-type questions: Safety in sport

There are 12 marks for each question.

1 (a) Suggest two general safety precautions to be taken for outdoor activities. *(2 marks)*

  (b) Give two examples of soft tissue injuries. *(2 marks)*

  (c) There are many symptoms when a major bone is broken. Give two. *(2 marks)*

  (d) In the RICE treatment, R stands for rest. What words do the other letters stand for, and what do they mean? *(6 marks)*

2 (a) Make two important points about protective clothing in sport. *(2 marks)*

  (b) What is meant by an overuse injury? *(2 marks)*

  (c) Explain why a player with a possible neck injury should be treated with great care. *(2 marks)*

  (d) Give six important points to remember when using mouth-to-mouth ventilation. *(6 marks)*

3 (a) Describe exactly where to place your hands for cardiopulmonary resuscitation. *(2 marks)*

  (b) What advice should be given to a player who has suffered concussion? *(2 marks)*

  (c) Give two important points to remember when treating shock. *(2 marks)*

  (d) Describe the recovery position and explain when it is used. *(6 marks)*

4 (a) Give one example each of accidental injury due to
  (i)   internal forces
  (ii) external forces. *(2 marks)*

  (b) What immediate action should be taken to deal with serious bleeding of the leg? *(2 marks)*

  (c) Name two symptoms of hypothermia. *(2 marks)*

  (d) In an emergency we can think of Doctor ABC. Explain what this means. *(6 marks)*

Answers are given in the World of Sport Examined Teacher Resource and Student Workbook.

8 The changing face of sport

The link between society and sport is very important. To look at the history of sport is to look at the history of society. Sport reflects the society in which it is found. Sport today is a world-wide phenomenon of great importance. Through television, sport reaches every corner of the world. Our screens are filled with the images of the stars. We share their successes and their failures as they happen. We dream our own sporting dreams.

The changing Olympics

page 176

The Sydney Olympics showed how much the Olympic Games have changed since the first modern Games in Athens in 1896. Thousands of competitors and officials are now involved in an entertainment extravaganza on a world-wide stage. The Games have survived 100 years, two World Wars, boycotts, killings, demonstrations and other near disasters. The Games in Seoul and Barcelona seemed to bring in a new era of sporting peace but this was shattered by the Atlanta bomb. Sydney once again fulfilled the Olympic aim of international goodwill and friendship through sport.

In the Olympic arenas of the past the champions competed for the glory of winning. They performed before the people of Greece and the Greek empire. Poems were written in honour of their victories. They inspired others to follow in their footsteps for a thousand years.

The contrast with today could not be greater. Yet sport has survived the centuries. To survive it has had to change as society has changed.

Developments in British sport

page 172

Before 1700, sports took place in the villages on feast days. These were local events, loosely organised and with simple rules passed down through the generations. The Industrial Revolution moved people into the cities, leaving behind their traditional sports and games. The public schools in Victorian times developed new highly organised sports. These were taken up by the masses, first as spectators then as enthusiastic players. In the twentieth century, improving standards of living and physical education in schools combined to boost sport. Today we all have the opportunity to take part in sport.

The role of the performer
page 182

The 'Gentlemen amateurs' of the nineteenth century would be amazed at today's highly paid stars, instantly recognisable as they jet around the world! They would also, no doubt, look in amazement at the thousands of runners of all shapes and sizes completing the London Marathon. The rewards for elite professional sportspeople are very great indeed. They are, however, the top of a pyramid whose base is made up of all the ordinary amateurs throughout the country who just play for fun.

New technology
page 186

The search for success in sport is never ending. Sportspeople have always looked to technology to improve their own ability. Dramatic changes have included the invention of the glass fibre pole for vaulting, the revolutionary design of racing bikes and the sharkskin suit for swimming. Other changes in materials, clothing, surfaces, buildings and equipment have not always had as much publicity but have been equally important. They have raised sporting performances everywhere.

Developments in British sport

The early days of sport

Before 1700, sport in Britain was a local affair. The games and competitions took place on feast days. They were organised by the people of the village and followed traditional patterns. Travel around the country was difficult and most people taking part were from the local area.

Patronage

At this time social position was fixed and a system of patronage existed. This meant that wealthy people were able to support talented people who were poor. Patronage helped many sports develop. For example, the Duke of Cumberland was patron to Jack Broughton, the prize fighter. Prize fighting led to modern boxing.

Gambling and the rules of sport

Gambling was linked to most sports. It encouraged cheating and the involvement of criminals because the results were so important. Prize fighting, cricket and horse racing all introduced rules to see that both the competition and the gambling were fair.

Industrialisation

During the Industrial Revolution large numbers of people moved to the towns and cities to work in the factories. They left behind their traditional games and sporting activities. Sports like mob football were often banned. People were worried about the lack of control and the damage to property.

Violence

Society was used to physical violence and brutality. Many sports were based on cruelty to animals, for example bear baiting and cock fighting. Bare-knuckle prize fights were only won when one fighter was unconscious. The first law to prevent cruelty to animals was not passed until 1822.

Sport in Victorian times

The foundations of modern sport were laid during Victorian times. At this time sport became important nationally. This was due to changing social conditions, the influence of the public schools and a better transport system. Sport changed so that it had to be:

- between two matched teams or competitors
- governed by rules
- for the honour of winning only
- played in a spirit of fair play
- without any gambling.

Changing social conditions

For most working people life was hard. Large numbers of people worked in the industrialised cities. Work occupied six days, with Saturday a full working day. There was a great need for physical recreation. People attended sporting events whenever they could. By the 1870s most workers only worked until lunch time on Saturday. This gave a great boost to both playing and watching sport.

The public schools

In the early nineteenth century, the public schools tried to stop their pupils taking part in traditional sporting activities such as hunting. Teachers were worried about the drinking and bad behaviour that went with the pupils' sport.

However, this attitude changed with the coming of a new form of sport. Dr Arnold, the headmaster of Rugby School, is often given credit for this development. Sport was encouraged as a form of physical religion, called 'Muscular Christianity'. Team games like cricket, rugby and football were played to develop such qualities as concern for others, unselfishness and leadership. Above all, these games were believed to prepare young men for their future careers.

The new games of football and rugby were developed by the public schools. In the early days many schools had different rules. They found it difficult to compete against each other until the Football Association in 1863 set out the rules of football and the Rugby Football Union followed in 1871.

The first university boat race between Oxford and Cambridge took place in 1829. The interest shown by the public helped to make rowing popular.

For most children outside the public school system education was very different. The state schools did not have the facilities, equipment or staff to provide a wide range of physical activities. Only exercises and drill were included at first, for disciplinary and health reasons. Later, Swedish gymnastics were introduced.

The transport revolution

Better roads helped spectators travel to sporting events. The railways allowed sports to develop nationally, for example horses could be moved quickly around the country for racing. Cricket teams toured the country. Football spectators and players travelled by rail to compete in the national Football League, which started in 1888.

International sport was also helped by easier and safer transport. The first England versus Scotland soccer match was played in 1872. The cricketers had started earlier, with a tour of North America in 1859.

British sport in the early twentieth century

In the early part of the century working conditions continued to improve. This left working people with more time and energy to take part in sport. Thousands regularly watched professional football games and attended horse racing, cricket and rugby league. For people with money there were now many more sports to play. Tennis, golf and cycling became popular. At this time, most women still did not take any part in sport.

After the First World War sport became part of the entertainment industry. There was still great interest in the major sports like cricket, football and horse racing. New sports such as speedway, greyhound racing, ice hockey and motor cycle racing started up. Wealthy people were able to take part in polo, sailing, skiing and motor racing.

In the 1930s there was a boom in outdoor activities including cycling, walking, camping and rambling. The Central Council of Recreative Physical Training (now the CCPR) was formed in 1935 to encourage sport and recreation.

In physical education at this time, drill had been replaced by exercises and games. In 1936 there were many changes based on the development of a healthy, efficient body. There was also a gradual move towards the idea of physical training for recreation.

British sport since 1945

The Second World War lasted from 1939 to 1945. Most people in Britain suffered a long period of hardship after 1945. Rebuilding the country was the first priority and therefore sport was slow to develop again. Changes in sport since the war have been due to:
- social changes
- commercialisation
- the media
- government involvement
- education.

Social changes

The standard of living for most people has greatly improved since 1945. Most people have more money to spend on leisure time activities. Basic working hours have been reduced, giving people more time for leisure. More recently, the rise in unemployment, part-time working and early retirement have all led to more leisure time. Work and housework have both become less demanding physically. The general health of the population has improved. The importance of a healthy lifestyle and the popularity of the fitness image have encouraged physical recreation. Facilities for sport and recreation have greatly improved through the efforts of the sports councils, the local authorities and now the National Lottery.

Commercialisation

Commercialisation means that a whole leisure industry has grown up around sport. This includes builders of specialist facilities, sports centre workers, equipment and clothing manufacturers and retailers. Today sport is an important part of the economy.

All sports try to develop their commercial potential. Sponsorship is very important for them. Sponsorship helps sport to reward its top performers, to pay for its events and to improve the sport itself.

The media

The media (radio, newspapers and television) have greatly influenced interest in sport. The arrival of colour television, for example, made snooker into a very popular sport. Sponsorship deals give sport much-needed money, especially when the sport is seen on television. Sponsorship, sport and television are closely linked today. The media can make stars overnight and ruin those who are seen to fail. Sport in the media usually means male sport.

The government

After 1945, the government became more involved in sport and physical recreation. The work of the CCPR was taken over by the Sports Council. In 1972 the Sports Council was given a royal charter and an annual grant from the government.

Government money has been put into sports facilities in run-down city areas to enable them to try to reduce their social problems. More recently, the National Lottery was set up and the present government's own ideas on sport, called 'A Sporting Future for All' were published in 2000.

In international sport, the government had a number of issues with which to deal. These included whether or not to have sporting links with South Africa during the Apartheid period and the right of the British team to take part in the Moscow Olympics.

Education

Education is also an area of government involvement. There were many changes in **physical education** in state schools after 1945. For example, local authorities had to provide facilities for physical education and games. Most importantly, physical education as a subject was accepted as being a vital part of all pupils' education.

Much more recently a number of changes have affected physical education:

- Surplus playing fields were sold off
- Many primary schools abandoned competitive sport
- The number of out of school sporting activities declined
- Health-related fitness programmes were developed
- Physical education was included in the national curriculum
- Time for physical education lessons was reduced in many schools
- GCSE and 'A' level physical education were introduced
- A great expansion in sport and physical recreation degree courses took place
- School 'Sports colleges' were established
- The appointment of Active Schools Co-ordinators

Colour television helped make snooker popular

The changing Olympics

In many ways, the changing face of the Olympics is an example of how sport changes over time to reflect changes in society.

The earliest known Olympic Games were held at Olympia in Greece in 776 BC. From this date they were held every fourth year, without a break, for over a thousand years. This is remarkable because the Greek city states were often at war. However, during the period of the Games there was a sacred truce.

The Games were not just athletics meetings. They were religious festivals of great importance. The Olympic Games were always held in honour of the god Zeus. The Olympic Games were one of four famous Crown Games, so called because crowns or wreaths were awarded to the winners.

How were the ancient Olympic Games organised?

Originally the Games lasted for only one day but were extended to five to allow time for making sacrifices, registering the athletes, taking the oath and prize giving. People came to see special works of art produced for the Games. Only Greeks and citizens of Greek colonies were allowed to take part. At first all competitions were for men, but later boys took part. They usually competed naked. Women and slaves were not even allowed to watch the Games.

Long jumper, discus thrower and javelin thrower

Which events took place at the ancient Olympics?

Athletic events, fighting events and chariot racing took place at the ancient Olympics.

Athletic events

The three main running events were:
- Short sprint, one length of the stadium (200 m)
- Double sprint, two lengths of the stadium (400 m)
- Long-distance race, many lengths (about 4800 m)
  These events formed the basic programme. Other events were included at different times:
- Pentathlon, which included five events – the long jump, discus, javelin, short sprint and wrestling. Three wins were needed for victory
- Long jump – weights were carried in each hand during the jump. They helped the athlete gain extra distance
- Discus – the discus was larger and flatter than it is today. It was thrown in a way similar to that used today
- Javelin – a leather thong held in the hand was wound around the shaft of the javelin to increase the distance thrown
  The marathon race was not held at the ancient Olympic Games. It was first included in the Olympics of 1896.

Fighting events

The three main fighting events were boxing, wrestling and the pankration.
- Boxers wore no gloves, but they bound leather thongs around their hands. They fought until one gave in or was knocked out
- Wrestling, like the event today, continued until one wrestler forced his opponent's shoulder blades against the ground
- In the pankration, competitors could punch, grapple, kick or throw. A submission or knockout decided the winner

Chariot racing

Chariot racing was held on a separate track, called a 'Hippodrome'. Races were very exciting and usually dangerous, especially at the turning posts at the ends of the stadium.

What do we know about the ancient Olympic Games?

About a hundred years ago excavations at Olympia uncovered the ruins of a large sporting and religious complex. The stadium was close by and contained a rectangular track, about 200 m by 30 m.

In the early Olympic Games competition was friendly and fair. As they became more important, so did winning. Athletes found trainers and specialised in one event. They trained very hard, even following special diets. Many cities offered valuable prizes to the winners.

Why did the Olympic Games stop?

The decline of the Olympic Games was gradual. The importance of winning and the large rewards given to winners changed the Games. There was bribery and corruption. The Romans conquered Greece in the second century BC. Although they kept the Olympic Games going they did not understand the Olympic spirit. Cruel events were introduced, eventually leading to contests between gladiators and fights with animals. In AD 393, the Christian Emperor Theodosius stopped the Olympic Games. He claimed they were a pagan festival. The sacred site of Olympia was very soon destroyed. First there were invaders, then an earthquake, and then a flood which buried the remains under mud and water. It remained lost for many centuries. It was not until 1896 that De Coubertin was able to bring the Olympic spirit to life again.

The modern Olympics

The modern Olympic Games were started by Baron Pierre de Coubertin, a French aristocrat, who became interested in sport and recreation. He visited England and was impressed by the sport he saw in the public schools. He organised a conference in 1894 with 79 members from 12 countries. They agreed to restore the Olympic Games. He wanted sport to help improve international understanding and promote world peace.

These are the cities which have hosted the summer Olympics.

1896 Athens

The Greek government was unable to pay for the Games but they were saved by a wealthy businessman and 13 countries took part – Australia, Austria, Britain, Bulgaria, Chile, Denmark, France, Germany, Hungary, Sweden, Switzerland, USA and Greece. Most competitors made their own way to the Games at their own expense.

There were nine sports and 311 male competitors

1900 Paris

This was held at the same time as the Paris Universal Exhibition. It was a near disaster, poorly organised and largely ignored. There were many new sports and women competed in golf and tennis.

1904 St Louis

This was held at the same time as the World Fair. It was a side show to the main event. Few countries took part and most competitors were American.

1908 London

Some pride returned to the Games when proper rules were used. However, there were arguments because all the judges were British.

1912 Stockholm

This was a very well organised event, without major problems. The number of competitors nearly doubled.

1916 Berlin

The Games were cancelled because of the First World War.

The 1948 Olympics were held at Wembley Stadium

1920 Antwerp

Europe had only just recovered from the war and many competitors had suffered during the war. Germany, Austria, Hungary, Bulgaria and Turkey were not allowed to compete.

1924 Paris

The number of countries taking part rose to 44, with over 3000 competitors. Germany and its war allies were still absent. The Winter Games started in Chamonix, France.

1912 Stockholm

1928 Amsterdam

De Coubertin, who was sick, sent a message of farewell, calling on the athletes to keep alive the Olympic spirit. Women took part in athletics and a number collapsed at the end of the 800 m.

1932 Los Angeles

Travelling costs reduced the number of competitors. There were high spectator attendances, with 100 000 for the opening ceremony. The first Olympic village was built for competitors.

1940 (Tokyo/Helsinki) and 1944 (London)

These Games were cancelled because of the Second World War.

1948 London

This was held in a blitzed city, by an exhausted nation after the war. 59 countries and 4500 competitors took part. Germany, Japan and the Soviet Union were absent.

1952 Helsinki

This was known as the 'Friendly Games'. Germany was still absent. The Soviet Union took part again after 40 years. These Games saw the start of East–West rivalry.

1956 Melbourne

East and West Germany combined into one team. Spain and Holland withdrew because the Soviet Union had invaded Hungary. Egypt and the Lebanon withdrew because of fighting over the Suez Canal. China withdrew because Taiwan was taking part. China considers Taiwan to be part of China and not a separate country. China only returned to the Olympics in 1984.

Jesse Owens

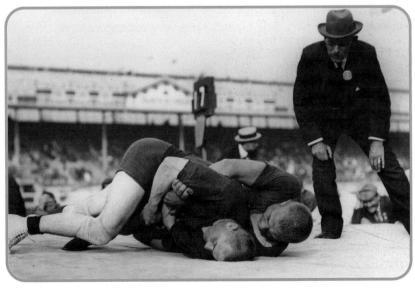

1908 London

1936 Berlin

Hitler's Nazi party was in power. Persecution of Jews and others had begun. However, the IOC insisted that the Games should take place. Hitler used the Games for propaganda purposes. He wanted to show the superiority of the German people. The black American Jesse Owens defeated Hitler's aim by winning four gold medals. Hitler congratulated the German winners but not Jesse Owens.

Coe, Cram and Ovett at the Los Angeles Olympics

1960 Rome

There were no political problems at the Games. Television showed the events world-wide. A Danish cyclist died after using drugs. An all-White team represented South Africa. Following the Games the IOC expelled South Africa from the Olympic movement. This was because of the system of Apartheid, which discriminated against the Black majority in South Africa. However, some non-Olympic sports, like rugby, maintained their contacts with South Africa.

1964 Tokyo

South Africa was banned because of their Apartheid system, as were Indonesia and North Korea for taking part in an unofficial competition. A total of 94 other countries took part. The Games were very expensive but very successful.

1968 Mexico City

A demonstration about poverty and the cost of the Games was brutally broken up and many people killed. East and West Germany entered as separate teams. There were drugs tests for the first time. Mexico's high altitude caused problems for distance athletes. During the medal ceremonies, Black American athletes staged a protest at inequality and injustice in the treatment of Black people in the USA. They raised black-gloved arms. All the athletes involved were sent home.

1972 Munich

The Games were technically brilliant. Rhodesia was sent home because of claims that they had been racist in selecting their all-White team. Black American athletes again protested during the medal ceremonies. Following the founding of the state of Israel in 1948, there had been wars between Israel and her Arab neighbours and there had been terrorist attacks against Israeli targets. At these Games Palestinian terrorists killed Israeli athletes and officials. The massacre in Munich was intended to bring publicity to the Arabs' cause and to gain the release of Arab prisoners in Israel. However, all the hostages were killed in a failed police rescue attempt. The Games continued after a memorial service although some teams and individual competitors decided to go home.

1976 Montreal

These Olympic Games were enormously costly. The French Canadians were angry at the Queen opening the Games and Taiwan was forced to withdraw because Canada only recognised China. There was a boycott by most Black African countries, who thought that New Zealand should have been expelled for playing rugby against South Africa. The IOC refused because rugby was not an Olympic sport.

1980 Moscow

These Olympics were successfully organised but with high security. There was a boycott by Western countries, led by the USA and including Canada, Japan and West Germany because the Soviet Union refused to pull its troops out of Afghanistan. The British government also wished to join the boycott but would not withdraw passports. A large British team decided to compete.

South Africa returned to the Olympics in 1992

1984 Los Angeles

This was highly commercialised, through marketing and sponsorship, and made a huge profit. Libya withdrew after two of its journalists were refused entry. The Soviet Union, Cuba and most East European countries boycotted the Games. Some American anti-Soviet groups had threatened violence before the Games. The Soviet Union said that the security of their teams could not be guaranteed. They also complained that the commercial nature of the Games went against Olympic principles.

1988 Seoul

This was superbly organised with a high profit. South Korea had no diplomatic links with communist countries. It was in a state of war with North Korea. There were no boycotts or disruptions at this event. Ben Johnson was disqualified for using drugs. Professional tennis players took part.

1992 Barcelona

This was a peaceful Olympic Games without incident. South Africa took part again after the release of Nelson Mandela from prison and the removal of Apartheid. Germany took part again as one country following the unification of East and West in 1990. The Soviet team was replaced by a 'Unified 'team and some independent countries. Yugoslavians competed for Croatia or as independent competitors following the break up of the country.

1996 Atlanta

Nearly all countries took part, 197 in all. Competitors numbered 10 788. The Soviet Union was replaced by the Russian federation and a number of new independent countries. Full professionals competed. A mysterious bomb shattered the peace in spite of high security.

Choosing the host city

The IOC chooses the host city through its members' votes. Cities, not countries, put their names forward. A number of scandals showed a great deal of bribery was involved in the process and new rules were introduced by the IOC in 1999. Cities cannot now be accepted as official candidates until the IOC Executive Board is satisfied that they are properly prepared in line with IOC guidelines. IOC member visits to such cities and gifts to IOC members are now banned.

Advantages for the host city

All summer Olympics since 1984 have made a healthy profit. There is status and publicity for both the city and the country. They must improve their facilities as well as roads, transport systems, guest accommodation and tourist attractions. Holding the Olympics provides other commercial opportunities because of the large influx of competitors and spectators during the Games.

2000 Sydney

199 countries took part, with East Timor competing under the Olympic flag. North and South Korea had a combined team for the first time. Women competed in all events, apart from boxing and wrestling. Testing for drugs was made more effective by the introduction of blood tests.
These Games were said to be the most successful ever.

Athens 2004

Even as the Sydney Games were drawing to a close, the IOC was worried that the Athens Games would not be ready in time!

Opening ceremony, Sydney 2000

The role of the performer

The status of players in the past

In the early days of sport in Britain, rewards and prizes were often given. Competitors accepted prizes if they won. Making money out of sport was not seen as a problem for either the organisers or those taking part.

In Victorian times, organised sport developed in the public schools. Boys from the middle and upper classes attended these schools. The boys came from families with money and they were prepared for well paid careers. Because they had no worries about money they were able to spend time playing sport. They were able to afford the costs of playing sport such as equipment, clothing and fees for joining clubs. These sportsmen were called 'Gentlemen amateurs'. This referred to their place in society. They were able to play sport as well as earn a living. They did not need to be paid for playing sport to earn a living. Rewards and prizes were not their reason for playing, although they could accept them if they wished. In fact, WG Grace, the famous cricketer, received a great deal of money from playing cricket. As he was a doctor by profession, he took part in cricket as a 'Gentlemen amateur'.

It was not so easy for working-class men to play sport. They needed to work very hard to provide a living for themselves. They had little leisure time and little money to pay for sport. Some talented sportsmen did play sport professionally. For instance, there were professional cricketers from the earliest times.

The problem for working-class sportsmen at the highest level was that they soon found that their sport stopped them earning a living in a normal job. They therefore needed to be paid to play sport.

W.G. Grace

As more people from all classes started to play sport, the rules about competitors changed. By the 1880s you were no longer an amateur if you accepted prize money or worked for a living at sport. However, not all sports were willing to accept professionalism. Payments and rewards needed controls. Business interests were growing. People running sport were worried that professionalism would bring major problems such as unfair practices, unfair competition and a loss of traditional values. In practice these problems did not get out of control because governing bodies of different sports made their own rules about the place of professionals in their sport.

The status of players in the twentieth century

Labelling sportspeople as amateurs and professionals continued for most of the century.

The modern Olympic Games were based on the ideal of the amateur sportsman. The IOC wanted only true amateurs to take part and made strict rules to define an amateur. They did not believe that sportspeople should make a living from sport or receive any financial reward. They saw the Olympics as competition between part-time sportspeople, who just played for enjoyment. The problem was that governing bodies in different countries could not agree about what was an amateur.

As international competition became more serious standards of performance rose. In the period after 1945, the traditional amateurs training just in their spare time found it increasingly difficult to reach a high enough standard to compete.

A number of different ways were found to get around the amateur rules.

American and Russian teams at the Winter Olympics at Lake Placid, 1980

College scholarships

In the USA sport is highly competitive and big business. Colleges are always keen to have good sportspeople studying and playing sport. Outstanding sportspeople were offered scholarships to join the colleges. This meant that not only were their fees for study paid but the college also provided very good facilities and coaching, together with top competition. These sportspeople were able to train full time but remain amateurs because they did not get paid.

State sportspeople

In the Soviet Union sport was an official activity. Success in sport was seen as a way of showing the superiority of their political system. There were no professional sportspeople. Instead, the state allowed people to stay in the armed forces or at college for the length of their sporting careers. They were given all the time they needed to train, together with first class facilities, coaching and competition. As students and soldiers they remained amateurs.

Trust funds and sponsorship

The UK had neither the college nor the state system but it did not want to be left behind in international sport. The first move to help top sportspeople came with the Sports Aid Foundation (SAF). The SAF collected sponsorship money from business. It passed this on to our top sportspeople, who were able to reduce or stop working in order to train more. The sponsorship paid for living, training and competition expenses.

Further help came when trust funds were set up, first of all in athletics. The arrangement was to put all sponsorship and prize money into trust funds for the sportsperson. During their sporting career they were able to use this money for their expenses. On retirement, the balance of the money went to the sportsperson. It was a form of delayed payment to allow them to remain amateur.

The status of players today

At international level, it gradually became obvious that ideas about amateurism belonged to the past. The IOC changed its rule on **eligibility** (the qualifications needed to take part). They decided that the international sports federation for each sport should decide on eligibility. The word 'amateur' was removed from the rules and no reference is now made to any rewards or payment. This has resulted in open Olympics with full-time professionals taking part.

Amateurs and professionals

Throughout the UK, thousands of people take part in sport in the traditional amateur way. At the same time there is a small group of professional sportspeople who earn their living by playing sport. In between these two extremes are many people who get help in playing sport or receive rewards for playing sport. This group includes part-time professionals, who are paid for playing but still earn a living outside sport. Sponsorship of all kinds helps both professional and amateur sportspeople.

Most sports today are called 'open', meaning that distinctions between amateurs and professionals have gone. A few sports maintain the traditional differences. For example, in boxing there are the Amateur Boxing Association and the Boxing Board of Control for professionals. The two parts of the sport take place quite separately and operate under different rules.

Rio Ferdinand cost a record £18 million in 2000, when he was transferred from West Ham to Leeds United

Amateurs

Amateurs take part in sport because of the enjoyment and satisfaction they get from the activity. Taking part is more important than the result of the game or competition. They train and compete in their own time, usually after work or at weekends. They are not paid. Above all, amateurs make their own decisions about sport. They choose to play. No one can force them to take part. Sport is quite separate from their work. It is a leisure time activity.

Professionals

Professionals are paid to compete in sport. Winning is all important. The more successful they are, the more money they earn. They usually train full time and devote themselves to their sport. Sport is their work. They sign contracts and must take part in competitions.

What are the advantages and disadvantages of being a professional sportsperson?

For most of us sport seems a very attractive career. The idea of spending all day taking part in sport and getting paid for it seems an ideal life. The advantages of being a professional sportsperson might include:

- high earnings
- luxurious living
- the attention of the media
- high-profile success
- popularity with the general public
- opportunities to travel around the world
- eventual retirement to a life of comfort!

However, this is not a typical lifestyle for most professionals. Most earn a living out of the limelight. They may have failed to get to the top for a number of reasons:

- Failure to fulfil early promise
- The effect of serious illness or injury
- Personal problems reducing performance
- Pressure from younger players
- Difficulties in handling the media
- Lack of determination in training
- Age may have overtaken them
- Pressure to win, leading to cheating – for example, taking drugs

Even someone at the top will have to look for a new career when they are only half way through their working lives. For those who achieve star status, it is often short lived.

There are a limited number of sports in Britain where professional players earn a living. Opportunities in professional sport are mainly for men. Only in tennis, golf and athletics are women, in any numbers, able to earn a living.

Justin Rose finished fourth in the 1999 British Open as a 17-year-old amateur. However, after turning professional he found success difficult to achieve

New technology

Improved performances in sport

Sportspeople are always looking for new technology to help them make the most of their ability, in order to improve their performances. Science makes advances all the time. Sports scientists watch the latest developments to apply the new ideas to sport.

Commercial companies need new markets and know that being involved with sport helps business. Governing bodies try to see that the changes are safe and within the rules. Sometimes the rules need to be changed.

Machines

Racing cars, motor bikes and power boats are so powerful now that rules have been introduced to keep top speeds down. In cycling frame design has revolutionised the sport. Modern materials keep racing bikes, hang gliders and sail boards both light and strong.

The speed of movement in some sports means that the officials need help. The 'Cyclops' machine checks if a tennis serve is in or out. Extra officials use television replays to decide run outs in cricket and tries in rugby.

In athletics, precision is essential because winning can be by the smallest amounts. Gauges are used to measure wind speed and markers to record distances automatically. For sprinting, the timing is electronically controlled. The gun and starting blocks are linked to register false starts.

Equipment

Players hit with greater power when using rackets with larger heads, frames of graphite and strings tightly strung. Many years ago the introduction of the glass fibre pole completely changed pole vaulting. With it came the need for better landing areas as heights increased. Highly aerodynamic javelins have been limited to reduce the distances they could be thrown and maintain safety for spectators. Changes to design and materials for skis, bobsleighs and luges have increased both speed and control. In archery, arrows of composite materials go further, faster and straighter.

Clothing

Improved materials make clothes lighter and give them different qualities:

- rain and windproof, for adventurous activities
- heat retaining, for sub-aqua sport
- heat removing, for distance athletes
- aerodynamic, for speed events
- hydrodynamic, for swimming events.

Shoes can be designed for each specific sport to improve performance, safety and comfort. Skiers need boots for skis, distance runners need shock-absorbing qualities and tennis players need grip for the different court surfaces. The use of light, impact-absorbing materials helps cricketers get protection yet keep their mobility. At the Sydney Olympics, swimmers used full-body suits to go faster. These are designed on the hydrodynamics of a shark's skin.

Facilities

All-weather artificial surfaces have helped many sports. Top-level athletics would be unthinkable today on any other surface. Hockey benefits from the speed and even bounce. League football experimented with artificial pitches. However, they changed the game too much and were returned to grass. Cricket is also a sport which needs a natural surface for the complete game. Only Wimbledon of the top four championships still uses grass. Most tennis at all levels is now played on a variety of synthetic surfaces.

Improvements in the design of specialist facilities have helped some sports. For example, gymnastics training has been made much safer by the use of landing areas placed below floor level.

Fitness clubs have the latest electronic machines. Personal programmes can be set up by putting in your personal details and requirements. During the exercise a constant stream of information, including heart rate and calories used, helps with motivation.

Modern all-glass squash courts have been built to make the game suitable for showing on television. Improved ball visibility and scoring changes have also been tried.

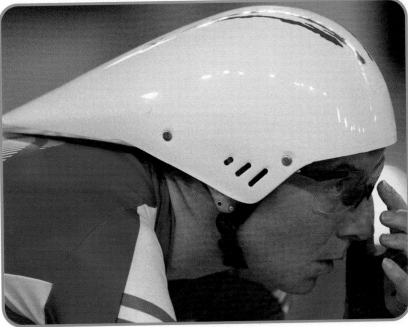

Training and coaching

Detailed scientific research has resulted in a greater understanding of how the body responds to exercise. Coaches and trainers are able to use computer simulations that show the likely results of different types of training.

Computers can also analyse the movement of a sportsperson in great detail. Specialists in sports mechanics can then suggest improvements to the performer's action. Individuals can also have instant video replays of their action during training. This helps them to change their action. Modern watches can also check pulse rates and blood pressure during training.

ICT and sport

Computer technology is constantly changing and improving our ability to communicate, view and record information. Satellite and cable television, computers using the Internet, interactive CD-ROMs and digital camcorders are now seen in homes throughout the country.

In some schools, students start their PE lessons by watching a video clip of a top performer. They then practise the skill, watch it replayed on a camcorder, critically analyse their movements and compare them with those of the top performer. Working with their teacher they can find specific ways to improve. Videos of team games can be used to analyse the effectiveness of tactics and strategies.

ICT equipment can take blood pressure, assess percentage of body fat and measure VO_2 max. This information can be used to assess a person's fitness and pinpoint ways of training more effectively.

Students studying sport can use the Internet to improve their knowledge – by, for example, finding out more about the Olympic Games, maximum oxygen uptake or any other part of the course. They may use interactive CD-ROMs to move around the human body or use computer games to play sport in the home.

Television

Through developments in satellite and cable television we are now able to watch a great variety of sports around the world as they happen. This gives sport a larger, more global audience and also allows less well known sports to be seen for the first time.

No corner of sport can remain hidden. Miniature cameras are placed in cricket stumps, in snooker pockets and on top of racing cars. This gives the viewer almost the same view as those taking part in the sport. Ultra-sensitive microphones pick up every grunt and groan – and lots more besides! Cameras can record the action from almost any angle and replay it instantly in slow motion. At the touch of a button the viewer can change the camera angle, view replays or follow an individual player.

Whilst this can record cheating and other unacceptable behaviour, it also enables people to question the officials' decisions. A football referee, for example, does not have the benefit of replays and views of the action from different positions. He or she must make the decision instantly only on the basis of what was seen.

Examination-type questions: The changing face of sport

There are 12 marks for each question.

1 (a) Name one sport where:
(i) amateurs and professionals compete together
(ii) amateurs and professionals compete separately. *(2 marks)*

  (b) Give one advantage and one disadvantage of being able to
view replays in sport. *(2 marks)*

  (c) Name two sports in which professional sportswomen compete. *(2 marks)*

  (d) Choose three technological improvements in sport.
In each case name the sport and state the improvement. *(6 marks)*

2 (a) Name two Olympic cities where major boycotts have taken place. *(2 marks)*

  (b) Give two advantages for a city hosting the Olympic Games. *(2 marks)*

  (c) Explain why South Africa was banned from international sport
for many years. *(2 marks)*

  (d) Give three advantages and three disadvantages of being
a professional sportsperson. *(6 marks)*

3 (a) There have been many changes in education which have affected PE.
Give two recent changes. *(2 marks)*

  (b) Name the groups of people involved in the 1972 massacre in Munich. *(2 marks)*

  (c) How has computer technology helped improve the accuracy of
results in sport? Give two examples. *(2 marks)*

  (d) Explain what is meant by amateur sport, professional sport and open sport. *(6 marks)*

4 (a) Suggest two ways in which the Victorian public schools influenced sport. *(2 marks)*

  (b) Explain the new rules introduced by the IOC to prevent bribery in the
choice of the Olympic host city. *(2 marks)*

  (c) Give two reasons to explain why there are no professionals in some sports. *(2 marks)*

  (d) In the past Britain, USA and USSR used different methods to enable their
top sportspeople to remain amateur. Explain what they did. *(6 marks)*

Answers are given in the World of Sport Examined Teacher Resource and Student Workbook.

9 Providing for sport

In the past in Britain, individual sportspeople, groups and clubs developed their own sports in their own ways. They had little contact with other sports. This freedom meant that there was no overall pattern for the development of sport. The sports clubs and their governing bodies have always protected their independence. The government was rarely involved.

Today the clubs and their governing bodies are still at the heart of sport in Britain. However, since the setting up of the Sports Council in 1972, the government has increased its influence. The Sports Council was given a government grant, and today the separate sports councils distribute vast amounts of National Lottery money.

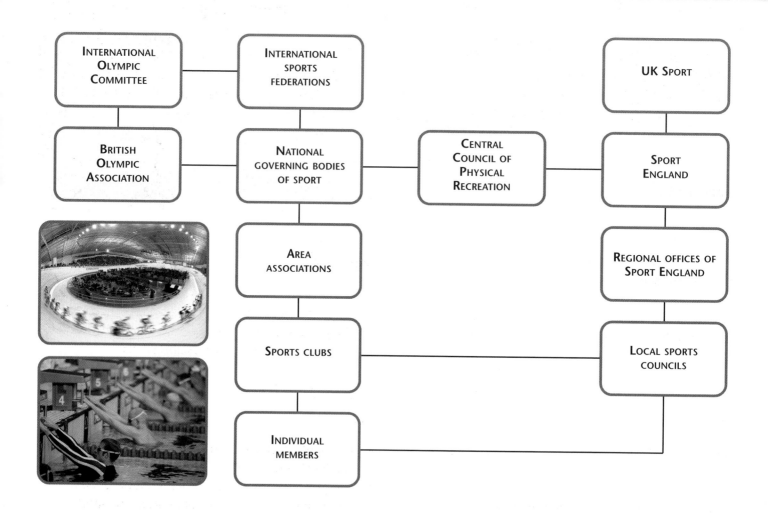

The structure of sport in England

In 1995, the government produced its plans for the future of British sport, which it called 'Raising the Game'. It mainly recommended and encouraged action by the organisers of sport. The present government's strategy – 'A Sporting Future for All', published in April 2000 – is quite different. It sets out exactly what the government wants to happen.

It states clearly that money will only be given if detailed plans are produced and targets reached. In future the government will be firmly in control of the direction of British sport.

Which organisations provide for sport?
page 192

- UK Sport
- Sport England
- The Youth Sport Trust (YST)
- National governing bodies (NGBs)
- The Central Council for Physical Recreation (CCPR)
- The National Coaching Foundation (NCF)
- The English Federation of Disability Sport (EFDS)
- Disability Sport England (DSE)
- The Women's Sports Foundation (WSF)
- The National Playing Fields Association (NPFA)
- The Countryside Agency (CA)

Who controls international sport?
page 202

- International sports federations (ISFs)
- The International Olympic Committee (IOC)
- The British Olympic Association (BOA)

Who provides sports facilities?
page 204

- The public sector – central government and local authorities
- The private sector – companies
- The voluntary sector – clubs and NGBs

Who provides the money for sport?
page 210

- The public sector – central government and local authorities
- The private sector – companies, including the National Lottery and the Foundation for Sport and the Arts
- The voluntary sector – clubs and NGBs

Which organisations provide for sport?

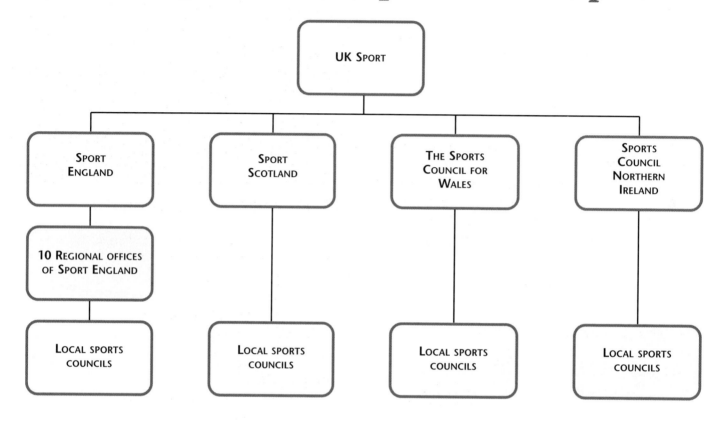

The original Sports Council was founded in 1972. The Sports Councils which developed later were themselves reorganised in 1997. Today we have five independent sports councils. The UK Sports Council, now known as UK Sport, looks after issues to be dealt with at UK level. The councils in England, Scotland, Wales and Northern Ireland are each responsible for sport in their own countries. In this chapter we will look at the work of Sport England, the brand name of the English Sports Council. The other home country sports councils work in similar ways.

What is UK Sport?

UK Sport has:
- a council of members appointed by the Secretary of State for Culture, Media and Sport
- a chief executive and full-time staff to put its plans into action.

What does UK Sport do?

UK Sport deals with high-performance sport at the UK level. It aims to achieve sporting excellence for Britain. To do this it
- gives full support to our world class performers through the World Class Performance Programme and the UK Sports Institute
- extends the UK's international sporting influence
- encourages the world's major sporting events to come to the UK
- promotes ethical standards of behaviour and provides an anti-doping programme.

Who pays for UK Sport?

The government gives an annual grant which funds UK-wide sporting projects. National Lottery money is given out to support excellence.

What is the UK Sports Institute (UKSI)?

The UKSI provides sports science, medicine, coaching and first-class facilities for elite sportspeople, teams and their coaches.

- A central services team is based in the London offices of UK Sport. It provides expert advice and support.
- Each home country sports council is responsible for the network of centres developed in its own area.
- The English Institute of Sport (EIS) runs ten regional institutes spread around England. These help the NGBs, and their elite sportspeople on World Class programmes, reach their medal-winning targets

What is Sport England?

Sport England has

- a council, whose members are appointed by the Secretary of State for Culture, Media and Sport
- a London head office with full-time staff to carry out the plans of Sport England

SPORT ENGLAND

- ten regional offices across England, which have close links with local authorities, local sports councils, area offices of NGBs and other organisations involved with sport and recreation.

The regional offices

The regional offices

- promote Sport England policy at local level
- keep Sport England in touch with needs at grass-roots level.

The local sports councils

The local sports councils

- are encouraged by Sport England but are independent councils
- bring together local people, clubs and groups interested in sport
- discuss problems, exchange views and plan for the future
- are only advisory but help developments in local sports in the best interests of the community.

What does Sport England do?

The objective of Sport England is to lead the development of sport in England. Its aims are:

- more people involved in sport
- more places to play sport
- more medals through higher standards of performance in sport.

More people

Sport England has developed new programmes to involve more people in sport:

- Active Schools – starting right
- Active Sports – getting more from your sport
- Active Communities – sport for all

More places

Sport England wants the right facilities in the right places and managed to the highest standards. To do this it deals with:

- Planning – what facilities do we need and where?
- Development – making sure the end result achieves the objectives
- Design – making sure the facility is fit for its purpose
- Management – putting the facility to work for sport

More medals

Sport England wants to develop excellence. It aims to do this through:

- The English Institute of Sport network of centres for elite sportspeople in England
- The World Class programmes – financial support from the National Lottery for talented performers
- National sports centres

Who pays for Sport England?

- The government gives a grant to each sports council
- Commercial activities, such as sale of publications
- It distributes National Lottery money

Sports development continuum
- Foundation – young people are taught PE and learn basic sports skills
- Participation – everyone is able to take part in the sport of their choice
- Performance – those interested have the chance to improve their sporting ability
- Excellence – talented performers can develop sporting excellence

How is Sport England trying to involve more people in sport?

Long-term national targets (for example, getting 20% more young people to take part in extra-curricular sport) were set out in the document 'England, the Sporting Nation' in 1997. Sport England is determined to involve the entire community in sport as participants, spectators or volunteers.

In 1998 it started three new nation-wide programmes:
- Active Schools
- Active Sports
- Active Communities

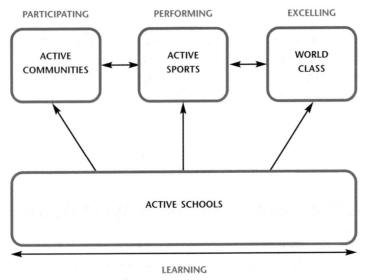

Active Schools
Sport England wants every child to stay physically active for life. This programme is built on the success of the National Junior Sport Programme. There are Sportsmark awards for secondary schools and Activemark awards for primary schools. These awards set schools targets for physical education and sport in the community. Teachers are given support, training and resources.

Examples include sports coaching for teachers, lottery-funded grants, workshops, booklets and study packs, TOP Play and TOP Sport in primary schools.

Active Sports
Sport England wants to do more to keep young people interested in sport. This programme targets nine sports – athletics, basketball, cricket, girls' football, hockey, netball, rugby union, swimming and tennis. It aims to help young people get more from their sport through participation, improvement and competition. Local action groups will offer young sportspeople coaching, competitions and opportunities to join clubs, taking over the role of Champion Coaching. They will all be encouraged to develop their ability further, leading to new development squads for those with talent.

Active Communities
Sport England realises that taking part in sport is difficult for many people. This programme will build on the work of the 'Sport For All' campaign. It will target grass-roots communities, especially those which are disadvantaged. It will do this by increasing the number of sports development officers working in the community, by extending the grants for small-scale sports projects, by providing funds to help priority groups and by developing new approaches to social exclusion through 'Active Community Projects'. It will create new 'Sports Action Zones'.

Equal opportunity for all
Sport England is also determined that everybody in England should have an equal opportunity to take part in sport. In the past some parts of the country and some social groups have lost out, for example girls and young women, Black, Asian and other ethnic minority communities, disabled people and people from deprived communities. Several new schemes will focus on these groups.

How is the government linked to sports organisations?

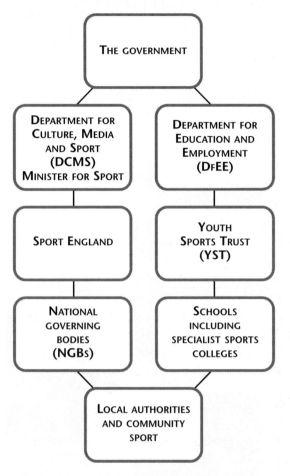

THE GOVERNMENT

DEPARTMENT FOR CULTURE, MEDIA AND SPORT (DCMS) MINISTER FOR SPORT

DEPARTMENT FOR EDUCATION AND EMPLOYMENT (DfEE)

SPORT ENGLAND

YOUTH SPORTS TRUST (YST)

NATIONAL GOVERNING BODIES (NGBs)

SCHOOLS INCLUDING SPECIALIST SPORTS COLLEGES

LOCAL AUTHORITIES AND COMMUNITY SPORT

The Department for Culture, Media and Sport (DCMS) appoints the Minister of Sport. The DCMS also appoints members to the five independent sports councils in Britain and gives them each an annual grant. The DCMS works for high quality and excellence in sport and to make sport available to everybody.

The Department for Education and Employment (DfEE) is responsible for the national physical education curriculum in schools. The DfEE works through the Youth Sports Trust (YST) to improve physical education and sport in schools. The YST also helps the DfEE to increase the number of schools becoming sports colleges.

What is the Youth Sport Trust?

YOUTH SPORT TRUST

The Youth Sport Trust (YST)
• is a registered **charity**, founded in 1994
• is governed by trustees
• has a mission 'to develop and implement, in close partnership with other organisations, quality physical education and sport programmes for all young people aged 18 months to 18 years in schools and the community'.

What does the Youth Sport Trust do?

The YST:
• has developed programmes for schools and the community
• runs the TOP programmes jointly with Sport England
• works on a programme for young disabled people called SportSability
• was appointed by the DfEE to work with schools interested in becoming sports colleges
• works with established sports colleges to assist their development
• takes on research, for example the Nike project to explore new ways to involve girls in PE and sport.

Who pays for the Youth Sports trust?

The YST gets funding from a number of sources:

• the DfEE
• companies
• trusts and foundations
• donations.

What are the TOP programmes?

These are a series of linked schemes, started in 1996, to help young people's sports development.
• TOP Tots – 18 months to 3 years: experience physical activity
• TOP Start – 3–5 years: learn through physical activity
• TOP Play – 4–9 years: learn core skills and fun sports
• TOP Sport – 7–11 years: introduction to sports and games
• TOP Skill – 11–14 years: extend sporting skill and knowledge
• TOP Link – 14–16 years: take a lead in organising sport
• Millennium Volunteers – 16–19 years: volunteer through sport
  All programmes provide equipment, activity resources and training.

What is the Institute of Youth Sport (IYS)?

The IYS is a centre for research and development for youth sport. It is a partnership between the YST and Loughborough University. It aims to turn research results in sport into development programmes for young people.

What are the government's plans for sport?

The government is committed to sport, especially the sporting needs of young people. Sport is increasingly being linked to social policy, for example health, crime prevention, social cohesion and community problems. It is not just seen as a good thing in itself.

In April 2000, the DCMS published the government's action plan for sport, called 'A Sporting Future for All'. This plan is quite different from previous plans. It states exactly what the government wants to happen in sport.

For the national governing bodies to receive money from the government:

- their plans must be in line with what the government wants
- their targets must be set out in detail
- their targets must be achieved.

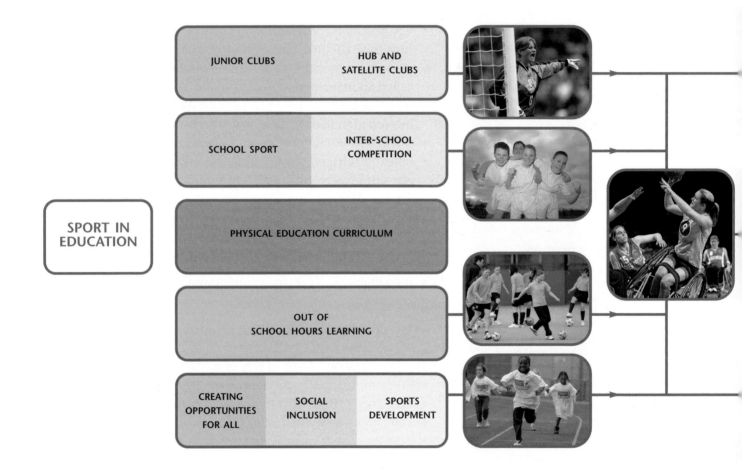

SPORT IN EDUCATION

JUNIOR CLUBS — HUB AND SATELLITE CLUBS

SCHOOL SPORT — INTER-SCHOOL COMPETITION

PHYSICAL EDUCATION CURRICULUM

OUT OF SCHOOL HOURS LEARNING

CREATING OPPORTUNITIES FOR ALL — SOCIAL INCLUSION — SPORTS DEVELOPMENT

Sport in education

The government will
- rebuild school facilities
- create 110 specialist sports colleges by 2003
- encourage after-school activities for all abilities
- appoint 600 school sports coordinators
- ensure talented sportspeople have access to coaching and other help.

Sport in the community

The government will
- prevent the sale of school and community playing fields
- spend money on community sports facilities, especially in the poorest areas.

Sporting excellence

The government will
- ask each NGB to create a national talent development plan
- ask sports colleges to offer a place to talented 14 year olds
- ensure that funding for individuals and teams is linked to target achievement
- encourage more and better qualified coaches.

Modernisation

The government will
- ensure that commercially successful sports put money back into grass-roots development
- change the role of Sport England to that of checking that grants are properly spent by the NGBs
- improve the running of sport by ensuring that NGBs:
  - have clear targets for participation and excellence
  - agree to accept money based on targets for their sports
  - agree to make social inclusion and fairness central to their work.

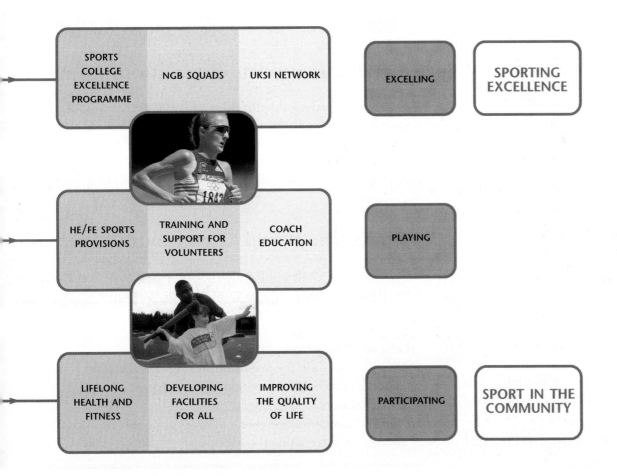

SPORTS COLLEGE EXCELLENCE PROGRAMME

NGB SQUADS

UKSI NETWORK

EXCELLING

SPORTING EXCELLENCE

HE/FE SPORTS PROVISIONS

TRAINING AND SUPPORT FOR VOLUNTEERS

COACH EDUCATION

PLAYING

LIFELONG HEALTH AND FITNESS

DEVELOPING FACILITIES FOR ALL

IMPROVING THE QUALITY OF LIFE

PARTICIPATING

SPORT IN THE COMMUNITY

Specialist sports colleges

A network of sports colleges will focus on elite sport. These colleges will have
- a commitment to the highest academic standards
- a fast-track route to National Lottery funds to develop world-class facilities
- access to their facilities for other schools and the community
- access to specialist coaching for pupils from other schools and the community
- a flexible day that allows time for high-quality training and learning
- links to the United Kingdom Sports Institute network centres so that talented youngsters can have access to the best sports science, medicine and coaching.

What are the national governing bodies of sport?

The national governing bodies of sport (NGBs):
- are voluntary organisations with democratic constitutions
- have members from clubs elected to make decisions
- use mainly unpaid volunteers
- have full-time paid officials to run them
- are independent of the government
- are usually members of the CCPR.

What do the national governing bodies do?

The NGBs:
- run their sports smoothly
- promote development of the sport
- organise competitions and events
- select teams at all levels
- arrange coaching and training
- organise award schemes
- enforce rules and laws
- see that they meet the rules of the international federation
- negotiate with television and sponsoring companies
- distribute funds for the World Class programmes
- produce detailed plans with clear targets for participation and excellence.

Who pays for the national governing bodies?

The NGBs are paid for by:
- members' subscriptions
- companies (through sponsorship)
- companies (for television rights)
- grants from the sports councils, National Lottery, Foundation for Sport and the Arts
- profits from spectator events
- partnerships with central government and local authorities.

How do area sports associations fit in?

The NGBs are responsible for their own sports throughout the country. Those that have large numbers of member clubs need to split up the country into smaller area associations. These area associations carry out the policy of the NGB. They organise coaching, training and competitions for clubs and individuals in their own areas.

What is the World Class programme?

The NGBs select outstanding sportspeople to receive funding from the National Lottery to support their training and preparation for international competition. It gives them the opportunity to be successful on the world sporting stage. Only sportspeople selected by their NGB will get help.
- World Class Start: for promising young sportspeople
- World Class Potential: for talented sportspeople with potential to represent their country
- World Class Performance: for elite sportspeople able to succeed in international competition

Denise Lewis received National Lottery funding

The Amateur Boxing Association is a member of the CCPR

What is the Central Council of Physical Recreation?

The Central Council of Physical Recreation (CCPR):
- is an independent **voluntary body** and was founded in 1935
- is the independent voice of UK sport and recreation
- has members who are mainly national governing bodies (NGBs). They are split up into six divisions based on their interests: movement and dance, games and sports, major spectator sports, outdoor pursuits, water recreation and interested organisations.

What does the CCPR do?

The CCPR has two main objectives:
- to improve and develop sport and physical recreation at all levels
- to support the work of the NGBs.

The CCPR:
- enables NGBs to meet to discuss common problems and the best way to develop their sports
- runs campaigns, for example against the loss of school playing fields
- advises government, local authorities and sports councils on sporting matters
- gives advice on sports sponsorship through the Sports Sponsorship Advisory Service
- helps professional sport through the Institute of Professional Sport
- runs the Sports Leader Award scheme
- encourages and supports volunteers who administer sport.

Who pays for the CCPR?

The CCPR is paid for by:
- Sport England
- donations from its NGBs membership
- sale of publications and other services.

Sports Leaders Award Scheme

This scheme was started in 1982 and
- trains young people as voluntary sports leaders
- aims to give young people the opportunity to become purposeful, positive and employable
- has awards at four levels – junior sports leader, community sports leader, basic expedition leader, higher sports leader award
- is financed by the British Sports Trust with donations from companies.

What is the National Coaching Foundation?

The National Coaching Foundation (NCF):
- is an independent charity founded in 1983
- has a board of directors to decide on policy.

What does the NCF do?

The NCF:
- co-ordinates coaching and coach education
- improves the skill and knowledge of coaches by offering courses at all levels
- provides a network of Coaching Development Officers in the home countries
- works closely with the sports councils, national governing bodies, the British Olympic Association, local authorities and education.

Who pays for the NCF?

The NCF:
- gets grants from UK Sport and UK England
- earns income from trading.

What is Disability Sport England?

Disability Sport England (DSE) is:
- the new name for the British Sports Association for the Disabled
- a national voluntary body, originally founded in 1961
- run by a national executive committee and a national advisory council.

Disability Sport England

What does DSE do?

The DSE:
- provides opportunities for disabled people to take part in sport
- promotes the benefits of sport and physical recreation for disabled people
- educates and makes people aware of the sporting abilities of disabled people
- improves the image, awareness and understanding of disability sport
- encourages disabled people to play an active role in the development of their sport.

Who pays for DSE?

DSE is paid for by fundraising and sponsorship.

What is the English Federation of Disability Sport?

The English Federation of Disability Sport (EFDS) is:
- a charity founded in 1999
- run by a board of trustees.

What does the EFDS do?

The EFDS:
- promotes disability sport
- aims to be the united voice of disability sport
- works closely with the seven national disability sports organisations: British Deaf Sports Council, British Blind Sport, Cerebral Palsy Sport, British Wheelchair Sports Foundation, British Amputee & Les Autres Sports Organisation, The English Sports Association for People with a Learning Disability, Disability Sport England.

Who pays for the EFDS?

The EFDS is paid for by Sport England.

What is the Women's Sports Foundation?

The Women's Sports Foundation (WSF) is:

- a national charity
- run by an executive committee.

What does the WSF do?

The WSF:

- increases awareness about the problems for women and girls in sport
- supports the involvement of women and girls in sport at all levels
- encourages better access to sport for women and girls
- challenges inequality in sport and tries to change things
- raises the profile of all British sportswomen
- advises many sports organisations about women's' issues in sport.

Who pays for the WSF?

The WSF is paid for by:

- Sport England
- subscriptions and sponsors.

What is the Countryside Agency?

The Countryside Agency (CA):

- is an independent, public agency
- was established in 1999 by merging the Countryside Agency and the Rural Development Commission.

What does the CA do?

The CA:

- looks after and improves the countryside in England
- runs the National Parks of England
- develops access for outdoor activities
- works with many organisations, like the Ramblers Association
- advises the government on all countryside matters.

Who pays for the CA?

The CA is paid for by the government.

What is the National Playing Fields Association?

The National Playing Fields Association (NPFA) is:

- a national, independent charity, founded in 1925
- open to membership by both individuals and organisations
- run by a council and trustees.

What does the NPFA do?

The NPFA:

- acquires, protects and improves playing fields, playgrounds and play spaces
- works for those who need play areas most – children of all ages and people with disabilities
- protects around 2000 playing fields across the UK.

Who pays for the NPFA?

The NPFA is paid for by:

- the public (through appeals)
- supporters (through donations)
- sales of publications and technical advice.

Who controls international sport?

| SPORTS CLUBS EACH CLUB CONTROLS ITS OWN SPORT UNDER NATIONAL RULES | AREA SPORTS ASSOCIATION EACH ASSOCIATION CONTROLS ITS OWN SPORT IN ITS OWN AREA UNDER NATIONAL RULES | NATIONAL GOVERNING BODIES EACH GOVERNING BODY CONTROLS ITS OWN SPORT IN UK UNDER ISF AND IOC RULES | INTERNATIONAL SPORTS FEDERATION EACH FEDERATION CONTROLS ITS OWN SPORT WORLD WIDE UNDER IOC RULES |

| BRITISH OLYMPIC ASSOCIATION RESPONSIBLE FOR ALL OLYMPIC MATTERS IN BRITAIN | INTERNATIONAL OLYMPIC COMMITTEE CONTROLS ALL OLYMPIC SPORT |

The international sports federations and the International Olympic Committee control international sport. The British Olympic Association promotes the Olympics in Britain.

What are the international sports federations?

The international sports federations (ISFs):
- are independent organisations
- are responsible for their sport world-wide
- have as members people who represent the NGBs in countries where the sport is played.

What do the ISFs do?

The ISFs:
- encourage the world-wide development of their sport
- control all international fixtures and competitions
- enforce and change the rules of their sport
- make sure their rules agree with the rules of the International Olympic Committee.

Who pays for the ISFs?

The ISFs are paid for by:
- companies (for televising major championships and international events)
- companies (through sponsorship of events)
- payments from NGBs.

Badminton Horse Trials

Sydney gold medallists

What is the International Olympic Committee?

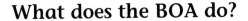

The International Olympic Committee (IOC):
- is an international non-governmental, non-profit organisation
- was founded in 1894 by Baron de Coubertin
- had 113 members in the year 2000. The members themselves elect new members.

What does the IOC do?

The IOC:
- is in complete control of everything to do with the Olympic Games
- works through national Olympic committees in the countries competing in the Olympics
- ensures the Olympics take place regularly
- strongly encourages women in sport
- is opposed to doping in sport.
  The main purpose of the IOC and the Olympic movement is 'to contribute to building a peaceful and better world by educating youth through sport, practised without discrimination of any kind and in the Olympic spirit, which requires mutual understanding, friendship, solidarity and fair play'.

Who pays for the IOC?

The IOC is paid for by:
- companies (for television rights)
- companies (from officially sponsoring the Olympics).

What is the British Olympic Association?

The British Olympic Association (BOA):
- is an independent organisation, founded in 1905
- is the National Olympic Committee of Great Britain
- has representatives from all Olympic sports as members
- allows its members to elect a committee to make decisions
- is totally independent of government and politics.

What does the BOA do?

The BOA:
- develops interest throughout the UK in the Olympic Games and the Olympic Movement
- runs the British Olympic Medical Centre to give medical help and sports science expertise to Olympic sportspeople
- helps the NGBs of sport to prepare their teams by, for example, providing warm weather training facilities
- organises the British team for each Olympic Games, including responsibility for travel, transport, insurance, health care, accommodation, food, training, publicity, documentation and behaviour at the Games.

Who pays for the BOA?

The BOA is paid for by:
- the public (through the British Olympic appeal)
- companies (through sponsorship)
- companies (for merchandise licences).

VIDEO: SCNI.

Who provides sports facilities?

Sports facilities are provided by the public sector, the private sector and the voluntary sector.

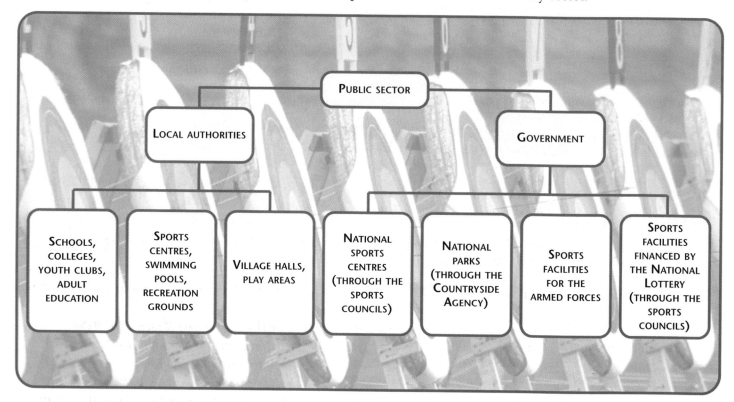

Who provides sports facilities in the public sector?

The government:
- gives grants to the sports councils for running national sports centres
- distributes National Lottery funds to the sports councils for projects, including facilities
- pays for the Countryside Agency, which runs the national parks
- pays directly for facilities for the armed forces.

National sports centres

There are 11 national sports centres, managed by the four sports councils. Priority is given to World Class Programme sportspeople, national team training and competition, and the training of leaders and officials.

National sports centres and their specialist facilities

Country	Centre	Specialist facilities
England	Crystal Palace	Athletics, swimming, diving
	Bisham Abbey	Tennis
	Lilleshall Hall	Football, gymnastics
	Holme Pierrepont	Water sports
	Plas y Brenin	Outdoor activities
Scotland	Cumbrae	Water sports
	Inverclyde	All purpose
	Glenmore Lodge	Outdoor activities
Wales	Cardiff	All purpose
	Plas Menai	Outdoor activities
Northern Ireland	Tollymore	Outdoor activities

Note: The National Cycling Centre at Manchester is owned by Sport England but run by the British Cycling Federation

National parks

The seven national parks of England are Dartmoor, Exmoor, the Lake District, North Yorkshire Moors, Northumberland, the Peak District and the Yorkshire Dales. The Norfolk and Suffolk Broads and the New Forest have similar status. They provide a wide range of opportunities for outdoor recreation.

English Institute of Sport Centres

The ten institute sites around the country will combine the best existing facilities with brand new facilities funded by the National Lottery.

The new English National Stadium at Wembley

The site was acquired by Sport England from Wembley plc. It will receive £120 million of National Lottery money. It will seat 90 000 and will be ready in 2004 if all the problems are overcome.

The new National Athletics Stadium at Lee Valley, north London

The new stadium is the result of a partnership between UK Athletics, Sport England, Lee Valley Authority and Enfield Council. It will have the potential to seat 45 000 and will be ready for the 2005 World Athletics Championships.

Local authorities

Wherever we live local authorities supply a variety of services such as education, street cleaning and leisure. If we live in a large city area, it is likely that all these services will be provided by one authority. In other areas there may be a county council responsible for major services such as education, and a district or town council providing others. In all areas there are small town or parish councils responsible for halls and open spaces.

Local authorities provide a wide variety of facilities

What are leisure and recreation departments?

Local authorities have departments to deal with their services. The policy of each department is decided by a committee of elected councillors. The councillors decide what should happen and professional staff in the departments carry out the council's policy. Most local authorities have a department responsible for leisure and recreation. Their committee will decide, for example, if a new swimming pool should be built.

What is provided?

Local authorities provide various sports facilities.
- Sports facilities for education must be provided by law
- Facilities for general leisure are not compulsory, although sports centres, swimming pools and recreation grounds are usually provided
- All facilities need qualified staff, good equipment and regular maintenance
- Leisure and recreation departments need activity programmes that people find attractive, accessible and affordable

Dual use and joint provision

Dual use is the use of school sports facilities by local clubs in the evenings, at weekends and during the holidays.

Joint provision refers to schools designed with purpose-built sports facilities to be used by the school and the community.

Both types of arrangement are supported by the sports councils.

Who provides sports facilities in the private sector?

PRIVATE SECTOR

COMMERCIAL VENTURES

FACILITIES FOR EMPLOYEES

SPECIALIST FACILITIES (FOR THE PUBLIC TO USE AT A PRICE):

- Commercial organisations may step in where there is a need but no facilities
- Facilities are usually friendly, modern and expensive
- They provide good value for money
- Attractive social activities are also offered
- Specialist facilities need to attract customers and make a profit to stay in business
- Examples include health and fitness centres, golf driving ranges, ten-pin bowling halls, ice rinks and tennis courts
- Purpose-built activity holiday centres attract families
- Hotels and country clubs offer high-class sports facilities as extra attractions

FACILITIES FOR TOP SPORTSPEOPLE (TO PERFORM FOR THE PUBLIC):

- Top sportspeople perform for spectators
- Vast crowds pay to see high-quality sports
- Facilities are usually purpose built for the sporting activity
- At race tracks, dogs and horses race for their owners and to provide betting on the result
- Major team sports attract loyal fans who watch regularly
- Individual sports such as athletics, golf, tennis, gymnastics and boxing also attract large crowds

- In the past, all large companies had social clubs
- These provided a range of sport and social activities
- This was free, but only for employees and their families
- Companies hoped this provision would encourage people to stay with them
- The upkeep of the buildings, courts, pitches and greens was paid for by the companies. It was expensive
- Today, companies are more likely to make arrangements with sports centres for special rates for employees or introductory fitness courses

A large crowd watching World Cup cricket at Lords

The Taylor Report

This was a report into the reasons for the Hillsborough football tragedy. In 1989, 95 fans were crushed to death during an FA Cup semi-final. The report suggested ways to improve the safety at football grounds. It recommended that Football League grounds should become all-seater, that fencing be made safer and that policing and medical facilities be improved. Today the Football Foundation gives grants to help with the cost of these improvements.

Who provides sports facilities in the voluntary sector?

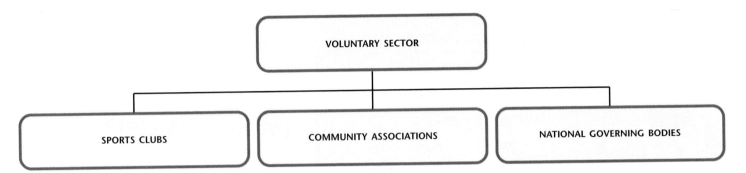

VOLUNTARY SECTOR

SPORTS CLUBS

COMMUNITY ASSOCIATIONS

NATIONAL GOVERNING BODIES

Sports clubs

For many adults taking part in sport means belonging to a local club. There are sports clubs in every town. Usually they are run by enthusiasts and concentrate on one sport.

Sports clubs need facilities. Those that have been going for many years may own their own facilities, for example golf, tennis and cricket clubs. Clubs that are new or do not have the money will need to hire facilities. These may be at the local sports centre, school, playing field or church hall.

Community associations

Not everyone wants to join a sports club in order to carry on with their sport. Sometimes groups of people in a village or part of a town get together to provide a variety of physical recreation for their local community.

These community associations need facilities. The village green may be available for cricket in the summer and hockey in the winter. Village and church halls can provide facilities for a number of indoor sports such as table tennis and badminton. Other facilities may be available for hire if necessary.

National governing bodies

Some NGBs have magnificent facilities – for example, the Rugby Football Union's ground at Twickenham. However, most of the NGBs formed more recently have no facilities of their own. Many use the facilities provided by the national sports centres.

Some NGBs have close historical links with an established club and use their facilities for its major events – for example the Marylebone Cricket Club (MCC) uses Lords cricket ground. The Football Association does not own its own ground but has used Wembley Stadium. This was owned by a private company but has been acquired for redevelopment by Sport England. Athletics and swimming do not have their own national facilities, and neither do many other major sports.

Village cricket is a British sporting tradition

Funding for sport – an overview

All sports need funding

To understand funding for sport, we need to look at why sport needs money and where the money comes from.

How important is spending on sport?

Today, sport and physical recreation are an important part of British life. Surveys show that around 36 million people, that is about two out of every three people, take part in sport and physical recreation at least once a month.

Sport is valuable to our society for economic reasons:

- it provides jobs for nearly 500 000 people
- it pays £3.6 billion in taxation
- it attracts £10.4 billion of people's spending.

Funding for sport

Public sector

Central government

Money comes in from:

- taxes
- betting duties
- National Lottery

Money goes out for:

- local authorities
- grants to – sports councils, Countryside Agency
- Youth Sport Trust
- Sportsmatch sponsorship
- Armed Services sport

Local authorities

Money comes in from:

- the government
- council tax
- business rates
- grants from – National Lottery, Foundation for Sport and the Arts, sports councils
- partnerships with business
- charges for sports facilities

Money goes out for:

- education facilities, equipment, staff for schools, youth clubs, adult education
- local sport facilities such as pools, sports centres, playing fields
- grants to local sports clubs or groups

Why does sport need money?

- We all need clothing, equipment, facilities and opportunities in order to take part in sport.
- We might also need teaching, training, coaching and competition.
- When we are at school, many of these things are provided without cost to us, but as adults we have to pay for them.
- Professional sportspeople expect to be able to pay their living, training and competition expenses. In addition they will expect payment and rewards for performing.
- Clubs and governing bodies need to pay for running costs, facilities, events, competitions and development projects.
- Local authorities need to provide leisure facilities for the community.

Where does money for sport come from?

The National Lottery is now the central funder for sport, although money comes into sport in many other ways. For example, the sports councils give grants to NGBs and distribute National Lottery money. There is much sponsorship by companies, and the selling of television rights brings in vast amounts of money for some sports such as football. Until recently all of these funders worked independently of one another. Partnership is now the key word in funding. Self-help by sports organisations aims to get more money into sport. The government's recent action plan ('A Sporting Future for All') explains how, for the first time, all organisations involved in sport must work together.

We have seen that facilities are provided by the three different sectors of society. In a similar way, money comes from these three sectors:

- In the public sector, the government and local authorities provide a service to the community
- In the private sector, companies work for profit
- In the voluntary sector, clubs and NGBs provide sporting opportunities for their members

Private sector

Money comes in from:

- profit from running business, including National Lottery profit
- spectators (paying to watch)
- merchandising

Money goes out for:

- direct sponsorship of individuals, teams and governing bodies
- sponsorship (through SportsAid)
- pools company money to the Foundation for Sport and the Arts and the Football Foundation
- payment for television rights
- National Lottery funds to government
- operating sports facilities

Voluntary sector

Money comes in from:

- grants from government (Sportsmatch)
- local authority
- sports councils
- governing bodies
- National Lottery
- Foundation for Sport and the Arts
- charitable trusts
- companies (sponsorship)
- subscriptions
- fund raising

Money goes out for:

- basic running costs
- development expenses

Who provides the money for sport?

Sports funding and the public sector: the government

The government raises money through taxes – taxes on personal earnings, on business profits, on sales of goods (called VAT) and many other taxes. Gambling is also taxed, so whether someone buys a National Lottery ticket, does the football pools or bets on horses, they will be paying taxes to the government. The government also gets money for good causes from the National Lottery company. This money is passed on to the sports councils for distribution.

Who gets government money for sport?

- Local authorities get a 'Revenue Support Grant' to help provide local services, including education and leisure
- The five sports councils get an annual grant from the government. In turn they give grants to NGBs and other organisations
- The Countryside Agency's costs are paid for by the government
- The government has put in place regional development agencies. These have money for economic and social development in their areas. Some sports projects may qualify
- The armed services. Physical fitness is essential for the armed forces. The government funds all facilities, equipment and clothing
- Sportsmatch scheme

The Sportsmatch scheme funds grass-roots projects

What is the Sportsmatch scheme?

This is:
- a grass-roots sponsorship scheme started in 1992
- run by the Institute of Sports Sponsorship.

What does the Sportsmatch scheme do?

The scheme:
- enables the government to give the same amount as the sponsor
- doubles the value of grass-roots sponsorship
- applies mainly to new sponsors and new schemes
- encourages new sponsors to become involved.

Who pays for the Sportsmatch scheme?

- The government
- The sponsor

Government policy and sports funding

- Grants to the sports councils have been gradually reduced over the years. They are now expected to raise money and reduce their own running costs.
- Local authorities, organisations and clubs are now all expected to find more of the money they need. They are expected to look for commercial sponsorship, apply for grants from, for example, the National Lottery and run their affairs cost-effectively.
- Following the publication of 'A Sporting Future for All' the NGBs are expected to produce detailed plans for development. These will include targets to be met. Grants will only be given if the targets are met.

Local authorities fund physical education in schools

Sports funding and the public sector: local authorities

Local authorities receive a 'Revenue Support Grant' from the government. They also raise money through the Council Tax and business rates. Today, local authorities often do not have enough money themselves to build facilities. They usually look for partnerships with grant-giving organisations, like the Sports Councils, National Lottery, Foundation for Sport and the Arts or business.

Who gets local authority money for sport?

Local authorities fund sport by building new facilities, improving old ones and paying for the running costs of activities in education and the community. The amount of money that local authorities spend on sport is very important. They provide about £960 million annually at present.

Education

The facilities for physical education in schools must be provided by law. The local authority may also provide money for sporting facilities for youth clubs and adult education. The local authority also pays for the costs of staffing and equipment.

Community

This money goes to the leisure and recreation department. Much of the money is spent on building and maintaining indoor and outdoor facilities. Some money may pay the salaries and costs of sports development officers and programmes. There are often small grants available to local clubs.

Compulsory competitive tendering

The government wants local authority sports facilities to be run efficiently and local authorities have to set out detailed plans for running their sports facilities to ensure this happens. Both commercial companies and the local authority's own leisure departments are allowed to bid to run the facilities. The contract is given on the basis of high-quality service at a competitive price. This is not privatisation – the facilities are still owned by the local authority, who decides how the facility will be run.

Sports funding and the private sector: companies

- The main purpose of running a business is to make a profit
- There are very many businesses involved in sport, for example companies making sports goods, shops selling sportswear and fitness clubs offering facilities. Many Premier League football clubs are now companies quoted on the Stock Exchange
- Professional sport today relies less on spectators paying to see the event than in the past. The sale of television rights and profits from selling merchandise (goods linked to sport) are now very important

Who gets company money for sport?

- Individuals, teams, NGBs and professional sports organisations receive sponsorship
- SportsAid receives sponsorship from companies
- The Foundation for Sport and the Arts gets money from the football pools companies
- The National Lottery gets money from the general public
- The Football Foundation receives money from the Premier League
- The NGBs and other sports organisations receive payment for the right to televise major events and to be official sponsors
- Local authorities get money through partnerships with business

What is the Football Foundation?

The Football Foundation (FF) was formed in 2000 to carry on and expand the work of the Football Trust. It is a charity, run by trustees.

FootballFoundation

football's biggest supporter

Professional sport is big business today

What does the Football Foundation do?

The FF works in three areas:
- Its main task is the development of football at grass-roots level. It provides money to improve facilities in parks and schools throughout the country. The Premiership pays 5% of its television agreement income into a new fund, which also receives government money
- It works in the community and in education to develop the game
- It continues the work of improving safety at professional grounds. These improvements were based on the Taylor Report into the Hillsborough tragedy

Who pays for the Football Foundation?

The FF is paid for by the Premier League, the FA, Sport England, the DCMS and the pools companies.

Sports funding and the private sector: the National Lottery and the Foundation for Sport and the Arts

Private-sector sports funding comes from the National Lottery and the Foundation for Sport and the Arts, as well as from companies.

What is the National Lottery?

The National Lottery:
- was started by the government in 1994
- is currently run by Camelot, a commercial company.

What does the National Lottery do?

It gives 'available' money to six types of good causes – sport (16.67%), the arts (16.67%), heritage (16.67%), charities (16.67%), the Millennium Fund (20%) and the New Opportunities Fund (added in 1998, 13.33%). After 2001 the Millennium share will transfer to the New Opportunities Fund.

The 'available' money is the money left after prizes (50%), tax (12%), retailer's commission (5%) and operator's costs and profits (5%) have been taken away from the sales figures.

Grants for sport are distributed by the five sports councils, totalling more than £200 million annually.

From 1997, grants have been made not only for facilities but also for running costs.

The New Opportunities Fund concentrates on health and education projects, including healthy living centres and after-school clubs.

The National Lottery only funds sports recognised by the sports councils.

Who pays for the National Lottery?

The general public pay by buying lottery tickets and scratch cards.

Stephanie Cook, gold medallist in the Olympic 2000 modern pentathlon, says: 'It's only because of Lottery money that I've been able to do it. There's no way I could have done the training that's necessary to get to this sort of standard without Lottery funding.'

What is the Foundation for Sport and the Arts?

The Foundation for Sport and the Arts (FSA) is:
- an independent, non-profit-making organisation, founded in 1991
- controlled by trustees from the pools companies, the arts and sport.

The Foundation for Sport and the Arts

What does the FSA do?

The FSA:
- aims to improve the quality of life of the community generally
- targets voluntary sports clubs, supporting grass roots
- offers grants, mainly for facilities but also for running costs
- gives about two-thirds of its money to sport and physical recreation (about £7-9million annually) and one-third to the arts
- supports SportsAid.

Who pays for the FSA?

The football pools companies.

Sports funding and the voluntary sector: clubs

Clubs need money to run their day-to-day affairs. They may also raise money to try to improve the club.

Basic running costs

Traditionally, sports clubs have been self-sufficient. They have been able to raise enough money from their members to pay the costs of their sport. These costs include such things as facilities, equipment, clothing, organising events and taking part in competitions as well as day-to-day expenses of running the club.

Clubs raise this money by:
- collecting membership subscriptions
- charging fees for taking part in sport
- running fund-raising events such as discos, raffles, quiz nights
- organising sponsored activities such as runs, rides and swims.

The money raised in this way is not very great but usually enough to cover the basic costs of the club.

Development costs

If a club wanted to build new facilities, improve what they have or start any other major development programme they would need a lot more money. In order to raise this money they would need outside help. These organisations give money to sport:
- The government (through Sportsmatch)
- Local authorities
- Sports councils
- NGBs
- The National Lottery
- The Foundation for Sport and the Arts
- Charitable trusts
- Companies (through sponsorship).

Dean Macey, decathlete, is supported by the World Class Programme

Sports funding and the voluntary sector: sportspeople

Over £16 million is given each year to help individual sportspeople competing from school level through to the Olympics. The government gives no direct help, but grants can be obtained from:
- The World Class Programme – this programme is organised by the NGBs and funded by the National Lottery. It gives grants for competition and living expenses to nominated elite and up-and-coming sportspeople
- SportsAid – sponsorship from companies is used to support sportspeople outside the World Class Programme
- NGBs – in addition to the World Class Programme, NGBs give help from their own funds and sponsorship

- The FSA – mainly gives grants to organisations, but a very small number are given to individuals
- Sports trusts and charities – a number of sports trusts and local charities support sportspeople, depending on their circumstances
- Companies – sponsorship is available from local and national businesses for sportspeople of all abilities.

NGBs provide top-class coaches

Sports funding and the voluntary sector: national governing bodies

The NGBs are voluntary bodies. They need money for many purposes.

Basic running costs

- Organisation of events and competitions
- Costs of providing training and coaching
- Achievement schemes for young people
- Supporting area organisations
- Upkeep of their own facilities
- General administration

Development costs

NGBs always need more money to improve their sport. Costs include building and running new facilities and developing new schemes for different ages and abilities.

Where do NGBs get their money from?

NGBs can raise money in various ways:

- membership fees from all their clubs and organisations
- grants from the same organisations as the sports clubs – the sports councils, the National Lottery, the FSA and charitable trusts.
- grants from the National Lottery to run the World Class Programme to assist elite and up-and-coming sportspeople
- working in partnership with the government (through Sportsmatch) and local authorities
- sponsorship from companies

Some NGBs run sports that are very popular and attract large crowds at major events and championships. Examples include the FA Cup Final, RFU international matches and the Wimbledon championships. They are able to sell the television rights for these events and also make a profit at the gate.

How is a sports club organised and financed?

Sports clubs exist because enthusiastic people have met together in the past to enjoy their sport. However, enthusiasm is not enough to keep a club going. To be successful, a club needs members, a committee, a constitution, facilities and finance.

Members should be:
- enthusiastic about their sport
- happy to take part with others
- willing to pay their share of the costs
- able to accept club rules
- available to play, organise, coach or be officials at competitions.

Committee members should be:
- willing to take on jobs
- ready to work on a committee
- able to make decisions for the club
- elected by the members at the club's Annual General Meeting (AGM).
  There are three essential jobs:
- Chair – controls committee meetings and acts as the club's representative
- Secretary – deals with the day-to-day business, arranges meetings
- Treasurer – deals with all the club's finances

Constitution
This sets out the rules of the club, which explain:
- how the club is organised
- how you become a member
- how people are elected to jobs
- how fees can be charged
- what happens if members break the rules
- how the club can be changed.

Facilities
These are needed for playing, training, meetings and social events. The needs of the club will depend on the type of activity and the size of the club. Facilities might be hired or owned by the club.

Finance
A club will need to pay for:
- hire or upkeep of facilities
- team clothing and equipment
- training and competition costs
- office expenses.

It can raise money through:
- fees and subscriptions
- fund raising
- grants and sponsorship.

Examination type questions: Providing for sport

There are 12 marks for each question.

1 (a) Name correctly two governing bodies of sport in Britain. *(2 marks)*

(b) Give two functions of the British Olympic Association. *(2 marks)*

(c) National sports centres specialise in different sports.
Give one such sport for each of these centres:
(i) Plas y Brenin
(ii) Holme Pierrepont *(2 marks)*

(d) Explain the main aims of Sport England. *(6 marks)*

2 (a) Give two functions of national governing bodies of sport. *(2 marks)*

(b) Name two essential posts in any sports club. *(2 marks)*

(c) Suggest two ways in which the manager of a sports centre could make it more attractive to young people. *(2 marks)*

(d) A local club wishes to improve its facilities. Name six different organisations to whom it could apply for a grant. *(6 marks)*

3 (a) Sport UK aims to achieve sporting excellence for the nation.
List two ways it aims to do this. *(2 marks)*

(b) Explain what the 'Sportsmatch' scheme is. *(2 marks)*

(c) Give two aims of the national sports centres. *(2 marks)*

(d) Describe the work and power of the International Olympic Committee. *(6 marks)*

4 (a) A talented sportsperson needs financial support.
Name two sources of grants. *(2 marks)*

(b) Name two aims of the National Coaching Foundation. *(2 marks)*

(c) Give two reasons why local authority leisure and recreation departments are important for sport in the community. *(2 marks)*

(d) List six major points from the government's action plan 'A Sporting Future for All'. *(6 marks)*

Answers are given in the World of Sport Examined Teachers Resource and Student Workbook

10 Taking part in sport

Different people take part in sport for different reasons. Some people decide not to take part at all but enjoy watching sport. For others, sport is of no interest and plays no part in their life. Why and how do we come to these decisions about sport? There are usually no simple answers. We are affected by many different factors in our lives. Society is made up of all sorts of people – men, women, different ethnic groups, able-bodied people, people with disabilities, people of different ages. If we belong to a particular group or groups of people, we may encounter a number of barriers to taking part

Leisure time
page 220

- How much time do we have for leisure activities?

Benefits
page 221

- Do we know what the benefits of sport are?

Home influences
page 222

- What influence do our parents, friends and peers have?
- What effect does our social class, financial situation and environment have?

School influences
page 224

- How does the status of PE in our school affect us?
- How do our PE lessons affect us?

School and community links
page 226

- Do we know where to find centres and clubs?

National campaigns
page 227

- Do national campaigns help us to get involved in sport?

in sport. Opportunities to take part in sport are not equal. Some groups of people will have more opportunities than others.

This is a complex issue. In order to be able to understand it properly, we need to understand why people take part in sports.

'The government has the highest aspirations for sport in this country. Our aims are clear. We want to see more people of all ages and social groups taking part in sport and more success for our top competitors and teams in international competition.'

Department for Culture, Media and Sport ('A Sporting Future for All' April 2000)

Gender and sport
page 228

Black and ethnic minorities and sport
page 229

Disability and sport
page 230

Older people and sport
page 231

- Are we influenced by our gender, race, culture, disability, age?

Careers in sport
page 232

- Would we like to work in sport?

Leisure time

Our day

We can put most of our daily activities under the headings of bodily needs, work, duties and leisure time.

- We have to do many things to stay healthy. Bodily needs include sleeping, eating and washing.

- We need to work to earn a living. Some unemployed people, mainly women, do not earn money but look after their home and children. This is also work. Pupils might consider time at school as work. Some activities are closely linked to work, such as travelling to work.

- There are a number of things we feel we have to do. These include duties towards our family and home. Many things may be called duties, for example washing up or taking the dog for a walk.

- If we take out of our day the time used up for bodily needs, duties, work and work-related activities, we are left with free time for leisure activities. This is the time when we have the greatest choice about what we do. During this leisure time we can take part in sport and physical recreation.

During our leisure time we can choose our activities

Today's patterns of work

Most people still work regular hours, and this sets the pattern for their lives. For these people their leisure time will be at weekends, in the evenings and during holidays. However, changing working patterns today have seen more weekend employment, flexi-time and working from home. Working long hours or overtime reduces our leisure time. People on night work or shift work may have to take their leisure time when other people are working. Our duties also take time and must be fitted in.

In the last 50 years there has been a great increase in the time people have available for leisure. Leisure time will continue to grow for almost all of us. There are many reasons for this:

- working careers have become shorter as we continue our education for longer and retire earlier
- we live longer in retirement
- paid holidays have increased
- working hours have become shorter
- housework takes less time
- unemployment, short-time and part-time work have increased.

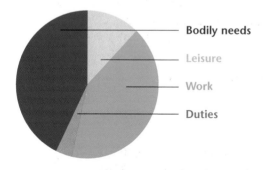

Average percentage split of a person's daily activities

Benefits

It is, of course, quite right that we should be free to choose our own leisure-time activities. We may be stamp collectors, bee keepers or voluntary hospital workers. All these activities have great value. Physical recreation and sport are different and offer other benefits.

Enjoyment

For most of us, enjoyment is the main reason why we take part in sport and physical recreation. We enjoy activities for different reasons:

- Dance can be enjoyed for the experience of moving to the music and performing complex movement patterns.
- Some players enjoy using up energy and aggression in activities such as judo.
- Archers get pleasure from being able to hit the target accurately.
- The thrill of going at speed over land, water and snow attracts riders, racing drivers, canoeists and skiers.
- Some people enjoy achievement, for example winning a match, recording a personal best or representing their area.

Health

- Taking part in physical activity helps us to maintain good health. We need to keep our bodies fit for the daily demands of life. The more active we are, the greater the physical benefits.
- Exercise is vital in weight control. Unfit, overweight people are more likely to have poor health than those who exercise regularly.
- Stress is one of the greatest challenges to health today. Physical activity helps us to feel and look good, improving our self-image whereas worrying can make us ill. Physical recreation will not solve our worries but it will help us to relax for a while, perhaps allowing us a fresh look at our problems.

Sport can be fun!

Social

- We all need daily contact with other people. Physical recreation gives us the opportunity to meet and talk to others. We have the activity as a common interest. This helps to stimulate conversation and encourages friendships to develop.
- Many activities take place in sports centres or clubs. We may attend regularly and develop an interest in a group or a club. Many people like being part of a team and choose to play together. Others work together to run the affairs of a club.

Work

A few very talented sportspeople can earn a living as professional sportspeople. Many more are able to make some money from sport as part-time professionals.

Home influences

Whether we take part in sport or not is influenced by many factors, including:
- our family
- our friends and peers
- our social class
- our financial situation
- our environment.

Family

Our family is a very important influence on us.
- If our parents play sport regularly then we will be brought up in a sporting atmosphere.
- Sporting parents and older brothers and sisters will provide us with role models to follow.
- Sometimes children with famous sporting parents will follow in their parents' footsteps. However, this is not easy to do and many will decide to do something completely different.
- Family influences can also be negative if there is little interest or encouragement to do sport.

Friends and peers

Our peers are the people who are the same age as us. Our friends are often our peers.
- What our friends do in their leisure time will usually affect us. Friends often have similar interests.
- We all need friends, and if our friends are not interested in sport we may drop out of sport too.
- On the other hand, if our friends take part in sport and enjoy it we might be willing to give it a try.
- In school, peer pressure can be very strong.

Social class

Social class refers to a number of factors, including type of employment, income level and family background. Our social class can affect the type of activity we take part in. For example, a middle-class person who is well off, lives in the country and owns his or her own horse is more likely to be involved in riding sports than someone who lives in a city and has a lower income.

Research shows that fewer working-class people take part in sport than people from other social classes. This is because people from other social classes have more time, money and opportunities to take part in sport.

From a young age, our friends and peers influence us to take part

Financial situation

- The amount of money coming into a family affects its standard of living and all the activities the family members do in their leisure time.
- Even for school PE we need quite a lot of sports clothing and equipment. Playing sport outside school time means we will have to pay even more for equipment, the hire of facilities and the costs of joining a club or centre.
- At a higher level, we need to pay travelling costs, training fees and all the expenses of competition. Although help is available to meet some of these costs, we are affected by our parents' ability to pay for our sport.
- If sports opportunities at school are reduced, children will miss out if their parents cannot afford the fees at sports centres and clubs.

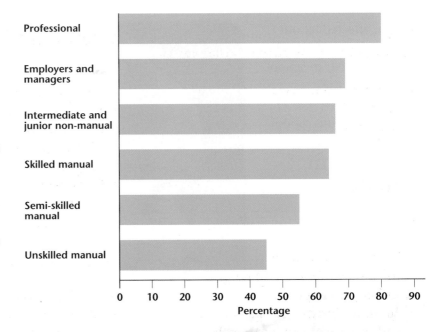

Participation rates for adults in all sports: Great Britain, 1996

Environment

Where we live affects some of the sports we can take part in.

- If we live near the sea, a large lake or river, there will be greater opportunities to learn water sports.
- Country areas might provide opportunities for outdoor activities, but they may be a long way from leisure centres and swimming pools.
- Inner-city areas will be short of open space but are more likely to have many indoor facilities within travelling distance.
- Cities and towns, because of their high population, may attract both commercial and private sports clubs.
- In some parts of the country there is a tradition for a particular local sport – for example, Highland wrestling in Scotland.
- We may need transport to get to facilities in order to play sport. If our parents do not have a car we will have to find the money for public transport.

Our financial and environmental situation affects our sporting activities

School influences

We are affected by our experiences of Physical Education (PE) in school and also by the importance given to PE and sport by our school.

Changes in education

Over the last decade there have been many changes in education that have had an effect on PE in schools.

PE lessons affect our attitude to sport

The National Curriculum

PE has always been a foundation subject in the National Curriculum. This gave PE equal status with other subjects. Targets have been set for each age group. The sports are chosen by the PE department from different categories and there are checks to make sure pupils achieve their targets. PE teachers decide on the best teaching methods.

Examinations in PE

Most pupils now have the opportunity to study PE at GCSE level and an increasing number can take PE at 'A' level. Many students continue with PE and sport studies at GNVQ, BTec and degree level.

Time given to PE

By law, schools have to teach the subjects of the National Curriculum. This means there is a lot of pressure to fit all of the subjects into the school curriculum. As a result time for PE has been cut in many schools, especially primary schools. The 'Young People and Sport' national survey by Sport England showed that overall the number of pupils spending more than 2 hours per week on PE fell from 46% in 1994 to 33% in 1999.

Open enrolment

Open enrolment means that schools are in competition with one another to attract pupils. The standard of PE in a school and the number of out of school activities will help the school's reputation. As a result PE in schools is especially important in attracting pupils.

Sports colleges

The government has allowed schools to specialise in certain subjects including sport. Sports colleges are at the heart of the government's plans to help talented young sportspeople raise the standard of British sport.

'A Sporting Future for All'

The government plans to put 600 school sports co-ordinators into communities where the need is greatest. They will link together primary and secondary schools with the specialist Sports College in their area. They will help provide opportunities for young people to compete regularly for their school and take part in a wide range of sports.

How do our PE lessons affect us?

PE has the same aim as other subjects on the school curriculum, in that it aims to contribute to the general education of all children. It does this by using physical activities of many kinds in PE lessons. Good PE lessons in school will encourage us to take part in sport after leaving school. There are three major factors which influence whether or not we take part in sport after we have left school.

'If it wasn't for my school coach I would never have heard of rowing. I'd have been a rugby player.'
Steve Redgrave

Skills

PE teachers:

- teach all pupils the basic skills of a variety of different activities
- develop these skills during our years at school so that we can take part confidently in the activities
- may also improve our abilities through coaching and training during after-school practices
- sometimes will be able to send pupils to local sports clubs or centres of excellence
- may offer pupils the opportunity to try for achievement awards in different sports.

Attitude

PE teachers:

- try to develop in their students a positive attitude towards an active lifestyle
- explain the advantages of life-long involvement in physical recreation
- use their own attitude and experience in their work as a role model for students.

Health

PE teachers:

- explain the value of regular exercise for health and fitness
- go through the important principles involved in training for different sports, in both theory and practice
- teach safe practices for all activities
- give advice for avoiding and, if necessary, dealing with injuries.

Research

The Sport England national survey 'Young People and Sport' found that the number of pupils taking part in sport after school (whether organised or just for fun) had increased from 74% in 1994 to 79% in 1999.

School and community links

Even if a school's PE programme is very good, the school–community link is vital in helping young people continue with physical recreation after leaving school. Pupils need to be introduced to the sports clubs, activity groups and leisure centres in their local community before they leave school. It helps if the community uses the school facilities regularly.

Bridging the school–community gap

Schools could:
- bring club members, centre managers and others involved in community sport into the school
- arrange for pupils to visit the clubs, centres and other facilities in the area
- explain how to find out about other sports not taught at school.

Clubs and centres could:
- run special introductory courses for young people at school
- ensure the clubs and centres are welcoming to young people
- provide coaching and training for young people
- help young people with the costs.

Leaving school

We need to leave school with:
- a sound basis of sports skills
- wide experience of different activities
- good understanding of the link between health and exercise
- a positive attitude towards physical recreation
- knowledge of local sporting opportunities.

Sport crosses all age barriers

'A Sporting Future for All'

The government will:
- prevent the sale of school and community playing fields
- provide National Lottery money to create new and improve existing outdoor facilities, especially in the poorest areas
- support Sport England's aim of using 75% of Lottery money for community sport over the next 10 years
- encourage local authorities to be at the heart of partnerships with private and voluntary groups to improve sporting opportunities in the community
- expect NGBs, in return for funding, to develop sport in the community by providing coaches, opportunities and detailed plans, especially for deprived areas.

National campaigns

In the past the Sports Council ran a number of national campaigns. They needed very strong links between the national message and local clubs to be successful. These campaigns had some success but are not used a great deal today.

'Sport for All'

This campaign was started in 1972 and for many years was central to the work of the Sports Council. Its main aims were to increase participation and improve performance at all levels.
Today it is to be found in Sport England's 'More People' and 'More Medals' campaigns.

'Sport for All'

Who has missed out?

Although more facilities were provided and the number of people taking part increased, not everyone benefited. Research showed that some groups missed out – including low-paid and unskilled workers, ethnic minorities, school leavers, parents of young children, women generally and unemployed young people.

'A Sporting Future for All'

The government stated in April 2000:
'... not everyone has the same access to sport. There are marked differences between men and women, between ethnic groups and particularly between different social classes... We want to reduce, over the next ten years, the unfairness in access to sport. To achieve this goal, we will invest in grass root facilities and make sure that everyone involved in sport makes a concerted effort to give opportunities to those currently excluded.'

Special campaigns

At different times the Sport for All campaign focused on different themes:

1975	Sport for all the family	Encouraged activities for the whole family
1978	Come alive	Emphasised good health through regular exercise
1981	Disabled people	Promoted sport for people with disabilities
1983	50+ All to Play for	Encouraged older people to take part in physical recreation
1985	Ever Thought of Sport?	Focused on the 13–24 year olds who were missing out on sport
1987	What's your Sport?	Produced detailed information about where to take part in sport
1990	Women in Sport	Concentrated on the needs of women in sport
1991	Year of Sport	Coincided with a number of international events in the UK

Gender and sport

Today it is possible for women to take part in almost any sport. Social changes have gradually given women more and more opportunities to control their own lives. This was not so in the past, as many sports were not open to women. The history of sport is mainly the history of men's sport.

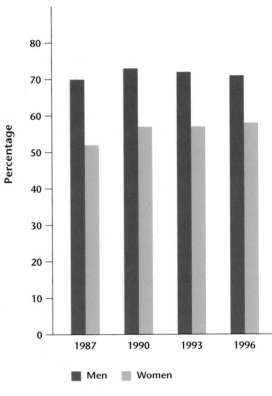

Participation rates for adults in all sports: Great Britain

What needs to be changed?

- Stereotyping means having a fixed image of a group of people. Girls in the past were encouraged to play with dolls, to learn to cook and to keep themselves clean. In contrast boys were encouraged to play ball games, allowed to climb trees and to get covered in mud.
- Children were, and still are, brought up to fit into these gender stereotypes – stereotypes for the different sexes.
- As a result, boys have greater opportunities to develop the skills of sports and the confidence that goes with them. Boys think a lot of their peers who are good at sport. Sport has high status for them.
- In contrast, many girls have been turned off PE at school and so do not consider sporting achievement to be important.
- Gender stereotypes continue into adult life. Some sports are still seen as unsuitable for women. Women often think that playing sport will make them unattractive to men.
- Married women are expected to take responsibility for the home and children. This reduces the time and energy they have for sport.
- Sport for a mother is a low priority in family life. The mother does not always have an independent income to spend on her sport or her own transport.
- Male sport dominates on television and in newspapers.
- However, these gender stereotypes are gradually being broken down.

What is being done?

The Sports Council has targeted women in a number of campaigns. In 1993 it published a policy and framework for action which still applies. It aims:

- to improve girls' skills and to develop a positive attitude to an active life
- to increase the opportunities for women to take part in sport
- to increase the opportunities for women to improve their level of performance
- to increase the number of women involved in the organisation of sport
- to encourage all organisations to have equal opportunities
- to improve communication about women in sport.

The Women's Sports Foundation supports women's sport (see page 201). In 2000 the WSF published a national action plan for women's and girls' sport and physical activity.

Black and ethnic minorities and sport

In our multicultural society, people of all races and ethnic backgrounds take part in sport at all levels. As a result of this, we often assume that they face no problems in sport. However, there is discrimination and disadvantage in sport as there is in everyday life.

What needs to be changed?

- Racism means not treating people of different races equally. Racists often hold stereotyped views about people from different ethnic backgrounds. Stereotypes lead to sporting myths about what different people can and cannot do. One example of a racist sporting myth is 'Black people can't swim at top levels'. This is nonsense.
- Personal racism is seen when Black and ethnic minority people are made to feel unwelcome by individuals at a sports club.
- Institutional racism is racism perpetrated by an organisation, rather than particular individuals. This kind of racism can often be seen in a lack of understanding, or a lack of willingness to understand and respond to, the problems faced by Black and ethnic minorities in an organisation.
- Racism is a major problem in spite of the efforts of many committed people who work to eliminate racial inequality.
- Socioeconomic factors include employment, pay and social class. In this country, people from the Black and ethnic minorities are over-represented amongst the unemployed and the poorly paid. One result of this is that Black and ethnic minority people often have less money to spend on sport and other leisure activities.
- There are many different cultures in Britain, each with its own set of beliefs about many important areas. Some of these beliefs will affect sport. For example, some women may not take part in mixed sports for religious reasons. Some people think this needs to change, but others disagree.

Tiger Woods

What is being done?

In 1993 the Sports Council published a policy and objectives which still apply.

Sports Council aim: To work towards the elimination of racial disadvantage and discrimination in order to achieve better quality sport for Black and ethnic minority people.

There are six main objectives:
- To raise awareness of racial inequality in sport.
- To increase the number of Black and ethnic minority decision makers in sport.
- To increase the number of Black and ethnic minority sportspeople involved in sports organisation.
- To improve skill and develop a positive attitude to an active life for young Black and ethnic minority people.
- To increase opportunities for Black and ethnic minority people to take part in sport.
- To increase opportunities to improve the level of performance of Black and ethnic minority people.

In 1993, the Professional Footballers' Association and the Commission for Racial Equality set up the 'Let's Kick Racism out of Football' campaign. It is still active but is now called 'Kick it Out' and is independent of the CRE.

Disability and sport

People with disabilities have much to offer the world of sport. As well as the top disabled sportspeople, there are many ordinary disabled people who can and do benefit from sport. Sport allows everybody to stay healthy and to meet people. However, people with disabilities do face serious obstacles to participation in sport.

What needs to be changed?

- It is not always possible for disabled people to get to events. Transport to facilities may be difficult. There may not be suitable doors and ramps at entrances to buildings.
- Plans for facilities, funding and events do not always take account of the needs of the competitors and spectators with disabilities.
- Planning should include training for the people to work with sports people with disabilities.
- Sports centres and clubs do not automatically make provision for everyone, including people with disabilities. Governing bodies do not usually hold events for disabled people within their able-bodied championships.
- People with disabilities may not be aware of organisations catering for their sporting needs.
- People with disabilities may have had little opportunity in the past to develop their sporting skills.
- People with disabilities may not be able to afford the cost of taking part in sport.
- The integration of school pupils with disabilities into PE lessons presents many challenges.

What is being done?

In 1993 the Sports Council published a policy and action plan which still applies.

Sports Council aim: To ensure equality of opportunity for people with disabilities to take part in sport and recreation at the level of their choice.

There are seven main objectives:

- To raise the profile of people with disabilities in sport
- To make sure plans for sport include the needs of people with disabilities
- To provide opportunities for people with disabilities to take part in sport
- To improve access to sport for people with disabilities
- To encourage involvement for people with disabilities in international sport
- To use all resources and to seek extra finance
- To make sure sport meets the needs of people with disabilities.

Full details of Disability Sport England and the English Federation of Disability Sport are on page 200.

Older people and sport

In general, people become less physically active as they get older. Research shows that in 1996 only 31% of people over 70 took part in sport and physical activities (including walking), compared with 86% of those aged 16–19. However, the percentage of people over 60 taking part in physical activities is increasing

What needs to be changed?

- If older people have not exercised for a long time it is hard to get their bodies working again.
- Some may not have had the opportunity to learn skills when they were young.
- Others may have had illnesses that mean they need to be cautious when exercising.
- Older people living on pensions may have only a limited amount of money for spending on leisure. Most sports centres do offer older people special rates, especially if they come along at off-peak times.
- Older people are less likely to be able to afford to run a car and may find it difficult to get to sports facilities.
- Sport in the media is dominated by young people but in many clubs veteran teams start at 35 or 40. There is not enough publicity for older people who achieve a high standard.

What is being done?

In 1983 the Sports Council started its campaign 'Sport for All – 50+ All to Play for'. It is still going. It encourages older people to take part in sport. It emphasises not just the health benefits but also the social benefits of an active lifestyle. Sport provides the opportunity for people to meet. In 1994 new guidelines were produced.

Local authority leisure and recreation departments usually offer a full range of activities for the 50-plus age group.

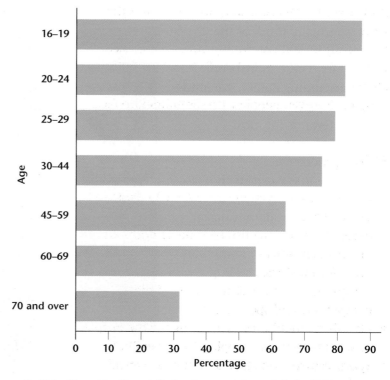

Participation rates for adults in all sports: Great Britain 1996

Careers in sport

When we talk about careers in sport we usually think of the glamorous lifestyle of the top sports stars. These sportspeople have outstanding ability. We must remember that they are the lucky few. The rewards for most professional sportspeople are much smaller.

There are many careers in sport apart from performing. Most of these jobs do not make the headlines, although they are essential to sport.

Sport as a career

Role	Example	Job description:	Main quality:
Performer:	Athletics, basketball, boxing, cricket, cycling, darts, equestrian, football, golf, motor racing, rugby, snooker, tennis.	Playing sport at a high level.	Outstanding ability.
Working with performers:	PE teacher, trainer, coach, instructor, team manager.	Developing sports skills in others.	Ability to analyse and improve skill.
Science and health:	Sports doctor, physiotherapist, sports psychologist, dietician, sport and exercise adviser.	Improving sports performance.	Understanding of sports medicine.
Organisation:	Centre manager, leisure officer, administrator, sports development officer.	Organising sporting activities.	Motivating others to take part.
Media:	Journalist, commentator, TV presenter.	Describing sport.	Communication skills.
Business:	Manufacturing, retail, sales, agent.	Applying business understanding to sport.	Ability to see potential for profit in sport.
Practical work:	Groundsman, mechanic, stable hand, match official.	Doing practical work of a high standard.	High level of practical skill.

Examination-type questions: Taking part in sport

There are 12 marks for each question.

1 (a) Give two reasons to show why we all have more leisure time today. *(2 marks)*

(b) PE encourages pupils to play sport. Suggest two ways in which this is done. *(2 marks)*

(c) Suggest two ways in which sports centres might ensure that their facilities are available to sportspeople with disabilities. *(2 marks)*

(d) We take part in sport because we enjoy it.
Give six other reasons why we play sport. *(6 marks)*

2 (a) Suggest two ways in which sports clubs might try to encourage pupils to join them after leaving school. *(2 marks)*

(b) Give two problems likely to affect older people wishing to play sport. *(2 marks)*

(c) Name two careers in sport involving the organisation of sport. *(2 marks)*

(d) Whether or not we take part in sport is influenced by many factors.
Describe six. *(6 marks)*

3 (a) Name two Sports Council campaigns from the past that were used to encourage participation. *(2 marks)*

(b) Give two reasons why our financial situation can affect our use of leisure time. *(2 marks)*

(c) Many people live in cities, others live in the country. Suggest two ways in which our environment affects our choice of sport. *(2 marks)*

(d) Explain why fewer girls and women than boys and men take part in sport. *(6 marks)*

4 (a) Explain what a stereotype in sport is and give an example. *(2 marks)*

(b) Suggest two ways in which our peer group influences our participation in sport. *(2 marks)*

(c) Give two reasons to explain why physical recreation is considered a worthwhile leisure time activity. *(2 marks)*

(d) The Government's action plan 'A Sporting Future For All' will aim to increase participation. Give six points from this part of the plan. *(6 marks)*

Answers are given in the World of Sport Examined Teacher Resource and Student Workbook

11 Sport as a spectacle

Sport has always been a spectacle.
Today, television and sponsorship
greatly influence our view of sport.

Sponsorship
page 236

Sports sponsorship is an agreement between a
commercial company and an individual, team or
sport. Sports people agree that in return for payment
they will advertise the names of the sponsors. The
detailed arrangements about the advertising are
worked out by the sponsors and the sport. The
sponsors also try to make their potential customers
feel good about them sponsoring sport. Sport is
attractive to sponsors because it involves young
people and exciting action.

The media
page 242

Sport is always worth reporting. At its best it is full of
drama, tension and excitement. By its very nature
there will be winners and losers. Through the media
we share in their happiness and their pain, we know
their successes and their disappointments. Uncertainty
accompanies sport, often to the finish, and keeps hope
alive until the very end. Above all, sport is about
people. For the media, sport makes bold headlines,
good stories and wonderful pictures.

Television

page 244

The sport we see on our television screens has been brought to us only after a lot of negotiating between many groups of people. These include the national governing bodies (NGBs), the sponsoring companies and people who work in television, such as producers, editors, presenters and commentators. The television companies need to keep the viewer happy, the sponsors require plenty of publicity, the NGBs expect a good picture of the sport and the sportspeople want good publicity, a winning performance and money. The viewer hopes to be entertained.

Sport, sponsorship and television – the future?

page 246

The NGBs need to control the demands of the television producers and commercial sponsors, who want sport to become increasingly like entertainment. The traditional idea of sport as being recreational has almost disappeared at the highest level. Today, professional sport is rapidly becoming part of show business. It demands stars and performances. The NGBs are in danger of losing control of their sports. They have become dependent on money from sponsors and television. They know that television coverage is essential for major events. Without television coverage there would be no sponsors, which would mean no money to attract top sportspeople. Without this money there would be no event.

Sponsorship

Sport sponsorship means that a company gives financial help in return for linking their name with an individual or team, or a sport in general.

- Companies exist in order to make profits. They do not have to make donations to charity or to sponsor sport, although many do so.
- Sponsorship is an investment. The company expects to get something in return for sponsoring a team or individual. Sponsorship helps the company to sell its products. The company wants to have an impact on likely customers. This impact comes through the link between the sporting activity and the product. The aim is to improve the business of the company.
- Donations are different from sponsorship; they are gifts. The company chooses to give money to sport. The company benefits by being seen to care about the community. There is no direct commercial advantage in giving money in this way.
- Sports sponsorship can work by promoting a sales message or by promoting an image.

Promoting a sales message

- At its simplest, sponsoring gives a company a chance to put over a sales message. such as 'Buy our product'.
- Sports stars are linked with a particular company's product.
- A team wears shirts with the company's name for all to see.
- Advertising hoardings at a televised sports event are caught by the cameras.
- A competition may carry the sponsor's name, for example the AXA FA Cup.
- Sponsorship aims to put the company's name in front of the public so that it is remembered.
- An example of sponsorship: Green Flag spent around £4 million over 4 years sponsoring the England football team. The public's awareness of the name went from zero to 53%. However, not many people knew what the company did! The company pulled out, having achieved its objective. It decided to explain its services by other means.

Advertising reaches new heights

Promoting an image

- At another level, selling a product can be a more subtle process... sponsorship is not linked directly to sales at all. Instead it tries to make the likely customer feel happy about the sponsoring company and its product. If the name of a company was on our favourite player, we might, without realising it, also feel good about the company.
- In this way, a company can transfer some of the values of the team or player to its own products. If the player or team is successful then this success is good for the sponsoring company also.
- High-level sport, in general, is played by young people. They bring energy, enthusiasm, excitement and skill to the activity. These qualities make a very helpful partner when marketing a product.
- Sponsorship is about getting the spectators to enjoy the sporting event and have a positive view of the sponsor. They are therefore likely to buy the sponsor's product.
- Example: Coca Cola tries to maintain its place as the world's favourite soft drink by being highly involved with the world's most important sporting events such as the Olympic Games or the Football World Cup. The company hopes that the excellence and achievement seen at these events will be linked with its product.

Deciding on sponsorship

When a company looks at sponsoring a sport, it must consider many factors.

It must ask questions about the sports organisation:

- Is it a respectable partner with the right image?
- Has it had sponsorship before?
- Is it run in a professional way?
- Will the company get value for money?
- Will our product go well with the sport?
- Will we reach our target audience?
- Will it be possible to extend the sponsorship?

It must also ask questions about publicity:

- How 'visible' will the event be?
- Will the company's name be given a high profile?
- Is the public interested in the sport?
- Will the individual, team or event be seen on television?
- Will there be publicity on radio or in the papers?
- Will lots of people attend the event?
- What type of people will attend the event (age, sex, social group, income)?
- Will the team or individual win?

The growth of sports sponsorship

- In 1980 sports sponsorship was worth only about £50 million a year.
- By 1990 this had risen to nearly £250 million a year.
- The latest figures are: 1997 – £322 million; 1998 – £353 million; 1999 – £377 million. These figures are likely to continue to grow.
- In 1999 grass-roots sponsorship of £3.5 million was doubled by the Sportsmatch scheme, making £7 million of new money for sport.
- During the first 6 months of 1999, 16 companies gave £70 million in sponsorship. This included the £20 million from Heineken for 4 years for the Rugby Union European Cup.

Exciting sports attract sponsorship

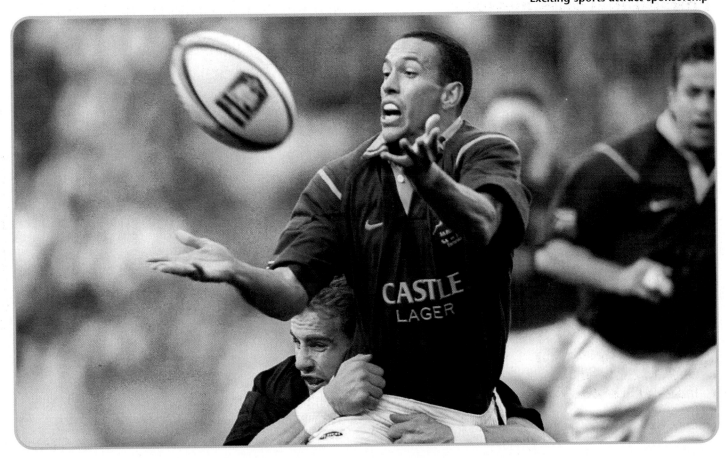

Who receives sponsorship in sport?

Today, sponsorship is available throughout the sporting world. And it is not only the stars of sport who are sponsored. Local teams and individuals can also find sponsors, often from the local community. Sponsorship is received by individual sportspeople, sports teams and groups, NGBs, coaching and achievement schemes, sporting events.

Individual sportspeople

- World champions and Olympic gold medallists can choose their sponsors. Successful sportspeople are in great demand. Sponsors hope that spectators will link the name of their product with sporting excellence.
- We forget sometimes that players advertise one product rather than another because of the money they are paid.
- Sponsorship, for professional sportspeople, adds money to their income from sport.
- For younger up-and-coming sportspeople sponsorship enables them to buy the best equipment and helps with the costs of training, competition and travelling.
- Top amateurs rely on sponsorship to pay their living expenses so that they can give up work or only work part time. Money is also available for equipment, clothing and travel, accommodation and the expenses of training and competition.

Sports teams and groups

- Successful professional sports teams attract a lot of sponsorship.
- Sponsors like to be linked with success and excellence.
- Sponsorship received by a team is used by the organisation responsible for the team.
- Amateur teams who are sponsored may have their equipment and clothing, training and travelling expenses paid.
- Sometimes sponsorship is given to teams at different age levels.
- Sponsorship of junior teams gives sponsors a good name.

National governing bodies

The NGBs receive sponsorship to develop their sport generally, for events and special projects.

Coaching and achievement schemes

- Most children are very happy to win a competition or achieve a standard in sport. Many sponsors support achievement schemes for young people.
- Sponsors pay all the costs of running the scheme, including badges and certificates. They receive publicity when the children take their badges and certificates home.
- They hope to get credit for encouraging young people to take part in sport and to improve their ability.

Sporting events

- International matches and championship finals are very popular with sponsors. These events are televised and the sponsor is guaranteed good publicity. Sponsors pay for the administration, organisation and expenses of the event. This allows the sport to keep any profit from television fees or gate money.
- Sometimes companies sponsor a league or cup competition that takes place over a period of time.
- Most major events depend on sponsorship in order to take place.
- Local events are also sponsored, with companies benefiting from local publicity.

Sponsors look for successful sports people

Which organisations assist sponsorship of sport?

What is SportsAid?

SportsAid is:

- a charity set up in 1998 to replace the Sports Aid Foundation (SAF). The SAF had supported top sportspeople, but this work was taken over by the National Lottery funded World Class Programme
- managed by trustees and governors.

What does SportsAid do?

SportsAid has two main objectives:

- to further educate young people through the medium of sport
- to encourage those with social or physical disadvantages to improve their lives through sport.

SportsAid:

- raises money through fundraising and sponsorship
- gives grants to young talented sportspeople nominated by their NGBs
- is a major supporter of sportspeople with disabilities.

Who pays for SportsAid?

SportsAid is paid for by:

- the Foundation for Sport and the Arts
- sponsorship from companies
- donations from individuals and organisations.

SportsAid supports sportspeople with disabilities

What is the Institute of Sports Sponsorship?

The Institute of Sports Sponsorship (ISS) is:

- a national non-profit-making organisation formed in 1985
- a group of companies who sponsor sport
- run by a committee representing the member companies.

What does the ISS do?

The ISS:

- helps increase sports sponsorship by bringing together sponsors and sports
- protects the traditional nature of sport
- helps companies get a fair return on their sponsorship
- has strong links with the sports councils, the CCPR and NGBs
- runs the Sportsmatch scheme for the government
- runs the Sports Sponsorship Advisory Service with the CCPR.

Who pays for the ISS?

The ISS is paid for by its member companies.

What advantages and disadvantages are there in sports sponsorship?

There are advantages and disadvantages to sports sponsorship for both the sports and the sponsoring companies.

Advantages for sport

For professional sportspeople and organisations sponsorship is just another part of their income.

For amateur sportspeople, sponsorship may:

- allow them to give up their jobs and train full time
- pay day-to-day living expenses
- pay for clothing and equipment
- pay for costs of training and competition.

For amateur organisations, sponsorship money can be used to:

- fund the running of events
- improve facilities
- organise coaching and training schemes.

Winter sports are heavily sponsored

Disadvantages for sport

The disadvantages of sponsorship for sport are that:

- once sponsorship is accepted the sport comes to rely on it. If sponsorship is removed, there may be financial problems for sport. This gives the sponsor a powerful hold on the sport
- sponsors may be able to change the sport. For example, professional rugby league has been changed to a summer game and completely reorganised
- some sports have little television appeal and so attract little sponsorship. They may find it hard to develop their sport without money from sponsorship
- the NGBs make agreements with sponsors. These agreements affect their sportspeople. They may be forced to wear their sponsor's clothing or use the sponsor's equipment. Their name will also be linked to the sponsor without them being consulted first.

Advantages for the sponsor

The advantages of sponsorship for the sponsor are that sponsorship:

- advertises the name of their product
- links the product with a popular activity
- provides exposure on television whenever the sport is seen
- ensures the use of the sponsor's name in the media
- improves a company's reputation because the company is supporting British sport
- transfers the spectators' good feelings about the sport to the sponsoring company's product
- reduces tax on the company, depending how they give the money to sport.

No advertising space is wasted in motor racing

Michael Johnson's golden shoes

Disadvantages for the sponsor

Sponsors have difficulty in deciding whether or not the sponsorship has been good value for money. They have to ask a number of questions, including:

- Has the sportsperson, team or event been successful?
- Has the publicity been good in the media, especially television?
- Does the public link our company with the sport?
- Does the public feel good about our company?
- Have sales increased or business improved?

Sponsorship agreements last for a period of time, sometimes years. Sponsors sign agreements. They cannot pull out quickly if things go wrong. From time to time the action of the sportsperson or teams brings bad publicity. This can happen because of their sporting behaviour or their behaviour in their private lives. The sponsor may want to withdraw its sponsorship.

Sponsors need successful people. Regular losers and weak teams attract few sponsors.

Sport and tobacco sponsorship

- Tobacco companies sponsor sport but smoking is a proven health risk. Sport keeps us healthy, so smoking and sport cannot go together.
- Some people argue that sport should accept sponsorship from any company. After all, it is accepted from companies that make alcohol and weapons.
- In 1998, the European Union voted to ban all sponsorship of sport by tobacco companies in magazines and newspapers by 2002, at normal cultural and sporting events by 2003 and at 'world level' sporting events, including Formula One, by 2006.

The media

When we talk about the media, we are referring to all the different ways that are used to bring us stories, news action and information.

Magazines

If we walk into any newsagent we will find dozens of magazines about sport. There is a wide choice of reading, which ranges from major activities like tennis to minority sports like the triathlon. Within the covers are pages packed with pictures, stories and news about particular sports. General sports magazines are very much rarer and in the past have not been successful over a long period.

Books

Successful books on sport are usually the life stories of current sports stars. At regular intervals, the histories of individual sports or their clubs are published in great detail. Coaching and training books help us to improve our sporting performance. Novels based on sport are much harder to find.

Sporting stars are always in demand

Newspapers

All national newspapers give several pages to sport and employ a large number of sports journalists. However, there is no national daily newspaper devoted to sport in Britain. The aim of editors is to sell more newspapers. This is reflected in the sports pages. Some newspapers carry more details about the private lives of the sports stars than they do about the sport itself. Newspapers are good at building up stars when they are successful. However, they are even better at knocking them down when they fail. Today, newspapers play a major part in forming our views about sport. The way sports writers present sport, and the pictures they use, affect how we think about sport.

Radio

Before television, the great advantage of radio was that it reported events live. The commentator described the action as it happened and the listeners felt they were there. In spite of television, radio still has its place. From the radio companies' points of view, it is much cheaper to report on radio, and uses a much smaller team of people. For the listener, radios are much cheaper and more mobile than televisions. This gives radio its great advantage – we can do other things at the same time as listening to the match, race or competition. It allows us to keep in touch with the sporting action, particularly when the events take some time to complete, for example cricket matches and tennis championships.

Film and video

Sport, being dramatic, full of heroic triumph and tragic tears, should make fabulous material for films. However, it seldom does. Films focussing on sport include:

- *Raging Bull* (1980): boxing in the 1940s and 1950s
- *This Sporting Life* (1963): rugby league
- *Eight Men Out* (1988): baseball story from the early part of the twentieth century
- *Hoop Dreams* (1995): basketball
- *Champions* (1983): a jockey overcomes cancer and wins the Grand National
- *Fever Pitch* (1997): experiences of a football supporter
- *True Blue* (1996): rowing

Video collections of great sporting occasions and outstanding individual performances are very popular. We can relive past glories whenever we like, in the comfort of our own home. There are also instructional videos for improving our sporting performances and to help coaches.

CD-ROMs and the Internet

CD-ROMs contain a wealth of information about a whole range of sporting subjects. For example, we can find out every detail about the modern Olympic Games from just one disc. Much of the information in this book has been transferred to a CD-ROM, together with interactive tests and animated diagrams of the body in action.

Through the Internet we can get information on sporting subjects from around the world almost instantly. This is the future for both sports fans and those interested in sports knowledge. You can go directly to a number of interesting web sites from *The World of Sport Examined* web site at www.worldofsportexamined.com.

The media can make successful sportspeople into celebrities

Television

Whether you love sport or hate it, you certainly can't get away from it on television! An ever-increasing number of hours are devoted to sports of very many different kinds. This is because sport is immensely popular and relatively cheap to produce for television. International sport does not have a language barrier either.

In the past, NGBs were not interested in having their sport shown on television. They were worried it would reduce the number of spectators going to events. The payment for television rights at this time did not compensate for this loss of gate money.

This situation was changed by a number of factors:

- Colour television pictures made sport look far more exciting as better cameras and other new technology improved the quality of the coverage.
- The banning of direct cigarette advertising on television forced tobacco companies to advertise in other ways. Tobacco companies decided to use sponsorship of sport as a method of advertising to get around this ban. As a result, money for sponsorship and television rights greatly increased.

How is sport shown on television?

Sport on television appears in many different forms.

- We can watch live events as they take place and then see edited highlights later.
- Interactive sport on digital television now enables us, when watching a match, to choose a particular camera angle, see the highlights, get extra facts or watch a particular player.
- News programmes bring the results of major events like the Olympic finals, as well as the latest stories.
- Sports quizzes, documentaries and magazine programmes are also popular.
- There seems to be no limit to the amount of analysis, discussion and interviewing we can see on some sporting subjects.
- Television also supplies sports information such as results, and it provides reports throughout the day and night on Ceefax, Teletext and Skytext.

Television cameras capture every sporting moment

Satellite television

Satellite television has had a great impact on sport. It allows us to watch sports events live from around the world. It also gives us the choice of a large number of channels. This has resulted in many minor sports being seen regularly on television.

Today people are worried that more and more of the major sports events are being bought and shown 'live and exclusive' by satellite television. This is because the satellite companies are able to offer sport more money than the other television companies.

In fact, satellite television now dominates sports coverage, as these 1999 figures show:

Sky	65.9%	ITV2	2.3%
Euro	20.1%	BBC2	2.3%
CH5	4.6%	BBC1	1.6%
CH4	3.6%		

The government decided some years ago that a number of events, including the FA Cup Final, the Scottish FA Cup Final, The Derby, The Grand National and Wimbledon, are too important to the nation to be sold exclusively to one company.

Of course, satellite sport is not free. It is only available if you have the money to spend on the equipment and the monthly payments to the company.

How does television affect sport?

Television benefits sport in a number of ways.

- Sport increases in popularity. This is especially true when a national team or individual does very well in international sport.
- Large amounts of money come into sport from the sponsors and television companies. This money can be used to pay the people taking part and to help the development of sport.
- Some sports have been saved from economic collapse by money from sponsors and television companies. These sports have needed money because costs have increased but crowds have decreased. Most sport has come to rely on sponsorship money. This makes it open to pressure from sponsors.
- Television increases the rewards for both individuals and teams. This in turn raises the standards of performance.

Sport has been changed because of television. Not everyone welcomes all of the changes that have occurred. Television causes the following problems for sport:

- Rule changes have made some sports more exciting for the television audience. Examples include one-day cricket, tie breaks in tennis and penalty shoot-outs in football.
- Changes have been made in clothing. For example, in some competitions cricketers wear multi-coloured clothes and not the traditional white.
- Starting times of events have been altered to increase the number of viewers – for example, Premier League football matches now take place on Sunday and Monday.
- Complete control and reorganisation of rugby league has passed to the sponsors. The company decided to form new league teams and to play the game in the summer.

- The authority of officials can be undermined when their decisions are examined in detail. They have to make decisions instantly without the help of replays and many different camera angles. Constant criticism of officials is not good for sport. Ways need to be found to help them make good decisions.
- Domination of television by a few of the most popular sports can lead to the impression that others are of little importance.
- The emphasis on winning produces sportspeople and teams who are desperate for success. This might encourage sportspeople to take part too often, to play when injured, to resort to unsporting play or to cheat by using drugs.
- Some sports have great difficulty in making their sport attractive for television. For example, squash is popular at club level but is only rarely seen on television. Television has tried to cover squash through using all-glass courts, special balls for the cameras to pick up and different scoring.
- Loss of television coverage has had disastrous effects on some sports in the past, for example table tennis and darts.
- There will be bad publicity for sport when such things as violence, drug abuse or personal problems make all the headlines.

Sport, sponsorship and television – the future?

Today, television, sport and sponsorship are very closely linked. What brings them together is money.

- Television wants to show major events because they are so popular with the public. The television companies are prepared to pay vast sums of money to win exclusive rights. This money is usually paid to the NGBs of sport.
- At the same time, companies want to sponsor the sports and sports stars who are likely to be seen on television. This is to improve the sale of their products. Vast sums of money are again paid to the sports organisations and their stars.

Who controls what we watch?

The NGBs are responsible for everything to do with their sport. However, the money paid by the television and sponsoring companies is so great that these companies can make their influence felt on the NGBs. This is because the NGBs have come to rely on money from television coverage and sponsorship to run their sport. Without this money they would be in financial trouble.

Many people believe that decisions are often made in the interests of sponsors and television producers. The NGBs have been willing to change their sports to meet the new requirements. For example, some football matches have been moved from their traditional place on Saturday afternoons to Sunday and Monday.

Sport on television is now an important part of the entertainment industry and has to respond to influences outside sport itself.

How does televised sport affect us?

Television viewers are affected by televised sport in a number of ways:

- The vast amount of sport on the different channels means that we all know more about what is going on in the world of sport. This means we have more detailed knowledge about our favourite sports and a better understanding of all the new and less popular sports.
- Sports stars can act as an inspiration for us all and as role models for young people. We hope that they will combine the highest skill with good behaviour, but this is not always the case.
- The gap between top sportspeople and us, the viewers, is getting wider. Their level of skill is now far beyond that of the casual performer. The financial rewards and lifestyles of top sportspeople are far different from those of ordinary people.

How do sports programmes affect our opinions about sport?

Our opinions about the world of sport are influenced by what we see on television. The responsibility for the programmes lies with the presenters, commentators, producers and editors. They are in a powerful position to influence us.

- The domination of sport on television by football and a few other sports reinforces their popularity. This makes it difficult for other sports to be presented as being of equal value.
- The way sport is presented on television affects our views about it. For example, a team may win a match well, but if the presenters concentrate on poor decisions by officials or bad behaviour by players they can change the emphasis of the match.
- So-called experts may praise a particular player or highlight a skill. We must remember that these are only their opinions and we should make up our own minds.
- Sport on television can also reinforce stereotypes. In the past, sport on television was dominated by young, able-bodied, male sportspeople. Today, older performers, sportspeople with disabilities and sportswomen are seen much more often. However, some commentators still comment on the appearance of women performers and whether or not they are married rather than their sporting achievements.

How does television influence us to watch or take part in sport?

The answer is that we are not sure. We can claim that television increases our interest in sport of all types. This has been true of sports such as snooker and show jumping. Sports from abroad, like American football and Sumo wrestling, have also become popular. Major events like world championships attract huge television audiences.

On the other hand, we can say that many people would rather watch sport in the comfort of their homes than go to an event. Good television coverage of sports means that there is little reason to go and watch it take place. This has been accepted in football – part of the television payment to televise the matches live goes to compensate the clubs for the reduced gate money.

Television certainly encourages us to be a nation of sportswatchers. It seems less likely that it will inspire us to put on our sports kits and take part.

The popularity of showjumping increased through television coverage

Sport and commercialisation

Sponsorship and television have combined to change sport and its performers at the highest level into a product to be sold. Sport is used to make money. Sport is no longer important for its own sake – it has become a business. Control of sport has moved away from the people taking part and towards the managers of sport, sponsoring companies and television producers. This is called the commercialisation of sport.

Sport, today, at the highest level, is like show business with its stars, very high salaries and need for spectacular performances.

Benefits of the commercialisation of sport
- Successful sportspeople can earn the money their talent deserves.
- The NGBs receive money to develop their sport.
- Sponsors get publicity for their products and companies.
- Television and newspapers bring a wide variety of sports into our homes.

Problems to be solved
- We have become a nation of sport watchers rather than participants.
- The NGBs have been forced to become professional and businesslike.
- Sportspeople are more tempted to cheat – using drugs, feigning injury, match fixing.
- The over-emphasis on success devalues the efforts of the people who don't win.
- The importance of national team success leads to xenophobia.
- There is emphasis on male, elite sport. Women, different age groups in sport, those with disabilities and most non-elite sport get less attention.
- Rules and sports organisations are changed for commercial reasons.
- There is an increasing gulf between elite performers and their fans.

The key issue
How can the true value of sport be protected whilst sport takes advantage of the money offered by commercial companies?

Examination-type questions: Sport as a spectacle

There are 12 marks for each question.

1 (a) What do we mean by sponsorship in sport?   *(2 marks)*

  (b) Talented young sportspeople need sponsorship. Give two reasons why.   *(2 marks)*

  (c) Suggest two ways in which television coverage of sport helps
the sports themselves.   *(2 marks)*

  (d) Give six reasons why companies sponsor sport.   *(6 marks)*

2 (a) Why do some companies sponsor coaching and achievement schemes?   *(2 marks)*

  (b) Sport has been influenced by coverage on satellite television.
Give two examples.   *(2 marks)*

  (c) Give two reasons why a company may wish to sponsor a sports event.   *(2 marks)*

  (d) List six examples of how sport has been changed by television.   *(6 marks)*

3 (a) What will a company look for in a sport before deciding to sponsor it?   *(2 marks)*

  (b) What does the SportsAid organisation aim to do?   *(2 marks)*

  (c) Give two advantages of listening to sport on the radio.   *(2 marks)*

  (d) Some companies sponsor individual sportspeople. Give three
advantages and three disadvantages for the sponsoring company.   *(6 marks)*

4 (a) How does the Institute of Sports Sponsorship help companies?   *(2 marks)*

  (b) Give two disadvantages of sports sponsorship for sport.   *(2 marks)*

  (c) Some sports accept sponsorship from tobacco companies.
Explain why many sportspeople object to this.   *(2 marks)*

  (d) Discuss this statement giving reasons for and against. 'Television coverage
encourages people to take part in sport.'   *(6 marks)*

Answers are given in the World of Sport Examined Teacher Resource and Student Workbook.

Glossary

abduction: limb movement away from the middle line of the body.

ability: qualities we have as a person that we have inherited from parents.

active stretching: extending limbs rhythmically beyond normal range. Thorough warm up essential.

adduction: limb movement towards the middle line of the body.

adenosine triphosphate (ATP): chemical substance that provides all energy needs of body. Must be reformed constantly.

adrenaline: a hormone that causes a rapid increase in heart rate.

aerobic capacity: see stamina.

aerobic energy system: system we use when enough oxygen available to satisfy demands of working muscles.

aerobic threshold: minimum rate at which heart must work in order to improve aerobic fitness.

aggression: in sport, intention to dominate others forcefully.

agility: ability to change direction of body at speed.

alveoli: small air sacs in the lungs where gases are exchanged.

amateurs: people who take part in sport for enjoyment.

anaerobic endurance: see muscular endurance.

anaerobic threshold: minimum rate at which heart must work in order to improve anaerobic fitness.

antagonists: muscles that work together with prime mover to control movement at joint. As prime mover contracts, antagonist relaxes.

antibodies: chemicals in blood cells that fight bacteria.

appendicular skeleton: part of skeleton made up of arms, shoulder girdle, legs and hip girdle.

arousal: intensity of desire to become involved in sporting situation.

arterioles: small blood vessels into which the arteries sub-divide, taking blood into the capillaries.

associative phase: learning period when improvers practice and get a feel for the skill.

atrophy: loss of muscle mass due to physical inactivity.

autonomic nervous system: part of nervous system that automatically controls many of bodily functions, for example digestion.

autonomous phase: when experts perform a skill automatically.

axial skeleton: part of skeleton made up of skull, vertebral column, ribs and sternum.

balance: ability to retain equilibrium whether stationary or moving.

basal metabolic rate: amount of energy we use to keep body alive and healthy.

blood pressure: force of blood against walls of artery caused by heart pumping blood around body.

body build: ability to carry correct amount of body fat and muscle.

body composition: relationship between fat and lean tissue in body.

body size: relationship between height and weight.

body type: use of somatotyping to describe body shape using terms endomorph, mesomorph and ectomorph.

capillaries: microscopic blood vessels that link arteries with the veins.

carbohydrate loading: eating greater amount of carbohydrate before endurance events. Increases amount of glycogen available to work muscles.

cardiac cycle: one complete cycle of the three stages of heart action.

cardiac muscle: heart muscle, which works without tiring.

cardiac output: amount of blood pumped from heart per minute.

cardiorespiratory endurance: see stamina.

cartilage: tough layer of tissue covering and protecting ends of bones. Also a shock absorbing disc between bones at a joint.

central nervous system (CNS): made up of brain and spinal cord. The CNS analyses information, makes decisions and starts action.

charity: organisation set up to help a good cause financially. Many sports organisations are registered charities.

choice reaction time: ability to choose an action and perform it as quickly as possible.

cholesterol: fat-like substance found in blood. Can build up on artery walls.

chronic injuries: injuries that have not been given enough time to heal. Will reoccur on a regular basis unless sufficient time given for repair.

circumduction: circular movement of limb about a joint.

closed skills: skills not affected by sporting environment, for example gymnastic vault.

cognitive phase: learning phase when beginners understand the movement clearly.

commercialisation: use of any activity for business purposes and financial gain.

concentric contraction: isotonic contraction in which muscle shortens.

conditioned reflexes: an automatic response to a stimulus, which has been learned.

continuous training: working for sustained periods of time.

coordination: ability to perform complex movements easily.

core stability: balance position with our centre of gravity over our base of support, ready for movement.

creatine phosphate: high-energy compound stored in muscles for instant energy.

creatine phosphate energy system: system that provides energy instantly but is used up quickly (immediate energy system).

decision making: we make sense of what is happening around us by using perception and memory. We use this process to make decisions.

dehydration: loss of body fluids, usually when working extremely hard in hot conditions.

donations: in sport, gifts to sporting individuals, teams or groups.

doping: use of illegal drugs to obtain unfair advantage in sport.

dual use: use of school sports facilities by local community during out of school hours.

eccentric contraction: isotonic contraction in which muscle lengthens while under tension.

ectomorph: body type with little fat or muscle and a narrow shape.

electrolytes: essential dissolved substances that maintain normal bodily activities.

eligibility: qualifications we need to take part in organised sporting activities.

endocrine glands: glands that produce hormones and release them into bloodstream when required.

endomorph: a body type, fat and pear shaped.

energy equation: diet, weight and energy needs are linked together. Changing one will affect the others, for example if we eat more we will gain weight unless we increase our exercise.

enzyme: chemicals produced in body that help in many bodily processes.

equilibrium: keeping our balance, with centre of gravity over area of support.

ethnic minority: relatively small group of people in a society who differ from majority because of race, religion or culture.

etiquette: special ways we are expected to behave in our sport.

excellence: in sport, performance at the highest level.

exercise: physical activity aimed at improving health.

expiration: breathing air and waste products out from lungs.

extension: limb movement straightening a joint.

extensors: muscles that contract to straighten joints.

external feedback: information from outside our body about the success of our sporting movements.

exteroceptors: organs that get information from outside body, for example from eyes.

extrinsic motivation: our desire to achieve success based on external rewards or pressures.

extroverts: people who are confident and socially outgoing.

fartlek: speed play – method of training in which we vary pace and training conditions.

fast twitch: muscle fibres that we use for anaerobic work. They provide fast, powerful contractions but tire easily.

fatigue: tiredness as a result of physical activity, caused by a build up of lactic acid in body.

feedback: information about outcome of performance.

fixators: muscles that steady parts of body to give prime movers firm base on which to work.

flexibility: range of limb movement about a joint (mobility, suppleness).

flexion: limb movement, bending a joint.

flexors: muscles that contract to bend joints.

force: muscular power used to move the body and anything in our hands.

formations: positions that games players take up on field of play at different times.

games: physical activities involving competition between opponents and played within fixed rules.

gender: being male or female.

glucose: simple type of sugar that is used for energy in body.

glycogen: chemical substance we use to store glucose in body.

goal: in psychological terms an ambition or target that we set ourselves.

haemoglobin: oxygen-carrying substance in red blood cells.

health-related fitness: fitness we need for good health.

health: state of being physically, socially and mentally sound and free from diseases.

heartbeat: one complete contraction of the heart.

heart rate: number of heart beats per minute.

heat exhaustion: state of fatigue in hot conditions caused by dehydration.

heat stroke: when the body becomes dangerously overheated through exercise in extremely hot conditions.

hip girdle: bones of pelvis and fused vertebrae of sacrum and coccyx.

hormones: chemical messengers produced by endocrine glands and sent around body.

hygiene: way we use good personal habits to keep ourselves clean and healthy.

hypertrophy: growth of muscles as a result of regular physical activity.

hypothermia: when the internal body temperature becomes dangerously low through exposure to extremely cold conditions.

industrialisation: change from a farming economy to one based on industrial production in towns and cities.

information processing model: theory about how we perform skills, with brain acting as a computer.

input: all information about a situation. We get this from senses.

insertion: the end of the muscle that is attached to the bone that moves.

inspiration: breathing air into lungs.

internal feedback: information from our senses about the movement and position of our body.

interoceptors: organs that get information from other organs inside body, for example digestive system.

interval training: any training using alternating periods of very hard exercise and rest.

intrinsic motivation: our internal drive to do well.

introverts: people who lack confidence and are socially shy.

involuntary muscle: muscles that work automatically.

isometric contraction: muscular contraction that results in no movement at joint.

isotonic contraction: muscular contraction that causes movement at joint. The movement can be concentric or eccentric.

joint provision: schools are designed with purpose built sports facilities for use by school and community.

knowledge of performance: form of external feedback that tells us how well we have performed regardless of the outcome.

knowledge of results: form of external feedback that tells us the outcome of performance.

lactic acid: waste product of muscular action that builds up if oxygen is not available.

lactic acid energy system: provides energy to working muscle when oxygen not immediately available (short term energy system). Lactic acid builds up in working muscles.

leisure time: free time after we have taken care of our bodily needs, our work and our duties.

lever: rigid bar that moves about a fixed point. Bones act as levers in body.

ligament: band of fibre joining bone to bone and stabilising movement at joint.

limited channel capacity: brain can only deal with limited amount of information at a time. Too much information will overload it.

load: the weight of the body plus racket, ball, dumbbell, etc.

maximum aerobic capacity: see VO_2 max.

maximum strength: maximum force that can be applied by a muscle group to an immovable object.

media: different ways that are used to bring us stories, news, action and information, for example television, radio and newspapers.

memory: process that helps us store and recall past events.

mesomorph: body type, muscular and wedge-shaped.

minute volume: amount of air breathed in, in one minute.

motivation: determination to achieve certain goals. Intrinsic motivation comes from inner drives. External motivation comes from rewards and outside pressures.

motor nerves: carry information to effector organs from central nervous system.

movement time: the time we take to move once a decision to move has been made.

muscle fatigue: a reduction in the ability of a muscle to work.

muscle tone: slight, constant contraction of skeletal muscles.

muscular endurance: ability of muscle or muscle group to work very hard for limited period of time (anaerobic endurance).

muscular power: ability to contract muscles with speed and force in one explosive act.

nutrients: basic elements of food that provide nourishment for body.

obesity: we are obese if we are more than 20% over standard weight for our height.

open skills: skills that are affected by whole sporting environment, for example hockey.

origin: the end of the muscle that is attached to the fixed bone.

ossification: growth and development of bones.

outcome goals: targets based on competitive success.

output: actions decided by central nervous system.

overload: principle of training that states that we must work our body systems harder than normal to improve them.

over training: continuing to train when body needs rest and time to recover.

over-use injuries: caused by using a part of body incorrectly over long period of time.

oxygen debt: the way we pay back oxygen deficit built up during anaerobic exercise, once exercise stops.

oxygen deficit: build up of lactic acid during exercise when insufficient oxygen available.

Paralympics: Olympic Games for people with disabilities.

passive stretching: using partner to slowly and carefully extend our limbs beyond normal range.

patronage: arrangement in which wealthy people supported talented people who were poor.

perception: the way we sort out information we receive, using our experience.

performance goals: targets based on improvements in personal achievement.

periodisation: method of dividing training programme into different parts.

peripheral nervous system: nerves and sense organs that send information to central nervous system and also send orders to working muscles.

personality: our unique qualities as a person, our character and temperament.

physical activity level (PAL): total energy used for all our activities.

physical education: a National Curriculum subject that uses physical activities for educational purposes.

physical fitness: ability of the body to carry out everyday activities with little fatigue and enough energy left for emergencies.

physical recreation: physical activity enjoyed in our leisure time.

pivot: a hinge (one of our joints) around which our muscles (force) and our body weight (load) work.

plan, perform, evaluate (PPE): an ongoing, effective way of analysing performance.

plyometrics: training method using explosive movements to develop muscular power, for example bounding and hopping.

pnf stretching: muscles are stretched immediately after being contracted.

posture: way in which body parts are positioned in relation to one another.

pressure points: blood flow can be stopped at points near surface of body where arteries pass over bones.

prime movers: muscles that are responsible for movement at joints.

professionals: people who take part in sport for payment.

progression: principle of training that states that amount of work we do must be increased in gradual way for improvement to take place.

public schools: private and independent education system for people able and willing to pay.

pulmonary circulation: movement of deoxygenated blood from heart to lungs. In the lungs, carbon dioxide is exchanged for oxygen and oxygenated blood returns to heart.

pulse: beating of heart, felt at arteries near surface of body.

racism: discrimination against individuals or groups of people on the grounds of race.

reaction time: ability to react to a stimulus quickly.

recreation: a way of relaxing and enjoying ourselves during leisure time.

repetition maximum (RM): the maximum weight we can lift a specified number of times, for example 1RM is the maximum weight we can lift once.

residual volume: amount of air left in lungs after we breathe out as hard as possible.

resistance: weight or load against which muscles have to work.

respiratory rate: number of breaths per minute.

reversibility: principle of training that states that any effects of training are not permanent and will be lost when training stops.

role models: individuals who set standards of behaviour and achievement for young people. Role models can be good or bad.

rotation: turning movement of body part about the long axis of a joint.

scholarships: in sport, money and support offered to talented sportspeople while they study.

selective attention: the ability to choose important information out of all input from our senses.

sensory nerves: carry information from receptor organs to central nervous system.

set: certain number of repetitions performed in succession when training, for example, one set = ten repetitions.

shoulder girdle: made up of two clavicle and two scapula bones.

simple reaction time: the delay between the stimulus and the action.

skeletal muscle: muscles of the skeleton that are under voluntary control.

skill: the learned ability to choose and perform the right techniques at the right time, effectively and consistently within a competitive game or activity.

slow twitch: muscle fibres designed for aerobic work. Provide slower, less powerful contractions than fast twitch muscle fibres but can keep working for long periods.

smooth muscle: muscles of the internal organs, which work automatically.

somatotyping: method of classifying body types.

specificity: principle of training that states that training must closely resemble sporting activity for improvement to take place.

speed: ability to move all or part of body as quickly as possible.

sponsorship: in sport, a company gives financial support in return for linking their name with an individual, a team or a sport in general.

sport: skilful physical activity in which we take part to meet particular challenge.

sport-related fitness: level of fitness necessary for success in a specific sport.

stamina (aerobic capacity or cardiorespiratory endurance): ability of the heart and lung system to cope with activity over a period of time.

static stretching: slowly stretching limbs beyond normal range and holding position for short period of time.

stereotyping: having fixed image of a group of people.

strategies: long term plans for success in sport.

strength: ability of muscle or group of muscles to overcome force or resistance.

stretching: extending movement of limbs about joints.

stroke volume: amount of blood pumped out by heart in each contraction.

synergists: muscles that reduce unnecessary movement at joint when prime mover contracts.

synovial joint: joint containing synovial fluid that allows wide range of movement.

systemic circulation: movement of oxygenated blood from heart to working muscles and other body organs and return of deoxygenated blood to heart.

tactics: methods we use to put strategies into practice in a game, race or other sporting event.

technique: basic movements in sport. We usually combine number of different techniques into a pattern of movement called skill.

tedium: principle of training that states we must vary training methods to prevent boredom and over-use injuries.

tendons: strong, fibrous tissue that joins muscle to bone.

tidal volume: amount of air breathed in and out during normal breathing.

tissue (hard tissue, soft tissue): one of materials of body, for example soft tissue (skin, muscles, ligaments, tendons and cartilage) and hard tissue (bones and teeth).

total lung capacity: vital capacity added to residual volume.

training: regular physical exercise aimed at specific improvements.

training threshold: minimum rate at which heart must work in order to bring about specific fitness improvements.

training zone: range of heart rate within which specific training effect will take place.

transfer of skills: we can learn techniques and skills more easily if we have learnt similar techniques and skills in the past. Transfer can be negative and can interfere with our skill learning.

venules: small blood vessels that take blood from the capillaries to the veins.

vertebral column: vertebrae of spine, which protect spinal cord.

vital capacity: maximum amount of air we breathe out after we breathe in deeply.

VO₂max: maximum amount of oxygen that can be transported to and used by muscles during exercise in one minute.

voluntary body: in sport, an independent organisation formed by individuals interested in one or more sports.

voluntary muscle: muscles that are under our direct control.

weight training: using weights as a form of resistance training.

xenophobia: irrational hatred of foreigners.

Index